Welcome!

You are about to discover positive uses of your emotions.

I'd like you to have some of the benefits of a live class by offering you some free audio recordings that take you through key practices.

Download these to enjoy personal instruction and guidance at: www.sensesofthesoul.com

→ *GuruMeher*

To all who feel!
May we live in
gratitude for life's
every high and low, and
find the way to transform
pain into peace.

Senses of the Soul

Emotional Therapy for Strength, Healing and Guidance

© 2013 Kundalini Research Institute

Published by the Kundalini Research Institute
Training ❀ Publishing ❀ Research ❀ Resources

PO Box 1819
Santa Cruz, NM 87532
www.kundaliniresearchinstitute.org

ISBN 13 978-1-934532-98-0

Project Editorial
Nirvair Singh Khalsa
Sat Purkh Kaur Khalsa
Rampreet Kaur
Jane Kupersmith

Interior and Cover Design
PranaProjects: Ditta Khalsa, Biljana Nedelkovska

Illustrations
Mandy Hurwitz

CONTENTS

A Handbook for Handling Emotions:
How to Work with This Book to Work with Your Feelings

I was feeling bad. That was not unusual; there was always a reason to be down on myself. This time it was that I had broken a promise and betrayed someone very important to me. A dark weight hung on me for months, with no relief. I decided to take counsel from a woman whose understanding of things I had come to respect. She helped me identify the bad feeling as guilt and suggested self-forgiveness as a remedy. It was such a relief to name *what* I was feeling, *why* I was feeling it, and *what* I could do about it to feel better. My mind now had a clear task it could understand and solve. Even better, in the future, I could use my knowledge of the nature of mistakes to learn to make corrections and move through similar situations more quickly. It seemed that bad feelings had a positive purpose. "Yogi Bhajan called emotions the senses of the soul," she told me. For a yoga master to give such a title of honor to what I understood to be unwanted weaknesses served as a koan—a puzzle—I have spent 15 years of personal and clinical practice trying to solve. What I have found is that emotions are an essential part of our very accurate sensory system; they are a source of information to avoid trouble, heal the past, and help access the peace and happiness that are the goal of every being. This practical understanding has brought such relief to every client and student with whom I have shared it, I now offer it to you with great hope for the help it will bring.

This book is a complete training in the benefits and use of your emotions. It contains both the information and the practical experiences you need to change and grow. Although some terms and concepts I use are also used in religious contexts, none of the information in this book requires a particular belief or spiritual viewpoint. My approach is, if it works, use it! Some ideas may be new to you, but they are all based on ancient, time-tested techniques applied to universal human conditions. In fact, many traditions and cultures have used techniques like these for thousands of years, and the simple, effective body–mind techniques have passed "clinical trials" with millions of people. The exercises are more relevant today than ever—pressures are high, and high-tech medicine that may fix our body has not soothed our souls. An open mind and a willingness to confront your own experiences with greater self-awareness, and perhaps some kind patience for yourself, are all you need. Gather your own conclusions through your experience.

This emotional training is designed for you to work steadily through each chapter from beginning to end. Since they all work together, becoming intimate with each emotion and its benefits stepwise has proven to give the best results. Chapter 1 offers a new way to look at what emotions really are. Chapter 2 deals with how to use those emotions to serve you. Chapters 3 and beyond explore the particulars of the main emotions, which are presented in a sequence that will help you build your skills sequentially. Of course, we all have our particular challenges and predominant emotions, so you may want to go right to the chapter dealing with your current feelings. If you then continue to work through every chapter in the order presented, you may find it all makes more sense, and you will gain the most benefit. In most cases, relief is immediate.

Get the Full Benefit from this Book—*Experience It!*

This is a workbook to be used, not just read. Designed for self-study and life-enhancing inner work, it is a combination of information and direct engagement. Information becomes knowledge when you internalize it through experience, but it becomes wisdom only when you live it. The concepts are important and helpful, but the practices will make all the difference. We are all self-contained, self-healing units, designed to solve problems and use challenges to become stronger and reach our full potential for happiness. Due to the poor and misinformed habits we acquire along the way, it takes some retraining to find and use the inner guidance you were born with.

Each set of ideas is followed by exercises structured to help you understand the material through your own experience. You will get immeasurably more benefit from this book by doing each exercise, which will typically have three elements. The first we call Getting Peaceful, which is a simple form of mindfulness while sitting still. Try it at the end of this introduction.

From that calm foundation, you'll begin instructions for a certain breath pattern, hand position, arm movement, mental focus, and sometimes a sound to vocalize. These exercises produce a balanced condition enabling you to more effectively deal with emotions. Specifically, they enhance clarity to help you know what you are feeling, give you the strength to handle those feelings, and offer the insight to understand what you need to do to feel better.

After these first steps, you will sit quietly and use your heightened self-awareness to learn about yourself. Most of the exercises continue with instructions to help you recall memories or visualize things, perhaps through a guided meditation or an inner journey. Many people find that as they gain skills, they begin doing the guided process during the exercise itself. You may be prompted either way; find what works best for you. A simple way is then given to finish each practice with a few deep breaths and stretching to slowly come back to activity.

You may wonder how you will be able to follow a lot of detailed instructions with your eyes closed. There are several ways to do this. You may read the first step, close your eyes, and imagine it; then read the next, close your eyes, and imagine it; and so on. Although this method works, the interruption can be distracting. It would be better to read through all the instructions for an exercise first, including the entire guided meditation. As you read, imagine and feel each part of the instructions. Then go back through the exercise meditatively from memory, opening your eyes to read and remind yourself of the next step as needed. Don't stress to get it just right; your own improvisations will be valuable. Of course, the easiest and most enjoyable way is to use the audio recordings offered with this book—just listen and follow along.

There are different learning styles, and some people are not visual learners. Even if you are not a visual learner, please do give the visualizations a chance; it may just take time to get used to it. You may also find that adding other sensory information, like sound and touch, enhances the visual experience.

Approach your study as a regular practice: find a reliable time and a place that is quiet and undisturbed. Read the text and then do the accompanying exercises. Have a notebook available to record your insights, which will prove more valuable than the advice anyone can give you. You will find a Self-Study section at the end of every chapter with suggestions for a daily practice that will maximize your understanding of the material and the benefits you will gain.

Be Responsible for Your Feelings

I have used every technique and idea in this book personally and with hundreds of people. Although it can be a bit scary to allow and work with strong feelings, I have never seen anyone hurt or worsen in the process. In fact, I have yet to see anything other than relief and gratitude, help and improvement, and permanent, positive, "lifesaving" changes. These results are why I want to share the concepts and exercises with you. Use them in your way, at your pace; if they don't serve you, retain your power to stop at any time. If you open a big issue that has lain dormant and then begin to pay attention and feel again, it can be intimidating. Your work will never create trouble; rather, it will reveal what has been there in need of attention. I assure you that you can handle it all; you are greater than your feelings, and they will serve you when you take conscious control of them. The goal is complete safety to be you and to handle all that this world brings you. We are all on a journey that includes learning to take better care of ourselves. Taking responsibility for our circumstances and taking initiative to improve those circumstances are vital steps that accelerate progress. You can do it, one feeling at a time.

If you do this work sincerely, it will bring you healthy changes physically, mentally, emotionally, and spiritually. It will, I hope, upset the status quo wherever it is not working for you now. That, in turn, will bring improvements to your moods and habits, relationships and environments. Your efforts can change things for the better, but old habits—even the dysfunctional ones—are comfortable. Like starting a new job, changing your habits can be both exciting and unsettling. Central to this entire work are the importance and value of listening to yourself and trusting what you hear. That's the only way to know your own limits while engaging yourself fully in transcending them. You alone can monitor and protect your sense of safety and adjust your activity accordingly. Thankfully, the age of blindly following anything is coming to an end. There is more benefit to taking full responsibility for yourself than to blindly following anyone else's advice. If you proceed with responsibility, then all success will be your achievement. Be courageous to experiment and grow.

I advise against the use of recreational drugs or the misuse of prescription medication while doing this work. Not on moralistic or fearful grounds—they just don't lead to permanent sustainable peace, nor do they solve problems. They complicate and confuse the task of figuring things out, and in extreme cases, they have caused harm when used in conjunction with transformational work. Largely used to feel good, they distract or mask what you actually need to be feeling in order to help yourself, and they can end up numbing your sensory equipment. If these drugs are dear to you, be open to losing interest and need for them as you develop your ability to feel good from within. However, you can safely do all of this work while on properly prescribed medication. In fact, many people have worked with their doctors to gradually reduce their meds as they feel better. Whatever your situation, you are in charge of your wellness.

Tim Tries It

I hadn't cried in forever. In this work, I have found myself exploring emotions that I had numbed and kept hidden so well that I didn't know they were there. The most surprising experience is that allowing them didn't kill me, nor did it take from me. But it did make me much more centered, clear, focused, and coming back into my own power. It worked for me to feel, to practice the meditations, and to read your notes to gain new insight about what my feelings are up to.

Getting Peaceful

Getting Peaceful is the basic practice we will use before every exercise in this book. Refer back to this section as often as needed until the practice becomes second nature. Getting Peaceful is basic mindfulness, a way of training yourself to be more aware of what's going on inside yourself and around you. Awareness is what solves problems. Learn to come easily into a mindful state to use with these practices or anytime you need some peace.

Getting Peaceful

Find a space to sit quietly at a time when you won't be disturbed. Sit comfortably in a chair with your feet on the floor or on a cushion with your legs crossed. Close your eyes and become quiet and still. Breathe slowly and deeply through your nose. Be aware of the sensations in your body. With each exhale, release tension throughout your body. Enjoy the full breaths and let them bring reassurance that all is well in this moment. Allow your body to be your own private place of safety, a cozy shelter from all that is outside yourself. Feel the chair or floor that holds you and accept its support and the stability it brings you. Let your breath, body, and the entire earth give you safety and strength. When you are calm and focused, and proceed to the next step in the exercise.

Beginning Your Practice—Tuning In

You will find that tuning in is indicated after Getting Peaceful only some of the time. This indicates that the practice that follows is an original kriya or meditation as given by Yogi Bhajan. And the practice of Kundalini Yoga as taught by Yogi Bhajan® always begins by tuning in. This simple practice of chanting the Adi Mantra 3–5 times aligns your mind, your spirit and your body to become alert and assert your will so that your practice will fulfill its intention. It's a simple bowing to your Higher Self and an alignment with the teacher within. The mantra may be simple but it links you to a Golden Chain of teachers, an entire body of consciousness that guides and protects your practice: *Ong Namo Guroo Dayv Namo,* which means, *I bow to the Infinite, I bow to the Teacher within.*

How to End

Another tradition within Kundalini Yoga as taught by Yogi Bhajan® is a simple blessing known as *The Long Time Sun Shine song.* Sung or simply recited at the end of your practice, it allows you to dedicate your practice to all those who've preserved and delivered these teachings so that you might have the experience of your Self. It is a simple prayer to bless yourself and others. It completes the practice and allows your entire discipline to become a prayer, in service to the good of all.

> *May the long time sun shine upon you*
> *All love surround you*
> *And the pure light within you*
> *Guide your way on.*
> *Sat Nam.*

Breath & Bandhas[1]

Kundalini Yoga incorporates profound praanayams throughout its practice. Understanding and mastering the breath is an important part of successfully practicing any Kundalini Yoga kriya. We have provided the descriptions of three of the most basic praanayams in the practice of Kundalini Yoga but as you work through the meditations and kriyas, please read the instructions for the breath carefully.

Long Deep Breath

To take a full yogic breath, inhale by first relaxing the abdomen and allow it to expand. Next expand the chest and finally the collarbones. As you exhale, let the collar bones and chest relax first, then pull the abdomen in completely. The diaphragm drops down to expand the lungs on the inhale and contracts up to expel the air on the exhale.
As you inhale feel the back area of the lower ribs relax and expand. On the exhale be sure to keep the spine erect and steady.

Breath of Fire

This breath is used consistently throughout Kundalini Yoga kriyas. It is very important that Breath of Fire be practiced and mastered. In Breath of Fire, the focus of the energy is at the solar plexus and navel point. The breath is fairly rapid (approximately 2 breaths per second), continuous and powerful with no pause between the inhale and exhale. This is a

---

[1] Adapted from *Kundalini Yoga Sadhana Guidelines, 2nd Edition.*

very balanced breath with no emphasis on either the exhale or the inhale, but rather equal power given to both.

Breath of Fire is a cleansing breath, renewing the blood and releasing old toxins from the lungs, mucous lining, blood vessels, and cells. It is a powerful way to adjust your autonomic nervous system and get rid of stress. Regular practice expands the lungs quickly.

Cannon Breath

Cannon Breath is a powerful continuous and equal inhalation and exhalation through the mouth, similar to Breath of Fire, but through rounded lips instead of through the nose. Very cleansing, this breath is invigorating, energizing and rejuvenating.

To consolidate the energy at the end of a kriya, many will call for a Cannon Fire exhale, which means we suspend the breath on the inhale and then use a single strong exhale through the mouth like a Cannon.

Bandhas

Bandhas or locks are used frequently in Kundalini Yoga. Combinations of muscle contractions, each lock has the function of changing blood circulation, nerve pressure, and the flow of cerebral spinal fluid. They also direct the flow of psychic energy, praana, into the main energy channels that relate to raising the Kundalini energy. They concentrate the body's energy for use in consciousness and self-healing. There are three important locks: jalandhar bandh, uddiyana bandh, and mulbandh. When all three locks are applied simultaneously, it is called maahaabandh, the Great Lock.

Jalandhar Bandh or Neck Lock

The most basic lock used in Kundalini Yoga is jalandhar bandh, the neck lock. This lock is practiced by gently stretching the back of the neck straight and pulling the chin toward the back of the neck. Lift the chest and sternum and keep the muscles of the neck and throat and face relaxed.

Uddiyana Bandh or Diaphragm Lock

Applied by lifting the diaphragm up high into the thorax and pulling the upper abdominal muscles back toward the spine, uddiyana bandh gently massages the intestines and the heart muscle. The spine should be straight and it is most often applied on the exhale.

Applied forcefully on the inhale, it can create pressure in the eyes and the heart.

Moolbandh or Root Lock

The Root Lock is the most commonly applied lock but also the most complex. It coordinates and combines the energy of the rectum, sex organs, and navel point.
Mul is the root, base, or source. The first part of the moolbandh is to contract the anal sphincter and draw it in and up. Then draw up the sex organ so the urethral tract is contracted. Finally, pull in the navel point by drawing back the lower abdomen towards the spine so the rectum and sex organs are drawn up toward the navel point.

Other Tips for a Successful Experience

Prepare for your practice by lining up all the elements that will elevate your experience: natural fiber clothing and head covering (cotton or linen), preferably white to increase your auric body; natural fiber mat, either cotton or wool; traditionally a sheep skin or other animal skin is used. If you have to use a rubber or petroleum-based mat, cover the surface with a cotton or wool blanket to protect and support your electromagnetic field. Clean air and fresh water also helps support your practice.

Practice in Community

Studying the science of Kundalini Yoga with a KRI certified teacher will enhance your experience and deepen your understanding of kriya, mantra, breath and posture. Find a teacher in your area at http://www.3HO.org/ikyta/. If there isn't a teacher in your area, consider becoming a teacher yourself. There are Aquarian Teacher Trainings all over the world. Go to www.kundaliniresearchinstitute.org for more information.

Chapter One

The End of Emotional Suffering:
A New Understanding of Your Emotions

Listening: A Problem and the Cure

Sometimes the best advice is the hardest to hear. We don't like anyone telling us what to do, especially if something difficult is required. It's worse when the message delivery is loud and harsh or dark and cold. But without that early warning, lesson, and correction, the agony of figuring things out from the after-the-wreck debris involves far more pain than listening to and obeying the teacher in the first place. This is the situation with emotions: They are an internal source of guidance. Whether sweet or sharp, they are relentless taskmasters; they are mentors that we may resist but that persist until we obey what is best for us. Cooperation with this intuitive wisdom is a skill that we all have and must develop in order to free ourselves from suffering.

I listen to people for a living. They bring me their problems, plans, hopes, and fears. They open their hearts and let me look inside their lives. They are often embarrassed by "what a mess" they are, but I let them know that though most of us manage to look fine, we all have an inner world that is often dark and difficult to navigate. They may come to me thinking that I will listen and give wise advice, but I just teach them to listen to themselves. That's where the answers are to be found. There is no authority other than you, no one who knows you better or who could have your best interests in mind. But your results and ultimate success all depend on what you are listening to.

When we are young, we are taught to listen to those we depended on and to obey the prevailing truths. We inherit a set of stories from our personal and collective history. What we come to be constantly listening to is a limited set of thoughts and feelings that become habitual and that define our reality. What we hear first from others we then come to repeat and believe: "I messed up. They don't like me. No one loves me. I'm not good enough. It'll never happen. I can't do this." These thoughts bring feelings of frustration, anxiety, embarrassment, loneliness, and despair that feel so real and become so habitual, we call it reality. There are two ways we get lost. The first is by not listening to and trusting ourselves, and the second is by listening only to the mind. When you learn instead to listen to your heart, to your Self, to your soul, to your emotions, you'll hear a very different story. That's where the truth is—it's where the answers are, where your answers are.

Emotions are a direct line of connection to your heart and soul. But they are intense, and they require your interpretation. By consciously listening to your feelings, even when they are unpleasant, you will discover what is wrong, what you need, and exactly what you can do about it.

Emotions are a direct line of connection to your heart and soul. But they are intense, and they require your interpretation. It's not an intellectual understanding; rather, it is an intuitive sense that we can all awaken. By *consciously* listening to your feelings, even when they are unpleasant, you will discover what is wrong, what you need, and exactly what you can do about it. When you respond not from the emotion but instead act through your consciousness—even though what needs to be done is daunting—you take care of yourself and handle your life. This restores Confidence and then Trust in yourself, even when these have long been lost; by listening to your emotions, you will be able to handle whatever life brings.

When you learn to listen to your heart—and everyone can—you will immediately hear a story that is very different from the one the mind has been repeating. You hear things more like, "I am beautiful. Everything's just fine. Relax and enjoy. I love you." This book is all about listening to *that* voice. When you know how to do that, things work out. You live with yourself 24/7 for your entire life, so it's time to work things out in that relationship. As in any relationship, it takes lots of quality time—paying attention, communicating, and listening.

The 15th-century master Nanak wrote a mystic poem to describe the benefits of listening within oneself and to encourage us to do so. He used the word *soo-nee-eh,* which is better translated as "Deep Listening." He taught that Deep Listening helps you easily focus; brings truth, patience, grace, and wisdom; destroys pain and error; makes the unknown known to you; reveals your path; is power; is worship; makes you a saint; and makes you God. Deep

Listening means quieting the mind and listening with all of your Self. The heart speaks with a different language—a nonverbal language that includes the sensations of your body, the feelings of your emotions, and the inkling of your intuition.

Emotions: Misunderstood Friends, with Benefits

How much of your time is spent doing what you can to be happy? And how much time do you spend unhappy? Seeking pleasure and avoiding pain is the main purpose in all you do, as has been true for people throughout history. But look around at human suffering: Why aren't we better at solving it by now? I'm not asking you to solve world hunger, war, and all disease; but why can't we solve the pockets of misery in our own lives? If we were all to do that, we would have world peace.

Most of human history has been focused on the problem of suffering. Religions have been founded on it, and the booming market that is self-help books, workshops, and retreats depends on it. We have gained great understanding of the body, have long pursued spirit, and are now scientifically probing the mind in order to gain well-being. But our self-understanding cannot be complete, nor can it advance in the pursuit of happiness, without expertise in dealing with the fourth cornerstone of our human "equipment" and experience—that is, our emotions. Emotions are the last frontier of self-awareness, our least understood faculty.

As modern Americans, we vigorously seek pleasure and avoid pain; we've never been more "full yet so empty." We are the most medicated, obese, and depressed generation in modern history. Chances are that each of us has enough of what it takes to survive—more comforts and resources than most humans have ever enjoyed—and yet our problems persist. The conclusions from our life of abundance couldn't be clearer: physical comforts don't guarantee happiness. Even in the best of conditions—beautiful house, perfect mate, beautiful life—we can become caught in the web of thoughts and feelings that create *unlimited* suffering.

Most people find that emotions bog them down. They think if only they could live without emotions, life would be so much easier! Unfortunately, I've found that when people try to eliminate their emotions, those emotions just get worse. Suppressing emotions doesn't work, and ignoring how you feel eventually makes you feel worse so that you usually end up in Depression. It's never the person or thing that's really the problem; it's the internal condition called "how you feel" about it all that creates or destroys your happiness. Emotions remain our least understood and most poorly used personal faculty. It may surprise you to discover that emotions are actually an indispensable key to resolving human suffering. Pain is part of life, but suffering is optional. Your personal pain actually contains the remedy to your suffering! So, it's time to learn how to use these "problematic" emotions as they were intended—to help you see the source of pain and guide you into peace.

You may be drawn to this work for several reasons. You may have the occasional "bad day" or bothersome incident and want to get over it. Or you may have persistent unpleasant emotions that seem inescapable. You may have shut down your feelings to survive and gone numb from lack of use, but now a desire for Love and Joy requires that you awaken. You may have suffered trauma, and that pain holds you back. You may have done a lot of work on your past and are now ready to leverage that to an even higher well-being. Perhaps you'd like a powerful set of tools to help others with their pain as part of your teaching and healing work. Whatever the reason, we all need a better working relationship with our emotions than that built by cultural misinformation and unskilled use. Remember that humans had hands long before they could use them with the skill of an artist or the capacity of a builder. Just so, work steadily and be patient on your way to advanced emotional skills.

The work in this book will help you experience a radical improvement in your relationship with your emotions, as well as a dramatic decrease in the time you spend feeling bad. You'll find an empowered new concept of emotions, practical information on how to use them, and simple techniques to safely resolve heavy feelings so you can feel relief and live lighter. Although you must do the work for yourself, know that you have the support of time-tested wisdom and the successful trials of many people—some of whom share their stories here. Ultimately you will learn to trust yourself—yes, to trust your feelings, too—and you will learn that you have all you need within yourself.

Happiness Is Your Natural State

I don't consider Happiness to be a distinct emotion; rather, it is the experience of one or more emotions that are enjoyed and seen as positive. This experience can vary greatly from person to person and from time to time. I have come to enjoy Sadness as a rich, bittersweet longing of my heart. Pain "for a purpose," like sacrificing for a greater goal, can bring happiness. More typically, however, security, tranquility, affection, and most pleasurable sensations are the kinds of conditions in which people will say they feel happy. By this definition, *finding happiness* is a matter of experiencing these "positive emotions." But I don't consider any emotion as being "better" than another; clearly there are more painful ones that cause suffering, while others are part of a higher quality of life and are thus more preferred. These "higher" emotions naturally arise and flourish, always available, whenever the heavier emotions are resolved. Thus, Happiness is your default experience.

When I was young, I read spiritual books that said Love, Joy, and Peace are the background energy that pervades the universe, always present and available. This sounded nice, but seemed as mystical and far-fetched as psychic powers. Maybe some had experienced that feeling, but what about us regular, troubled people? Well, 30 years later, I am a believer— not because of indoctrination or faith, but from my own experience. Actually, I'm not a believer; I am an experiencer. All that good stuff is there for me, as long as I have taken care of anything that interrupts my ability to enjoy it. I'm not saying I don't have dark times, but they are now the exception rather than the norm. Years of work to understand myself and how things work not only inside myself but also here on earth have paid off. I encourage you to continue your work to clear the remaining obstacles to the flow of your Happiness. In time, life will shift from pain with intermittent periods of relief to serenity with occasional challenges. Can you imagine reaching an inner stability such that nothing could disturb your inner peace? That can occur when Happiness is no longer dependent on circumstances; it can happen when Happiness is internally controlled! If that sounds to you like a distant reality, know that it once seemed so to me as well—but feeling is believing. It can happen to you when you are clear and strong, and that takes some personal training.

The concepts in this book can change everything about how you use emotions, gain control over your life, and enjoy an ever-increasing happiness. But it can't be done simply by reading and thinking it can happen. You must practice and experience directly. You can read about an exotic paradise, watch a movie, and even imagine you are there, but until you have the direct living experience of being there, you don't really know it. This is your life, not mine. They are your feelings; no one made you have them. They are your problems; no one is going to solve them for you. Likewise it is your sweet victory to claim, your success to enjoy, your bliss to relish. Once you have achieved that for yourself, nothing can take any of it away. The ideas and practices in this book have helped all who have used them. With a little guidance and support, you too can have your heart's desire.

Throughout the book, I'll share some information, and then I'll invite you into a practice. As David Gonzales wrote in *Deep Survival:* "You think you know what you think, but you really only know what you feel." You must have your own experience in order to learn.

Here is your first experience—a brief visit with a few key emotions. The following exercise is typical of the experiences offered in this book. For maximum effect, read through the entire process before you begin; then, if you need to check and read the next instruction, it will be brief and less interruptive. (Remember: Following the recorded version is the easiest way to go.) As explained earlier, the exercise has three main elements. The first is always Getting Peaceful (page xi), which prepares you for the experience to follow. The second is an exercise (or set of exercises), using breath, posture, and sometimes sound. If you are new to this type of exercise, it may feel awkward at first. Just remember, these are all thoroughly time-tested practices; simply relax and follow the instructions as you allow yourself to have the experiences they are sure to bring. You will then be able to use the clarity and fortitude the exercises produce for the third element—the guided visualization. The imagery in the visualization is designed to reveal the wisdom and answers you need, which is always with you—these techniques just help you to hear it.

A New Relationship to Your Feelings

❶ Begin with Getting Peaceful (page x).

❷ Long Deep Breathing. Focus on your breath. Feel your belly rise and fill out. As the belly reaches its limit, expand the ribs and chest. Continue filling and finally "top off" the lungs with a slight lift in the clavicle and shoulder area. Slowly reverse this, releasing the shoulders, allowing the chest and ribs to contract next, and then smoothly pulling the belly backward. Continue this rise and fall of the breath like a wave. Once you have it going calmly, count to 8 in a steady cadence as you inhale, and similarly take a full 8 seconds to exhale. It may help to have a ticking clock to pace yourself. Continue this deep, measured breathing for a full 5 minutes. Then move on to the scenarios in the guided meditation.

❸ Use Your Senses: Picture This.

a.   Recall a fond memory from childhood. It can be anything important to you that felt then—and feels now—warm and sweet. If nothing comes to mind, focus on someone or something you like or love a lot. Just relax and enjoy the thoughts and feelings, while letting everything else in the world be unimportant for a full minute. Don't care about anything but the pull toward that wonderful experience or deep love of yours. Enjoy this feeling for a few moments or minutes as you wish, then take a deep breath. As you exhale, let the memory go.

b.   Turn your attention to your immediate senses—a sound, smell, or bodily sensation. Focus minutely on just that sensation. Get curious and explore it. Use that initial sense, other senses, and your mind to gather all the information about it that you can. What might you do with this information? Might this sensation motivate you to take action? Are you drawn to want more of it or to get away from the objects of your attention? When you have explored that sufficiently, take a deep breath and clear away those thoughts and feelings.

c.   Imagine you are driving on the freeway in heavy traffic. Check the rearview mirror, the side-view mirrors, your speed, the cars to the side, the road ahead. How do you feel? Now imagine you are driving at night or in the rain. Are you worried and tense, or are you wide awake but relaxed and confident? Once you have felt this clearly, let it go with a deep breath.

d.   Remember a time when something bothered, irritated, or frustrated you. Go through the event in detail and feel it all over again now. Feel your energy shift inside. Can you name any physical sensations that arise? Do you feel like you want to do something about it? Observe carefully for a minute or two; then wash these images away with your breath.

e.   Think of a time when you confidently handled a lot of demands, like a gym workout, fully participating in a conversation of varied ideas, or a time working with great productivity and accomplishment. Take note of your body and any subtler feelings. Enjoy this fully for a minute or two. Carefully observe the sensations in your body and the emotional sensations.

f.   Pull back from these experiences with a deep breath. Can you recall each of the five experiences again at once and feel the many contrasts and differences?

You Have Control! With this guided meditation, you have proven that you have control of your emotions by way of your thoughts. In each step, a suggestion was made, but then you chose the thought—a memory is one type of thought. That thought created an emotion that you felt, partially in your body but also more subtly in what we could call your "emotional body." Because you didn't have to deal with much outer stimulation for each step, you were more easily able to work with your emotions. Of course, it's harder to focus this way when someone is in your face and the situation is dire, but we do learn to crawl long before running a marathon. These simple skills of awareness and conscious guidance that you just practiced can be developed into great expertise: you can learn to master the equipment you have. Do you find it surprising that what you felt in the first scenario is a facet of Sadness and Grief, that the second and third are examples of your Fear working, and that the fourth and fifth are two of the many forms of Anger? As you move through this book, you will find that emotions all have a painful side you don't like, as well as an invaluable service you need and enjoy.

> Sometimes we operate under the misconception that we can control the circumstances of the outside world. What we can do is control our inside worlds. That is a gift given to us. And that is where we must start.
>
> → *Yogi Bhajan*

Emotional Liberation: A Very Practical Goal

Freedom is a deep, fundamental, even primal need: freedom from restrictions and to do as you like; freedom to be in your body and to experience happiness; and freedom to be yourself. But life, relationships, gravity, your body—everything comes with restrictions. The trick is to experience freedom within the limitations of the world. You can't be free of pain entirely, but you can be free of self-created pain and limitations, free of mental and emotional suffering, and free to grow, excel, and be victorious over any challenge—you can even be free from the fear of death. The old preacher used to say, "Everybody wants to get to heaven, but nobody wants to die." But when you are truly liberated, you experience heaven on earth. And emotions can help get you there.

Emotional Liberation means learning to use your sophisticated, powerful, life-enriching emotions to create safety and then confidence, and to eventually know and love yourself completely.

Emotional Liberation is not about getting rid of emotions. Yes, emotions are unwanted sometimes, especially when they make life hard by making you feel bad and do things you later regret. But you no more want to deaden or rid yourself of your feelings than you want to lose your five senses: sight, sound, smell, taste, and touch. Emotional Liberation means learning to use this marvelous, sophisticated, powerful, life-enriching equipment to create safety and then confidence, and to eventually know and love yourself completely. Only then can you live fully and freely. That is Liberation.

Emotions: Why You Have Them, Why You Need Them

You have five senses that get you where you need to go, help you avoid potentially harmful things, and guide you toward perceived good things. When injured, your sense of touch demands your attention—you follow the pain to the problem, figure out what's causing it, and begin to remedy it. When you solve the source of pain, you are rewarded with being comfortable again. *Pain brings your awareness to harm so you can stop both pain and harm.* Although we may not like painful nerve signals, it's detrimental to ignore them. And we certainly don't consider blaming them, do we? So, why do we blame our emotions?

Emotions are a parallel sensory faculty. As such, they provide situational information designed to protect your body, mind, and heart from harm. Emotional pain—just like physical pain—is meant to get us to stop, focus, and attend to a situation. However, because we have many more judgments and reactions to emotional pain, we tend to ignore, override, or let the emotional pain compel us to do more harm. But what would happen if we listened to the pain and let it show us the cause?

Emotions are just as accurate as nerves. They just take more awareness and skill to interpret. Medical science has helped us more accurately connect pain to remedy; now we must similarly learn the best responses to emotional pain. Don't judge or question your emotions; instead, seek their source and their solution. The emotion of Fear, for example, alerts you to a threat to your well-being on some level. When you follow that feeling to the source of your discomfort and deal with it, Fear, having done its job, subsides, and you feel safe and comfortable again. However, this simple purpose of Fear is interrupted when we don't work with this emotional information, when we ignore our fears rather than address them.

Whereas the five senses are mostly limited to physical reality, your emotional senses work with the mind to address the much larger world of thoughts, dreams, impressions, and projections of the past and future that are unseen and unlimited by time and place. Because of our inability to "locate" emotions in the same way that we can "locate" pain in time and space, emotions seem unreal and unreasonable. And yet, this same quality is the source of an inherent capacity to guide us through unknown territory, to access more than the mind can know. Emotions are a component of intuition.

Emotions bring a vast amount of information, all in one instantaneous feeling. The meaning and significance of a person, thing, or situation are unique individual perceptions based on countless past experiences. A hundred different people can all see the same thing but "feel" a hundred different ways about it, resulting in very diverse stories, each of which is an absolute reality to the viewer. Our past perceptions, captured and conveyed as feelings, determine how we respond and interact. "A picture paints a thousand words" is a truism that reveals how much data can be compacted into a single image—just check how much larger a JPEG file is compared with a DOC file. Now imagine someone you strongly love or hate; notice how all the many years of memories instantly arise and merge into a unique gut feeling about that person. This gut feeling, in turn, determines how you behave with that person. Just as one image contains a thousand words, one feeling contains a million pictures!

Emotions heal trauma. A normal day brings challenges, small and large, that disturb your pursuit of happiness and shape your future approach to things. Most lives contain disappointment, hurt, loss, betrayal, danger, hard choices, upsets, and shocks of all kinds. The earlier in life or more unprepared you are to handle those shocks and the more intense the invasion of your peace and sanctity, the deeper the impact is on your personality and behavior. That lasting mark is called *trauma*. Emotions have the remarkable ability to help us optimally navigate trauma in real time, to learn from past events so that we can better handle similar ones in the future, and to heal trauma-induced dysfunction.

Your emotions exist to guide and heal. As loyal messengers, they persist even when ignored. A cut to the skin can heal if you work with the body's ability to repair it by keeping the cut clean and protected. Before infection was understood, however, many people died from such simple wounds. Similarly, we have a healing mechanism for trauma, but how to work with this healing system is not widely known or taught. Rather than learning and growing stronger from trauma, the negative effects snowball from one violated generation to the next. But now it is time to heal—and our emotions will show us the way. Let's explore these concepts directly.

Your Sensory System: Feeling for Information

Begin with Getting Peaceful (page xi). Then proceed with these visualizations.

a.   Imagine you're in a dark room with no sight, no sound, and no ability to feel, touch, or taste. You can't interact with your environment at all. Just try to be there. How do you get anywhere? How do you know where you are? Imagine going through your typical day tomorrow the same way, with none of your five senses. Impossible!

b.   In the same dark room, imagine you now have only the sense of touch. Feel your skin and the temperature and movement of air around you. Just allow these sensations to exist as pure data. If it gets too cold or too hot, then so be it. You simply have that information coming in, but you have no preference for anything. You don't have any preference for what you feel.

c.   Now add the dimension of all five senses, picking up real-time information about each while still remaining dead to reaction. Absolutely nothing matters; you just take it all in like a computer. Imagine going through your home and your day with all your senses but no sense of it all. You don't prefer anything; you don't reject anything. It's just like a TV with no one watching. It is just data. Does it feel more peaceful or dead? Is it a bit familiar or very foreign to you?

d.   Relax and let go of all the sensations and breathe. In a moment, you will flash your eyes open just long enough to take a "snapshot" of whatever object your eyes meet, without holding back any reaction. Go! Now, close your eyes again. Holding that picture in your mind, what do you feel? Is a sensation generated in the body somewhere? Examine and describe that sensation. Notice how with every piece of data that comes in, you have a reaction.

e.   Again, open your eyes to look at the same object, but this time hold your gaze on it as you let all your feelings about that object flow as you continue to look at it. No thoughts or words—just feel what you feel about the object. Your feelings are so instantaneous and move so quickly that it's almost hard to keep up with them. You can feel information about the object faster than you can think about it.

f.   Now shift your focus to another object. No words! What do you feel about that object? Notice how much information there is in that one picture. This information moves fast and can be overwhelming. Just let the mind relax; be quiet and just observe. Now move to a third object. Remain closely aware.

Can you feel, in your body, whether you have a mild attraction or repulsion that changes from one object to another?

g. Close your eyes and picture in your mind your mother. Feel the flow of information, the variety of pictures, the feelings, your history and understanding of her, and the sum total of her effects on you up to this very moment. Inhale deeply and wash it all away.

h. Now picture in your mind a person you fear or loathe and allow all that to flow again for a few moments, just as you did in the previous step.

i. Finally, picture in your mind a person, animal, or place in nature that you adore. Just let the richness of that thing that you love come in to you. Let it touch you deeply. Let your felt information flow.

j. Inhale deeply and hold a few moments. Exhale with a sigh and shake your body all over for a moment.

Sensory System Groundwork. Write a few notes of your experiences. Reread the paragraphs before this exercise. This is just a little groundwork to help you marvel at this thing called your sensory system and how vitally important your emotions are. As soon as you sense something external via senses or internal via thought, an emotional component is there, adding information, responding or reacting. The emotional component makes life rich; so, don't go around blocking it out. All living things seek more pleasure and less pain. These things we call *feelings* were developed to detect and navigate to achieve that end. An insect has feelers to know what it's running in to; we have feelings to know what we have hit, how to recover from it, and how to avoid that pain in the future. When we steer clear of all that unnecessary pain, happiness naturally fills the void; we feel good.

The Purpose of Emotions

Emotions are the part of your sensory system that brings in information about how things are going for you. Their purpose is to let you know what's blocking your path toward increased wellness and what to do to move toward that well-being. When emotions achieve this purpose, they give you positive feedback. You feel better!

Thus, the purpose of emotions is to help successfully guide you through life by doing the following:

Sending you messages about how things are going for you
Bringing you information, remedies, and solutions to avoid or diminish suffering
Giving you the appropriate energy to take action
Rewarding you with well-being, happiness, and fulfillment

Emotions Revisited: They Hurt in Order to Help

The purpose of emotions is quite different from what most of us believe or experience. Your "heavy " emotions come uninvited. Just when all is fine, they show up and spoil your day. They seem uncontrollable, unreasonable, and cruel. They lurk around for years; then suddenly, they arise, stir up the past, and cause trouble. An incident from years ago leaves a strong, lasting mark that changes everything for the worse. A memory makes life a living hell long after the event is over. No relationship is trusted after that betrayal. No place is safe after that accident. Life is forever clouded by that loss. You wonder whether you'll ever feel good again. But emotions are also a most valuable and powerful gift.

The times we live in demand greater refinement and skill in using our emotional faculties to survive and thrive amid life's pressures. When environmental changes create pressure, a species must adapt in order to thrive. If that species cannot change to meet the times, some or all are weakened or die. You—we all—are currently under such pressures: the accelerating pace of life; the tremendous volumes of constantly streaming information; 24-hour news and overstimulation; constant change; instability; diverse ideas, opinions, and choices; diminished privacy and downtime; great and swift consequences to mistakes; less time to relax and more difficulty doing so. These "new normal" conditions create a constant demand on the human nervous system, which evolved in a much calmer rhythm. But we all have the tools to cope, if those tools are applied correctly.

Here's a breakdown of how we experience the heavy emotions (negatively), along with why they work that way (positively).

❧

Emotions don't feel good . . .

>*"Anxiety, depression, and anger are no picnic; they ruin my day, my health, my life. I just want some peace, not pain. I'd like to get rid of them forever."*

. . . because emotions feel bad to get your attention.

Just like ambulances are loud and flashing so that we'll get out of the way faster.

> **Lesson: You only feel pain when there is something to gain.**

❦

Emotions can't be trusted . . .

> *"I have irrational fears from my past, unnecessary jealously, shame for my body, inappropriate outbursts of anger, stupid fears of tomorrow. I give up and feel helpless. How can I believe that mess of mixed messages?"*

. . . because you don't know yourself well enough to trust your emotions.

Emotions arise always and only in response to some need you have. However, you may not understand the connection between the emotion and its purpose. We have been misinformed and untrained in the purpose and language of emotions, and mistrust is a common reaction to things we fear or don't understand. In any relationship, trust and confidence are gained through communication and by gaining familiarity. So get to know yourself and your emotions and then build Trust in both.

> **Lesson: Your emotions are *right*, even when they are wrong.**

❦

Emotions won't quit . . .

> *"Sometimes my emotions get stuck, keep coming back to torture me, beat me up, and wear me down."*

. . . because emotions are loyal friends; let them help you.

Emotions are loyal servants of your happiness. When something's not right, they have a job to do, and they won't quit until things are better. Just as an alarm rings until help arrives, memories and feelings return when improvement and healing are still needed. Peace returns when the work is done.

> **Lesson: Emotions persist because they insist that you get better.**

❦

Emotions cause trouble . . .

> *"Emotions make me mess things up. They make me do things I regret, like hurting others, destroying relationships, avoiding action, and missing good opportunities."*

. . . because emotions demand change.

When something isn't working right in your world, you may not know it or may have ignored it, but your protective emotions sound the alarm to wake you up and get you figuring it out. When you take care of it, emotions leave you in peace.

> **Lesson: Emotions are not the problem; they point to the problem.**

❧

Emotions are out of control . . .

"My emotions take over like some alien in my body; I feel like their slave."

. . . because emotions require your guidance and conscious cooperation.

Like wild beasts, emotions need training and direction to harness their power and become refined workhorses for your wellness. You can be their master, but you must understand their job and let them do it. Emotions do arise automatically from our instinctual animal nature, but that primitive relationship can and must come under your conscious control.

> **Lesson: Emotions are controlled by your awareness.**

❧

Emotions change rapidly and unpredictably . . .

"I feel like I'm on a roller coaster: up, down, and jerking me this way and that. I loved you yesterday; I hate you today. I liked my job, but then I quit when I got mad. I lost my confidence, and now I'm scared to try. I am so sad over losing my lover, I can never be happy again. I did feel good; why can't I get it back?"

. . . because emotions respond immediately to changing conditions.

Life is a constant flow. Your needs change, and the circumstances around you are in flux. When you work well in real time with your feelings, they have the most up-to-date and relevant information for you, so that you can be in the moment and take care of it. Even emotions from a distant memory mean there is something needed now.

> **Lesson: Emotions indicate real-time needs that must be addressed.**

Emotions wreak havoc with my energy . . .

> *"Fear makes me run around crazy. Next thing you know, I'm depressed and then so angry, I pick fights with everyone. Now I'm just sitting around sad and lonely."*

. . . because the amount and kind of energy emotions bring, they provide direction and motivation to do what is needed to resolve them.

Fear gives you the energy to wake up to danger, Sadness slows you down so you can let go, and Anger brings the intensity to act with Strength. The right kind and amount of energy needed for the solution are built into every emotion.

> **Lesson: Emotions bring you the right energy for the job.**

Emotions are a weakness . . .

> *"I've been told, 'You shouldn't be angry, don't be scared, there's no reason to be upset, don't feel bad, you'll get over it, be nice, smile. Don't be emotional, keep it together.' Everyone knows that emotions are bad."*

. . . because the power in emotions can help or harm, depending on how wisely they are used.

When emotions are misunderstood and misused, their intended benefits are replaced with harm. When you experience the pain, persistence, subjugation, chaos, and damage of emotions, they certainly do weaken you and may seem a liability. Strength results from the wise use of energy, and you can learn to use yours. Your feelings are real to you. No one can fully understand your experience and why you feel what you do, so no one can tell you what you should or shouldn't feel.

> **Lesson: Emotions are a source of wisdom, strength, and healing.**

The specific advantages that emotions give you, when used well, perfectly meet current pressures. Seen and used in these new ways, our emotional liabilities become tremendous assets—just in time!

Dinosaur or Adapter: Which Will You Be?

Emotions evolved from our instincts, from the period when humans had to instantly call on past experience in order to survive. But when emotions are used that way today—like an animal—we create drama, trauma, and most of what appears in the news cycle, entertainment, and media. To automatically attack when angry, mate when horny, withdraw when hurt—all without thoughtful awareness—makes us animals on two legs, subject to unplanned and undesired consequences.

You have that animal reactivity, but you also have a most sophisticated sensory system designed to avoid suffering and to guide you to ever-increasing peace. This equipment includes your five senses, plus your somatic body awareness, intellect, emotion, meditative mind, and intuition. The collective information from all of this is currently increasing in sensitivity as an adaptation to social and environmental changes. Emotions are vital to your survival, and upgrading how you use them is essential to living either in Stress or in Peace.

> A Sensory System will develop, a new system where the individual will find him-or herself complete. It will be automatic that one will find satisfaction through the self-sensory system, which people will develop in the coming 50 years... And the sensory system which will develop automatically out of us will be our archangel protecting us and glorifying us...
>
> Our creativity will be our sensory system. And through this sensory system we will be overflowing with energy, touching the hearts of people, and feeling their feeling, and filling their emptiness. We will act great and our flow will fulfill the gratefulness in the hearts of others.
>
> → *Yogi Bhajan, from The Aquarian Teacher*

Let's explore the purpose of the sensory system to imagine how emotions have evolved, so we can continue to advance in our skills and consciousness.

The Development of Your Sensory System: A Guided Journey

1 *Start by Getting Peaceful* (page xi). Then quietly look into the darkness behind your eyelids and creatively imagine each state of sensory awareness below.

a. You are unformed, undifferentiated, boundless, pure energy. Part of everything, knowing all without any thought, pure existence, no effort, desire, or action. What is it like to just Be, without any restriction, preference. You think nothing but are aware for everything. You are complete.

b. After eons, you seek and form. You are a rock on the newly formed earth. Whatever consciousness you can imagine is in solid massive mountains, unmoving for millions of years. No senses, thoughts, or sensations. This is the extreme opposite of your pure energy state. However, all of that former being and consciousness is there in every swirling atom of you as a rock. You're in darkness with no feeling, no touch; there's no stimulation at all—it's just void. You have no sensory input or mental processes. This is very different from what you are used to; as a rock, you are aware of existence, but nothing more. There is no striving; you exist like this for millions of years. Recall that previous state of pure energy and compare it with this experience. Feel a connection and a longing to return to it, as well as a "desire" to evolve into a more active state that is further removed from the previous boundless state.

c. After tens of millions of years, you find yourself effortlessly floating in fluid. There's life in you, and you want to keep it. To survive, you need the right conditions. So, from being completely unaware of your surroundings, you now grow this amazing ability to sense temperature and pressure. You notice that if things get too hot or too cold, it's not good for you. You seek a certain temperature and pressure that is just right for you. This is the ancient beginning of your sense of touch, as well as your reaction to (or "feelings") about things.

d. Much later, you are a primitive organism that needs nutrients from the environment. Maybe they come through a simple opening or just through your cell walls. You notice that some items that come into you are favorable, while others are harmful. Done with wasting away in harmful conditions, you develop a preference for and the ability to move toward the sweet bath of chemicals that sustain you and away from the bitter acidic waters that weaken you. This is the beginning of taste, as well as of hunger, needs, and desires.

e. Now you find you are a complex deep-sea creature in the dark, deep sea. You have additional life-prolonging sensors to help you find the ideal conditions for growth and to avoid perishing. To sense those beneficial and toxic substances early and pursue or avoid them, you have developed the ability to taste at a distance—the beginning of smell. You can also feel vibrations of food or danger at a great distance—this is your early sense of hearing.

f. Now you find yourself able to detect light and dark shades close by. Then comes distance and color. This changes everything. You see things at a distance and with such detail. So much information about things coming at you—friend or foe—means you can travel fast and far with safety. You explore the world and find greater delight. You learn faster. You feel your brain growing more complex to process all that information. You have vision.

g. Now you are on land. You have many more needs to maintain this animal body and to reproduce. The environment is complex and dangerous; there are others like you, as well as many more unlike you, and they are all competing for their needs. It is complex to navigate through and survive these environs. Over millions of years, your desire to get what you need and avoid harm has developed the five senses, along with feelings like Fear to warn and Anger to attack. Notice how closely sensory information is linked to automatic emotional response. These feelings hold a vast amount of information from your past.

h. Fast forward through many species. Now you are an early Neanderthal. You live socially as a survival advantage, and it's very complex. Survival is no longer just about getting food for yourself; it now depends on working within the group and discerning subtle signs, like a lifted eyebrow or a hand gesture. Your emotional response to your senses is so sophisticated and complex that you know the difference between a "huh" and a "heh"—one tone means all is well, and the other means trouble is coming. The five senses and the dozens of emotions and thousands of thoughts help you read subtle clues of acceptance in the clan, receptivity of mates, changes in weather, and habits of food sources. But the advantage of this tangle of elaborate internal feelings has become a challenge as well. For example, you may react with an uncontrollable burst of fear or rage that can bring unanticipated negative results.

i. Another half-million years of human development pass like a dream. You are here in your present body. Just imagine the vast bank of experiences you have within you: thoughts about the past, present, and future; ideas, visions, and fantasies; things that have never really been. Every one of those thoughts, real or imagined, has a feeling component. It's a powerful and tricky way of knowing about the world. Survey what it is like to be you, a summary of the experiences of this lifetime, all that you have seen and felt. Bring it all to one crystallized summary of how you feel about yourself. How do you feel about your life?

j.   Now look forward from where you stand. It has been eons since you first moved from energy into form. You can conceive and begin to perceive that formless state, perhaps even remember it. Something in you longs for it. You are so subtle that you can feel that same consciousness that has been the constant witness to this entire process. Your most advanced skills are ready to be used to navigate this world with great safety, ease, and joy. Your thoughts can find peace by connecting you to the energetic source that you share with all other material objects and beings. Your soul developed these emotional sensations to guide you from suffering to peace, back home. A strong or uncomfortable emotion is simply a road sign: "Danger, stay away from this hazard," or "Pay close attention here," or "Take action immediately." The sign is not the problem; it is a blessing. You have become the wise person, the sage, the seer. You are now ready to read these signs, know what they mean, and use them to steer clear of harm to the body, heart, and soul. You now cultivate a healthy relationship to your own self-care.

❷ Inhale deeply, relax, and slowly come back to the present as you open your eyes.

❸ *Capture Your Gains.* Take your time to recall and record any important impressions from the experience. What do you see in the relationship between the physical senses and your feelings? How do they work together, and do they do so well or poorly? How can they serve you better?

Emotions Serve the Challenges of Our Times

From this view of the evolution of emotions, we look at their continued refinement in our times. Beyond our animal components of feeling and instinct is the human mind, which has brought about most of humankind's progress in the past several millennia. Intellect, reason, and science have produced greater control of our environments and broader access to physical comfort. Though much suffering remains due to unequal access to resources, there is also unprecedented abundance. And yet, even in the face of such broad-reaching prosperity, preventable, self-created suffering has risen. As Albert Einstein said, "We can't solve problems by using the same kind of thinking we used when we created them." The mind has created as many problems as it has solved; the mind is not enough. Stress, exhaustion, and depression indicate that we can't use the mind alone or in the old way to address the amount of suffering we have created.

Effective use of emotions is key to your psychological well-being, if not your absolute survival. It is impossible to sort through the huge amount of conflicting ideas and information that constantly bombard you in order to find what is true and best for you. But the signals to what is right and true for you are always right inside, if you will only learn to listen.

It is impossible to sort through the huge amount of conflicting ideas and information that constantly bombard you. But the signals to what is right and true for you are always right inside, if you will only learn to listen.

Changing times require better tools. We're overloaded with information and overwhelmed with choices. What we know, how we know it, and what is considered important are all challenges we must interpret and discern every moment of the day. Our every human faculty has to be brought fully to bear, combining intellect with intuition, knowing the facts while trusting our heart, balancing our "gut instincts" with neutrality, using the left and the right brain equally.

Access to a Higher Self: The Sensory Self

The great yogis and masters of the ancient East were scientists of the mind. They described humans as having three aspects: (1) the automatic and instinctual animal, (2) the thought-filled human, and (3) an even subtler faculty that can be called our angelic or divine nature or higher consciousness: our spirit or soul. We have a greater capacity beyond thinking that can be described as intuitive awareness; it is a way of knowing without thinking. Emotions are an avenue to this kind of knowledge. With so much conflicting information coming loudly at you, emotions can help you listen within and instantly know what is right and best for you. This is direct knowledge. *Emotions give accurate, real-time information in immediate response to rapidly changing conditions.* Thus, they are a good match to the rapidly changing conditions of these accelerated times.

Greater Sensitivity Is the Problem and the Solution

The pace of life and information today both require and increase our ability to feel. People desperately want to connect, but they find it painful to do so. We're so "touchy," easily upset, feeling the upsets of others, taking them on as our own, or reacting to the mental-emotional pain around us. For some, this creates mass hysteria and major uprisings, while others become overwhelmed and withdrawn. There is a lot of fighting—in the media, within and between countries, and in our homes. Everywhere pride, insults, hurt feelings, and retribution cause more pain.

There are people with heightened sensitivity who can help and heal others, but many of them are suffering from this same gift of empathy and caring that should help. This is because it hurts more when you feel everything vividly. And yet this ability to accurately "feel" the deeper truth beneath the conflicting details, to compassionately understand the unspoken, often unknown, pain behind a person's story, is exactly what we all so urgently need. Imagine trying to get through a crowded market without the help of your five physical senses. Awareness of a situation is crucial to managing it well. You need the entire spectrum of awareness, including emotions, to get through life's challenges. The work in this book will help those of you who suffer *because* of your sensitivities to discover that you have much-needed gifts. It will also show you how you can use and enjoy them. *Where there is pain, there is something to gain.*

Faster Learning

In the half-million years since *Homo sapiens* first appeared, we have advanced by trial and error, which is a very slow process of learning by repeatedly making mistakes until discovering something that feels better and works better. More time then passes for this new way to be widely adopted by the entire species. But it is now possible—and required—for us to learn and change more rapidly and easily. The speed and amount of information flowing at us require a faster response. The swiftness and magnitude of consequences from mistakes are greater. Together, these pressures are creating a change in us—not only in increased sensitivity, but also an awareness to learn faster and more efficiently.

Emotions play a key role in that they help us quickly and accurately determine what is happening, what is needed, and how to respond for the best outcome, all without the limitations of ineffective beliefs and habits from the past. With emotions, we become able to learn and apply a lesson in one experience or, better yet, to apply our intuitive capacity to use the slightest clue of what is to come in order to completely avoid the calamity that was once needed to learn something. We all have this ability, and we better hurry up and learn to operate this machinery of ours; otherwise, we'll be left behind like the dinosaurs!

Desperately Seeking Stimulation

Emotions are problematic, however, in part because we enjoy and want to feel a lot! *Emocionante* in Spanish translates into English as "exciting." Just count the ways, from morning coffee to evening news, that you seek stimulation. Like any addiction, ever-greater doses are needed to reach the same high and to block out all pain, but the damage also increases. In this love/hate relationship with feelings, "ups" are followed by and matched with "downs;" you fatigue from both, and pain persists. But there is a higher octave of pleasure that is subtler and more sustaining. The experiences at this higher level are considered spiritual goals: Peace, Joy, Bliss, Unconditional Love. These are boring when compared with action movies and family fights, but they become more appealing as we detox from living in constant motion and commotion. They become the main desire and goal of what we call saintly beings, and these sublime experiences are feelings that we all deeply long for.

Senses of the Soul

Just as your five senses relate to the body, emotions relate to the soul. They tell you what your heart longs for, and they convey pain when you don't get it. They bring fierce energy when your peace is disturbed so that you can protect your sanctity. All the big yet invisible experiences that determine your quality of life—Love, Peace, Contentment, Beauty, Grandeur, Hope, Inspiration—are *felt* inside. These inner experiences are known through the same sensory system that brings you Anxiety and Hate. "Negative" emotions are, in fact, warning signals pointing to whatever it is that is interfering with your preferred "positive" states. Emotions are the Senses of the Soul. They lead you to light. They let you know where you are on the pain-to-peace scale, alerting you away from pain and toward deep and sustainable pleasure.

As you begin to use emotions to clear up trouble rather than cause it, you will spend more time feeling good and happy. This will become your new normal.

As you begin to use emotions to clear up trouble rather than cause it, you will spend more time feeling good and happy. This will become your new normal, and inner peace will become your natural home. Suffering arises to awaken you to whatever has blocked it or knocked you off your game. You are then rewarded for handling those blocks by feeling better. Deep and constant peace is constantly available to you. Due to its soft and subtle nature, however, it cannot be felt over the "noise" of those exciting and painful emotions.

Soul and God are only known by feeling them. Perhaps they are just words that attempt to describe the ultimate "felt" experience. Religions all began with the purpose of attaining and living that highest possible human experience. Someone felt that feeling inside and tried to teach or train others to enjoy it. Religions don't always achieve that goal—it's a tricky job—but the desire and ability to achieve it is built into each of us.

The work in this book requires no particular beliefs in God or Soul. Our foundation and approach is this: direct experience is the source of your knowing, and that knowing is the guide to your happiness. For this work, I define *Soul* simply as a warm and elevated experience of clarity, knowingness, and deep peace. Emotions are the senses that help guide you to that experience. Whatever your past experience and belief, just be open to feeling better.

Increase Peace

Here is a quick, effective way to manage emotions. When you don't know how to get control of thoughts and feelings, you can first control the body with the simple breath pattern. Since body and mind are linked, the mind follows the body's calm lead. It then becomes easier to direct the mind to the images suggested in the Simple Practice to Increase Peace, and there you are, feeling better. Drink some water before you start.

❶ *Begin by Getting Peaceful* (page xi). Tune in with the Adi Mantra and continue.

❷ *Emotional Balance Breath.* This exercise begins with a basic breath technique for emotional calmness. It is also excellent to do before bed to let go of the worries of the day. Inhaling through the left nostril stimulates the brain's capacity to reset your framework of thinking and feeling, allowing new perspectives. Exhaling through the right nostril relaxes the constant computations and cautions of the brain, which helps break automatic patterns. Regulating your breath pattern in this way sets a new level of brain functioning, which establishes emotional balance and calmness after periods of intense stress or shock.

a. With your eyes closed, press gently up and to the center, focusing at a point just above where your eyebrows meet.

b. Use your right thumb and right pinkie to close off alternate nostrils: Close off the right nostril with the right thumb as you inhale deeply through the left nostril. When the breath is full, close off the left nostril with the right pinkie finger and release the right nostril as you exhale smoothly through the right nostril. The breath is complete, continuous, and smooth. (An alternative method is to use the thumb and index finger.) Continue with long, deep, regular breaths for 3–31 minutes. To end,

inhale and then exhale completely; then hold the breath out and squeeze the lower lock. Relax completely.

❸ *Simple Practice to Increase Peace.* During or after the breathing exercise, follow this imagery:

a. Maintain your awareness of the safety of your groundedness to breath, body, and earth, as well as your connectedness to everything vast. Float and be carried; do nothing, as there is nothing that needs doing. Just be; just experience. Feel the subtle pleasure of it all.

b. From this expansive viewpoint, view your human body sitting between Heaven and Earth. You will safely be able to view any human problem from here. As you continue, accept any and all thoughts and feelings that arise, even if they are different from what is suggested.

c. What you are feeling is a taste of the experience we call soul; define soul as that which you are feeling. It's not a lucky taste of heaven out there somewhere; it is always in you to be enjoyed whenever the noise and pain subside. This experience is wonderful, available, and patiently and lovingly awaiting your interest and attention; it's certainly preferable to the pain. When you care, it is there for you, but it does not intrude or impose itself. However, it does let you know when you are moving near to or far from it. Pain means you are farther away and looking in the wrong place; persistent pain is a loving, loyal message for you to awaken, pay attention, and move!

d. Can you feel your direct access to the most accurate and immediate truths about yourself, right now—what you need and what you need to do to get ever closer to maintain continuous contact with that deep peace and refined pleasure? Compare this type of pleasure to all you have been doing and wanting and seeking most of your life. You have suffered and learned so much. You are ready to have it all come together now; you are ready to leave pain behind by learning from it quickly and accepting the peace. Feel the great strength of it. From this expansive viewpoint, view your human body sitting on a mountaintop as a wise sovereign, poised between Heaven and Earth. You will safely be able to view your entire human life from here. This is the wisdom and clarity you can always access to guide your decisions and actions; it is a way to establish yourself to safely work with your emotions, however intense and difficult.

e. This experience is known through your emotional senses; embrace it as good. Imagine now that your soul is calling and drawing you in with these feelings, like proverbial breadcrumbs to guide you home. You want more of this, so you figure out how to follow the trail to get more.

f.   All the pleasant feelings, such as Love, Peacefulness, Tranquility, Well-Being, Safety, and Security, are your natural state, your home. Everything less than that is like a signpost that says, "No, no, no, don't go there, come back home." Although you may now live your life primarily in uncomfortable feelings, these feelings are trying to help you remove what's bothering you, to help you take care of yourself by clearing up situations so you can return to your preferred peaceful state. If you are living in a backlog of unfinished business and clutter of past issues, peace may seem unattainable. Life will always have ups and downs, but your soul sees the way through and guides you using emotions and intuition. Suffering is not the human condition; it is an earlier developmental stage of the human condition. You have the inherent nature and the opportunity to live in that more peaceful state. Simply listen to the messages that drown out the peace; they are alerting you to what's not working so you can deal with them directly until the good stuff returns.

g.   Observe and enjoy for as long as you wish. To finish, inhale deeply and stretch your body, and then open your eyes.

Emotions are your friends, but they have had a lot of bad press, arising from misinformation and misuse. I hope these concepts of what emotions are and how they can serve you have initiated a more positive relationship with your emotions. Chapter 2 will discuss specific emotions and, more importantly, will provide practice on how to use them. Begin retraining yourself now.

Self-Study: Establish a New Relationship with Emotions

❶ What insights have you had throughout this chapter about your emotions and how they work? Use awareness and simple observation of your feelings during the day. These ideas and experiences will begin to alter how you view and relate to emotions. You might be realizing that emotions are not so bad after all.

❷ Spend at least 6–11 minutes or more in focused practice daily. Use the Emotional Balance Breath with the Simple Practice to Increase Peace (page 24) to increase feelings of safety and control with your inner world, while also increasing your awareness. Practice going deeper into that soul feeling. Here is a short version of the Simple Practice to Increase Peace that you might like to incorporate into your regular Getting Peaceful exercise: Sit comfortably and close your eyes. Breathe long deep breaths through your nose. With each breath, relax your body. Notice all the sensations in your body. Be very present. Continue to relax and let the thoughts in your mind slow down. Enjoy the reassurance of each breath, which creates safety for your life. Let the breath connect you to the body as you continue to relax. Feel your body supported by the chair where you sit and the floor and the earth below them. Through your breath and body and earth, feel well supported, comfortable, and safe. Retain this grounded feeling as you focus at your forehead and above your head. Imagine you have access to the space above you, the sky above that, and the whole universe beyond that. Expand to fill and be part of this vast space, leaving your small, earthly concerns behind. Feel the expansive vastness of all space and all time and let that give you a feeling of clarity, certainty, and power.

❸ Once you feel clear and calm, allow feelings from recent events to arise. Fully feel everything. Observe without indulging or resisting. Be fully aware as you let your mind be quiet and observe; just totally feel. The breathing will help you handle it all. Finish with the breathing and visualization as needed to end your session feeling calm.

❹ Afterward, record any thoughts and feelings you had.

❺ Take time daily for a review of how and what you felt throughout the previous 24-hour perioid. Note the predominant and recurring emotions. When do they arise, and how do they retreat? After working through this chapter, you may be feeling more, or you may simply be more aware of what you are feeling.

Ideas to Use: New Truths to Remember about Emotions

You only feel pain when there is something to gain.	Emotions feel bad to get your attention.
Emotions are *right*, even when they are wrong.	What you feel is real; learn to trust yourself.
Emotions persist because they insist that you get better.	Emotions are your friends; let them help you.
Emotions are not the problem; they point to the problem.	Emotions demand change.
Emotions are controlled by your awareness.	Emotions require your guidance and conscious cooperation.
Emotions indicate real-time needs that need to be addressed.	Emotions respond immediately to changing conditions.
Emotions bring you the right energy for the job.	The amount and kind of energy gives a clue for what you need to do.
Emotions are a source of wisdom, strength, and healing.	The power in emotions can help or harm, depending on how wisely they are used.

Chapter Two

Getting Emotions to Work for You
Use Your Feelings as the Senses of the Soul

Seeing emotions as assets is the first step, and that alone will begin to change everything for you. Now we're going to talk about *how* to use your emotions so that you can practice and enjoy their benefits. First, let's look at how they are misused.

Feelings: Devilish or Divine?

Emotions and their many effects have long been feared and condemned by institutions and individuals. The Seven Deadly Sins are said to keep you out of heaven and to be the root of all bad behaviors—and every one of them is an emotion or emotion-driven behavior. Although it's clear that pleasure and pain can both cause lots of damage, so far no church, law, or therapy has been able to stop the flood of feelings or to produce the ability to control ourselves. The world still lives largely in a tired and powerless cycle of denial, giving in to indulgence, followed by regret. Western religions and Eastern philosophies alike have a history of seeing the human body and experience as an impure and unholy impediment.

The 7 Deadly Sins: Emotions that keep you out of heaven.

Lust
Gluttony
Greed
Sloth
Wrath
Envy
Pride

This view coincides with imbalance in the male–female archetypical influences known as patriarchy, where rules, judgment, and self-denial dominate over intuition, acceptance, and enjoyment. Such imbalances always create more suffering. For example, guilt, shame, and punishment for natural human sexual behavior have only increased the obsession with its pleasure, without diminishing its potential harms or increasing its lasting joys. Although tantric philosophy, introduced in medieval India, initiated the acceptance of the body and its pleasure, to this day, even with the continual liberation of sexual mores, we still deeply fear the power in our passions. With so much past abuse, we don't yet trust ourselves with this power. So do our emotions make us a devil, or are they, as Senses of the Soul, really divine? It all depends on how you use them.

Misuses of Emotion: Reaction and Repression

Emotions are not to be blamed for the trouble they cause, any more than nerves are the villains when they inform you of a bodily injury. *The problem with emotions comes from our misuse of them.* We misuse our emotions in two main ways that are polar opposites of each other. At one end is repression: ignoring and not feeling them. At the other end is unbridled expression and unfiltered reaction. Both approaches cause trouble, and both result in the bad reputation of emotions.

Emotional Reaction

Rather than viewing human behavior as either good or evil, let's view it as a threefold model of our inner nature: animal, human, and divine. Our animal nature has a primary instinct to survive, and we inherit that instinct's advantage of immediate reaction to a threat or an opportunity. This animal aspect seeks immediate gratification or safety, with no filters on behavior or regard for long-term outcome. If it tastes good, you eat it; if you're horny, you have sex. Desire is acted upon regardless of the consequences. When hurt, you attack, even when doing so will harm you or push those you love farther away. Fear has you run and hide from the opportunities that you want but find challenging.

Reaction is an action with an unplanned outcome. You may explain it away by saying, "I can't stop myself" or "I couldn't help it." In reaction, the emotion is in charge and takes control of your words and actions, while the real you is temporarily lost. Whenever you are in survival mode, which can last moments or a lifetime, you lose touch with reality to some degree, whether slightly or dangerously. All our moral and cultural demonization of emotions is attributable to the misuse of emotions in this automatic way. Using the unprocessed information of emotion as a basis for action is like using the raw data in an experiment as a final conclusion. Although you still need the beast in you to run from lightning and stomp out fires, most often you will have time to consider the consequences before taking action. Thus, it is not the emotion but the reaction that causes your suffering.

Emotional Repression

To our animal nature, we have added "human" capacities that allow us to rationally decide what to do with sensory information from the environment. The messages contained in emotions become extremely useful when combined with our ability to strategically delay response, interpret what is happening with an awareness of desired outcomes, and strategize the best way to achieve those outcomes. In short, we use self-control. The ability to call on brute instincts as needed, while also managing that power judiciously, has given rise to civilization and to those who have succeeded in it. Where impulsiveness once led to ruin, patience and planning became great advantages. What a fantastic discovery! But with the gift of control came our ability to suppress or cut off the valuable information that feelings bring.

> In his book Artificial Unhappiness: The Dark Side of the New Happy Class, Dr. Ronald Dworkin tells the story of a woman who didn't like the way her husband was handling the family finances. She wanted to start keeping the books herself, but she didn't want to insult her husband. The doctor suggested she try an antidepressant to make herself feel better. She did feel better, but in the meantime, the woman's husband led the family into financial ruin.
>
> → **Atlanta (CNN)**

Because emotions have been uncomfortable, uncontrollable troublemakers throughout history, people have spent a lot of time devising ingenious ways to not deal with them. The main strategies involve creating some other "noise" as a distraction or ignoring them and becoming numb. The diversions of pleasure and pain, physical or mental, create trouble that is somehow preferable to the original feelings and their source issues. Food, shopping, gambling, sex, drugs—just about any pleasure—can begin as a relief from discomfort that is then used in ever greater and more desperate amounts as a single remedy to drown out, or repress, the original discomfort. We run from these bothersome messages, and we hide them from others. Other people are as uncomfortable with our feelings as they are with their own, and they don't want to deal with anyone else's emotions or the intensity they bring. Poor attempts to control someone else's emotions are heard in such phrases as, "Don't be afraid. Good girls don't get mad. Big boys don't cry. Don't get upset. Get over it. Don't be a baby. Don't worry."

A layer of difficulty is added when emotions are made wrong. To the first emotion that had a true purpose, others may be added that complicate and obstruct relief: you feel embarrassed for being afraid of your feelings or angry at yourself for your feelings. Children are commonly punished for being angry rather than given help to understand or resolve the frustration. As you can see, there is plenty of motivation and reward for stifling emotions. With no information and poor role models, it often seems like the best choice.

But don't mistake the alarm for the fire, and don't blame the pain for the problem. When you have a sharp physical pain, you go to the doctor, who will help resolve the source, rather than simply numbing you out and letting the disease go unattended. Emotions will not be denied their purpose (which is to help you); when the flood of loyal emotions is dammed up, pressure builds until it finds some other way to be released. Repression leads to hidden agendas, manipulation, unresolved issues, elaborate coping mechanisms, addictions and obsessions, or medication. Nature abhors a vacuum, and revolt eventually follows oppression. Anger, for example, goes "postal" or becomes self-destructive in some quiet way. When our very natural sexuality is repressed under Shame and Guilt, it smolders under the cover of secrecy and denial and often balloons desires into uncontrolled obsession and addiction. Even with public disclosure and mounting evidence of priests and politicians acting out, this denial is maintained. The legacy of emotional dysfunction is passed on generationally—abuse creates abusers (expressers), while repressors invite abuse and spawn more uncertainty, unassertiveness, and distrust around them. Repression ultimately fails because your mind is a thought- and feeling-producing machine.

Our natural desire for pleasure is a positive motivating force, which, when used consciously, leads us to ever-increasing well-being. The force behind wanting to feel good, when guided by clarity and perspective of our ultimate purposes and aims, creates good for all. Puritanism and rejection of emotions, whether of Joy or Anger, have set up an unwinnable war between our self and concepts of who we should be. Health, Happiness, and Dignity have long been the casualties of that battle.

Do you tend to express emotions regardless of the damage? Or, alternately, do you tend to repress them at any cost? The unwritten rules and favored strategies for "dealing with" emotions are learned culturally and within families, though they may change generationally. Latin and African cultures tend toward strong expression, while Anglo and Asian cultures tend to keep it all in, though repressors do explode or vent secretly. Which do you use most often, and what is your opinion of people who use the opposite? Can you see the origins and influences of your emotional coping strategy in your family and culture?

My Dad's Difficulty Dealing with Feelings

My father was a man of his generation—a 1950s' male, breadwinner for his wife and four kids. He drank every night but handled it well; we didn't call it alcoholism until the 1980s, but now it's clear to me how depressed he was. When I was little, it was the occasional intense outbursts of Anger that scared me the most. This Anger was sometimes directed at me—spanking was standard punishment in those days—and more embarrassingly at others in public. My dad slowly withered over decades, from a handsome, competent, ambitious young adult to a chronically smoking, drinking, withdrawn, unhappy older man, sitting and watching TV until cancer quietly took him deeper into, and then out of, his pain. Yet now I can see the softness of his heart and his fragile but rich inner world that found no expression. His culture said that men are men; gender roles then were narrowly defined, and his role modeling came before the 1960s, when men began to grow long hair and spoke of Peace and Love. Although he did early work in the human potential movement, which explored new areas of experience, he still couldn't find himself—meaning he couldn't match his inner experience to the concepts and expectations life presented. Most of all, he didn't know what he was feeling or why. He didn't know that it was okay to intensely feel, nor did he know what to do with those feelings. So he tried exciting distraction, then got bored, drank, got numb, and slowly pulled away from everything as a way to seek shelter.

→ *GuruMeher*

You Are Not Alone:
Emotional Pain by the Numbers

If you suffer because of emotions, you are not alone. I invite you to be compassionately astounded by the statistics that follow, as indicators of our collective emotional pain and lack of ability to manage it. Most of us keep it together on the outside. But inside?

Feeling Bad

- 1 in 5 Americans 18 or older experienced a diagnosable mental, behavioral, or emotional disorder in 2011. The rate was 29.9% for those aged 18 to 25.[1]

Depression

- An estimated 1 in 10 U.S. adults reports depression, and the number of patients diagnosed with depression increases by about 20% annually.[2]
- In 2012, 8.6 million adults had suicidal thoughts.[3]

Fear

- Anxiety disorders are the most common mental illness in the United States, affecting 40 million people ages 18 and older, or 18% of the U.S. population.[4]
- Forty percent of U.S. workers report that their job is "very or extremely" stressful.[5]

Sadness

- More than 44 million people in the United States, or 15% of the U.S. population, describe themselves as lonely and are ashamed of their loneliness. That shame hinders their efforts to meet and bond with another person.[6]

Anger

- In 2010, 6,628 hate crimes were reported to the FBI.[7] Hate crimes are motivated by biases based on race, religion, sexual orientation, ethnicity/national origin, and disability.
- Every nine seconds in the United States, a woman is assaulted or beaten. Domestic violence is the leading cause of injury to women—more than car accidents, muggings, and rapes combined.[8]
- Up to six million women and six million men in the United States are victims of "intimate partner violence" each year.[9]
- One in four U.S. women reported being raped or physically or sexually assaulted in her lifetime.[10]
- Of women assaulted since the age of 18, 76% said that an intimate partner had committed the assault.[11]

- One in five female high school students reported abuse by a dating partner.[12]
- On average, more than three women and one man are murdered by their intimate partners in this country every day.[13]
- Of the men who frequently assaulted their wives, 50% also frequently abused their children.[14]
- Approximately 3.3 million children witness some form of domestic violence annually.[15]

Not Dealing Well with Feelings

Medical Help

- Of Americans age 12 years and older, 11% take antidepressant medication, 60% of those have taken it for two years or longer and 14% for more than 10 years.[16]
- One in five U.S. adults is on behavioral medication! More than 20% of American adults took at least one drug for conditions like anxiety and depression in 2010, including more than one in four women. [17] (This is just meds prescribed by doctors!)

Self-Medicated

- In the United States, 15% of the population are considered "problem drinkers."[18]
- In 2010, an estimated 22.6 million Americans aged 12 or older, or 9% of the total population, had used an illicit drug or abused a psychotherapeutic medication. The most commonly abused drug is alcohol, followed by marijuana, prescription painkillers, cocaine, and hallucinogens.[19]
- America has only 5% of the world population yet consumes more than 60% of illegal drugs in the world.[20]

Out of Control

- Violent behavior attributed to alcohol use accounts for roughly 49% of murders, 52% of rapes, 21% of suicides, and 60% of child abuse.[21]
- Up to 24 million people of all ages and genders in the United States suffer from an eating disorder, such as anorexia, bulimia, and binge eating disorder, and 35.7% of adults are obese.[22]
- The prevalence of websites offering information and help for addictions indicate some of the leading behavioral forms: food (eating), sex, pornography, gambling, using computers and/or the Internet, playing videogames, working, exercising, spiritual obsession, pain (seeking), cutting and other self-injury, and shopping.

Can't Stop the Feeling

We live in a time when the majority of our suffering is generated inside ourselves or by another person as a result of his or her own inner torment. In developed countries, we have done well in terms of our physical survival, but in the realm of emotional wellness, we are beginners. Someday people will look back at these behaviors with sympathy for our lack of ability to control the inner world, just as we now view primitive cave people who worked without our modern skills and tools. We have not developed the ability to use our internal equipment—but we must, because feelings don't and won't stop.

You can't stop the flow of feelings for long, nor would you want to. Stuffing your difficult feelings makes you equally numb to the good stuff and the bad stuff. The desire to quell pain leads to collateral damage, such as the inability to feel loved or to experience deep satisfying Joy. When life goes gray, extreme effort is needed to break out of what is called Cold Depression. If you go out and "paint the town," you inevitably fall into the same pattern of repression, compulsion, and regret—there is not much real sensitivity and awareness when painting the town. You feel a lot of things, but you don't understand—kind of like sleepwalking. You lose the innate sense of what is right for you; you question your judgment; you become indecisive or make poor choices for yourself. As you can see, you need to know what you feel about things, as this is an essential part of your sensory guidance system.

> **You can't stop the flow of feelings for long, nor would you want to. Stuffing your difficult feelings makes you equally numb to the good stuff.**

Emotions won't go away; just like your heart and lungs, your thoughts and feelings are continually working to take care of you. They cannot be stopped or interfered with impunity. The yogis, who for thousands of years have explored the science of mind and meditation, found that the mind produces a constant stream of thoughts—"1,000 per wink of the eye." That's a lot of live streaming data! Thoughts ripen into feelings and then into desires, which motivate actions, and all of that can be automatic; you are not in control. When the flow of sensation, thought, and emotion becomes a tsunami, we often drown in it. But like it or not, we live in an ocean of emotions, so we must learn to swim!

Although we can't not feel, we can learn to use emotional information skillfully. Powerful tools are dangerous in untrained hands, but in expert hands, they produce results. Knowing that our emotions are inevitable but purposeful will lead us to better solutions than our impossible attempts to ignore or stop them will.

Emotions as Allies

Emotions are your allies, guides, and healers. They are the voice of your deepest needs, hopes, and truths. If you try to understand emotions as the way your own loving soul speaks to you, this one idea can change everything. Even when they feel really bad, your emotions are serving you, trying to get your attention, bringing information, offering solutions, and demanding that you take action. Better than your Mom or your best friend, they always have the best up-to-date answers that are perfectly suited to you, with no other agenda than your own happiness.

If you try to understand emotions as the way your own loving soul speaks to you, this one idea can change everything.

So loyal are these allies, your emotions, that even if you don't listen and learn, they never give up—even if it means prodding you nonstop. Like a friend screaming at you to get off the train tracks, you have to look at the message and its purpose, not just the immediate experience. If you trust that the screaming friend has your best interest in mind, if you know that she is always right, and if you have seen how much she has helped you every other time, then you move! You get out of harm's way and go about your day; when the danger is past, your friend's unpleasant screaming stops, because it served its purpose. And you can say, "Hey, thanks for the obnoxious warning. Let's move on." This is exactly how your emotions want to serve you. If you learn to work with them, you can be happier—and even safer.

How to Use Your Feelings

As we've seen, there is no way around emotions; Peace can only be found by going through them. Reaction means the emotion directly initiates action; in repression, part of you is lost. Both reaction and repression reduce awareness—you become less conscious, you are asleep at the wheel. Either way, emotions are in control of you. They lead you somewhere you don't necessarily want to go. When you exercise your conscious ability to interpret emotions, when you analyze the raw data before making a decision based on them, you have something to say about where you end up; you get the results you desire. When clear understanding is the basis of your action, that is wisdom. That is called *conscious control*.

What does *conscious control* mean? *Conscious* is an adjective defined as "awake and responsive, keenly aware, appreciating the importance of something, done with intention, sensitive to something, fully active mental faculties, known to oneself, interested, well informed and understood." The meaning of the word *control* has a bad reputation these days—as in a control freak or a controlling person. No one likes to be under that heavy hand that comes from Insecurity and an underlying lack of Trust. But the opposite of being in control is being out of control, which is a familiar feeling when emotions take over.

> **Definition of Emotions:**
> The Senses of the Soul
>
> **The Purpose of Emotions:**
> To help successfully guide you through life by:
>
> 1. Sending you messages about how things are going for you
> 2. Bringing you information, remedies, and solutions to avoid or diminish suffering
> 3. Giving you the appropriate energy to take action in order to increase your well-being, to know your life's purpose, and to experience fulfillment

The approach in this book will not be overbearing. In place of failed attempts to fight for control through denial and constraints on our feelings and behavior, our approach will be to accept those feelings and behaviors and allow them to do their job. We can gain control by allowing emotions to deliver their information and achieve their purpose. Then, and only then, will they leave us in peace. I call it, control by allowing.

Because emotions are linked to thoughts, we can study them similarly. To learn conscious control, we can look to the well-developed science of working with thoughts—that is, meditation. A common meditative approach to working with thoughts is to calmly observe them with a minimum of distraction (sitting quietly with eyes closed). Then, rather than just "having" thoughts, you observe them. This trains you to detach and choose what to do with those thoughts—typically, to let them go, rather than following a thought wherever it leads you. This is simple to learn but difficult to master; it is a method of training the mind to obey the conscious you. Like the bumper sticker says: "Don't believe everything you think!"

For those new to meditation, know that it is a natural and scientifically validated process that you can easily learn in a few minutes. There is no such thing as not being good at meditation. To those with experience meditating, you may have approached it only through thought and not with emotion. You will now welcome emotions into the meditative experience as a valid and essential part of the process.

Mary's Meditation

Mary is a long-time meditator with a committed regular practice of more than 30 years in an established and effective system of meditation. She came to my workshop to better deal with some issues with difficult relationships at work. She admitted to being embarrassed that she had so much Anger, and she thought it invalidated her years of spiritual work. I observed that she went very deep into meditation and could expertly attain physical and mental poise. The trouble was in her nonmeditative state, which is most of the day. In this awake and alert state, situations with coworkers got quickly frustrating and built up over time to become quite enraging. I assured her that she had the necessary skills; she simply hadn't let emotions into her meditative practice. Her teacher had not specifically excluded feelings, but the focus had always been on thought and images. And consistent with our culture and Eastern tradition, emotions were not smiled upon in general. It was quite a relief for her to allow her Anger to be a legitimate addition to her practice that could then be processed through her meditation rather than ignored.

The same clear state that meditation offers us to see thoughts without being caught in their web is exactly what we need to approach emotions and to stay present long enough to make use of their benefits. So, our approach will include observing both thoughts and feelings. I have found that despite years of excessive or repressive use of emotion, most people learn to listen to their emotions quickly and easily, with only a little instruction and reassurance. Read about the emotional map to learn a bit of the science behind how this works.

The same clear state that meditation offers us to see thoughts without being caught in their web is exactly what we need to approach emotions and to stay present long enough to make use of their benefits.

Our Emotional Map

In the old brain, the amygdala maps out the world in terms of survival. We are hardwired to instinctively run, fight or hide; that particular neuro-pathway does not require thought or even conscious recognition. In this way, we can act on an emotion in a few milliseconds. We feel in charge, in control, when we are on automatic—partly for our own survival. If our environments are fairly stable then this works well. Unusual things are noticed, experienced and encoded in our memory along with emotional tags—somatic markers—that immediately cue our bodies and our minds to deal with whatever is happening as we have before. In fact, much of our memory and perception depends on that emotional map. However, if our environments or circumstances change rapidly, or if we are affected by things beyond our immediate surroundings, tribe, time or space, then those emergency maps become the emergencies themselves. We can't seem to turn off our alarms. We start to imagine monsters in the dark, serpents in the sea, and evil all around us. Thankfully, our feelings don't come solely from the amygdala, the old brain. We can also generate thoughts and feelings from the neocortex. Our frontal cortex associates thoughts, objects, feelings and events. We assess what is happening, apply beliefs and decide if something is a threat or an opportunity. We can train this part of our mind. In fact, if the frontal brain is strong, the autonomic system responsive, and our glands healthy, we can override the emotional and instinctual reactions of the old brain. We can decide the bear is too far away to be a threat, or that lightening will only hit the hill above us. This capacity to assess situations, to generate a response and not just a reaction, is the core of mental strength and the key to handling our stressors. In this way, we initiate healing, rather than generate more stress and trigger a stream of reactions that snowball beyond our control.

→ *KRI International Teacher Training Manual Level 2: Vitality & Stress*
(Kundalini Research Institute, 2008)

Mind's Proper Place

The science of meditation describes the role of the mind in terms very different from terms used in Western belief. Western belief defines mind as our highest power. And, yes, the mind is incredible—it is the most complex single thing we know of—but it is better at content than it is at context, or understanding the entire picture at once. Intuition is a process by which we can know more than the known facts. Emotions serve intuition by helping us know—in our gut, in our heart, in our soul—what the truth is, what's right, and what's next. Mind's considerable power can only debate the pros and cons until, exhausted, we make a choice. Mind's skill lies in its ability to compute and execute the logistics necessary to accomplish that heartfelt directive. People ask, "How do I know whether it's my mind or my soul speaking?" The short answer is, "Practice!"

The long answer is to begin with this simple guideline: the mind speaks to you in words; the soul speaks through emotions and feelings. You ask questions from your mind, and then you feel the answers. The mind will try to rush in so fast to interpret everything, that you may be talked out of the things you feel: "Did I really hear that? That will never work. Impossible! I have a better idea. Just do it the old way." In the following exercises, encourage your mind to relax and observe. It loves to help, so reassure it that you will ask it to do that later. Mind is not the originator, but the interpreter, of these deeper messages.

> Working by your heart means using your feelings and emotions to lead you to your spiritual sense of existence.
>
> ⇥Yogi Bhajan, February 15, 1984

Emotion as Intuition

❶ *Begin by Getting Peaceful* (page xi). Tune in with the Adi Mantra and continue.

❷ *See Clearly.* This powerful breath exercise for clarity will prepare you for the SOS Method that follows. You must know your reality by intuition, not by information.

a.   Place your hands flat against each other at the chest. Keep the index fingers extended as you interlock the other fingers to clasp your hands together. Cross the thumbs and place the fingertips a little below your nose so you can see them through the one-tenth opening of your eyes.

b.   Inhale in 4 powerful strokes through your mouth, with the lips formed in a firm ring—an "O" rather than a pucker—at the rate of 1 stroke per second (that will be a 4-second inhale). Then exhale in a single powerful stroke through the nose at the same rhythm for a 1-second exhale. Continue for 16 minutes.

c.   To end, sit straight, inhale, hold your breath 20 seconds, and stretch your arms straight out to each side, arms parallel to the ground and palms facing up. Exhale. Then inhale deeply again, hold your breath 20 seconds, and stretch your arms again horizontally as you stretch your spine vertically, making a rigid "T" with your body. Exhale. Inhale deeply, hold your breath 20 seconds in the same position, but this time open up your fingers, making them like steel and tightening your entire body. Imagine you are squeezing energy up and into your arms. Exhale, lower your arms, and relax.

❸ *The SOS Method: Simple Steps for Working with Emotions.* This method is designed to help you discover the underlying cause of an emotion you are having or have had and to resolve the situation that triggered it, this wil bring relief from both the problem and the emotion that arose to solve the problem.

a. **Stop and Feel.** Call up the feelings you have strongest and most often— whatever is there right now. A memory of anything that bothers you will trigger the emotion. Relive that memory and pay close attention to your feelings—you will feel the same emotions in present time. Get interested in those emotions. Allow them; let yourself fully feel the bodily sensations. Sit with the discomfort and discover that you can handle it. Explore your own experience, as a scientist would. Fully feeling the emotional message is how you listen to it.

b. **Find the Source.** Address the sensations as you would in any intelligent communication. Something has disturbed your well-being, so ask your feelings, "Why are you here? What do you want? What is wrong here that I need to know?" Ask any question that occurs to you. The answer often comes immediately, but don't expect it to come in words—it may be a feeling, an impression, an image, or a "sense." It may take a bit of practice to hear this subtle message directly before the mind steps in to analyze, judge, deny, or reject the message. Just trust what you hear and feel, even if it doesn't make sense to you or if initially you disagree.

c. **Ask for Solutions.** Once you understand what's disturbing you, ask your emotions what they need for things to be right: "What must I know, do, or say to take care of this, for you, my bad feelings, to feel satisfied so that I can feel better? What will it take for you to feel complete?" If the answer is not clear, ask again. Learning to hear that quiet voice is part of the training; so, if it is not immediately clear, keep trying. Ask the mind to quietly listen to the feelings and to not interfere.

d. Finish with a few deep breaths and stretch to slowly come back into normal activity.

❹ *Capture Your Gains.* Take time to write down what you experienced and learned just now—it is most valuable, even if it may take time to understand or act upon. What did you learn about yourself? About the situation? Did you get solutions? What did you learn about how to work with emotions? Does some of the information presented here make more sense in light of this experience? Can you begin to see some value in your emotions? This was just a first attempt to listen consciously to your inner voice through feelings. Be patient. Remember, you learned to crawl and then to walk before you could run.

❺ *Take Action.* Act on the needs and solutions you've gathered to resolve the situation.

Shortened SOS Method

Once you've done this exercise a few times, you can prompt yourself through it when needed by remembering this shortened version:

❶ *Feel It.* Consciously allow the emotion.

❷ *Ask It.* Why is it here? What does it want?

❸ *Solve It.* Let the feelings, not the mind, solve it.

❹ *Do It.* Use the information you receive.

Feel better and repeat as needed.

And even simpler to remember is this: *Feel the emotion and ask what it wants.*

A longer version of this exercise, with more explanation, is provided in the Resources (page 327). Whichever version you use, this exercise works with all emotions and, over time, will become natural to you. In the chapters that follow, you will learn the specialized purpose of each emotion, which will add depth to your skills.

How Tracie Used the SOS Method with Her Anger

I had been really angry lately at everything and everyone. My process of using your method went something like this:

❶ What was I feeling and why? *Frustration with my daughter when she misbehaves.*

❷ The thought? *I should be more patient.*

❸ What is the feeling of Anger protecting me from? *The idea that I'm not good enough as a mother; that I'm not providing the emotional support my daughter needs from me.*

4 What is the action or info needed? When I asked this last question, I had several realizations:

a.   Apparently I'm not done working on keeping my ego in check. I was taking my daughter's behavior as being all about me.

b.   She doesn't need to get it all from me all the time. She has two parents.

c.   I need to accept that there are no perfect parents.

d.   If I can stop the cycle between the initial frustration with her and the guilt/frustration with myself for having that feeling, then I can get over it faster.

e.   I really need to take the time to read something about parenting and discipline techniques, because I feel like I'm flying blind sometimes.

Four of these five are internal changes, and one is an action. I can do this!

Reorientation

If you are like most people, you are now in foreign territory. There are several common responses to the SOS Method, and all are normal. You may feel nothing, or you may be confused, because these are your patterns. Or you may be intimidated by your feelings and hesitant to let them flow. If so, remember that you can always stop. But also remember that I have yet to see anyone hurt themselves when they consciously address their emotions. You may be overwhelmed—because like me and my emails after vacation, you may have a lot of unattended messages to deal with. You may be embarrassed by what you find—just remember that it's normal; be kind and compassionate with yourself. You may not believe what you found, but gaining trust takes time and proof. So be sure to revisit some of these practices at the end of the chapter to help you adjust and tune your ability to handle your feelings.

Energy Management

In addition to becoming aware of your emotions and learning to listen to them, it's important to understand that emotions come with their own energy source. The distinct quality and quantity of physical and emotional energy in each emotion is key to using them well. These energy signatures can (1) help you identify the emotion and the job it has for you and (2) give you the appropriate energy to do that job. You have felt these varied energies of emotions: Fear brings you sharp, busy energy that is needed to think and act quickly. Anger brings a strong, hot force to break down barriers or put up walls. Grief brings damp, dark, introspective energy, while Despair drops the bottom out of your ability to hold any energy at all. Each *type of energy* is exactly what you need to handle the situation that gave rise to the emotion in the first place.

Furthermore, the *amount of energy* generated at any time by an emotion matches the job at hand. For example, Anger can escalate through a scale of intensities to match the size and urgency of its assigned task, moving from displeased to bothered to frustrated and on through irritated, mad, really pissed, furious, raging, and explosive. These levels of energy can fluctuate instantly with changing conditions and needs. Without an understanding of the intended purpose of Anger, you are hostage to volatility and unpredictability. But by training to consciously cooperate with these energetic resources, which are the gift of emotion, you always have the right tools for the job. In the chapters that follow, you will learn more about each emotion's special purpose so you can put its energy to work.

Any emotion will intensify over time as needed to get your attention, to override your resistance to the feeling, and to motivate you to deal with it. For example, your friend says or does something slightly bothersome, and you brush it off. The next time it happens, you have a stronger reaction but decide to "ignore" it for the sake of getting along or for fear of her reaction. After days and years, it becomes a very big issue; you want to "kill her." Eventually you can't stop yourself from doing something—whether hurting your friend, the relationship, or yourself—in order to release that pressure. A happy ending requires awareness to consciously direct the energy toward the outcome the emotion arose to achieve: a close friendship free of obstacles to deep connection.

> **Any emotion will intensify over time as needed to get your attention, to override your resistance to the feeling, and to motivate you to deal with it.**

If you've put off dealing with a situation, the first few times you stop to fully listen to the message, it may be more intense than needed to do the actual remedy. In the first step, Stop and Feel, your emotions may swell in intensity once you allow yourself to feel them. But usually within a few minutes, those feelings subside slightly. The energy decreases as a result of the emotion having accomplished one goal—it got your attention. Being less disturbed, you are now in a better position to hear details. In the next step, Find the Source, when you identify why you are feeling Anger, it is another win for emotions, and they back off a little more. When you learn what you need to do to make it right in the third step, Ask for Solutions, you talk to your friend and ask her to change her behavior—then you feel much better. Anger has almost filled its mission. But until you Take Action and the harm stops altogether—the last step of the method—that Anger will creep back in, because it is still needed. When your friend changes her habit and you feel protected and honored, the Anger is gone ... until the next time something disturbs you.

The Four Roles Emotions Play

Emotions are here to help us through the varied conditions we encounter in life. There are four types of situations and four roles that emotions take to address them.

Present Situation: Requires Immediate Response

Emergencies require in-the-moment responses—sudden retreat from a biting dog, instantaneous action to save a falling child, sudden blush and cover to a public embarrassment. For these, your leap-before-you-think instincts are best for the job. However, these instincts can become ineffective and numb or hyperactive and volatile from physical imbalances, mental interference, and trauma-induced emotional disconnectedness, all of which can be remedied through practice.

Future Situation: Calls for Anticipation and Preparation

When your immediate survival is not at risk, you next seek security or the assurance of continued safety in the future. The mind helps you imagine what might be coming so you can make plans and take action for the desired outcome. Most people spend very little time in life-threatening emergencies, so most of our emotional life is of this type. "Will I keep my job? Will he leave me? What if I get sick? Will the economy recover? What will climate change do to me?" These are Fear's attempts to obtain or avoid something in order to ensure your continuing comfort. Stress and chronic anxiety are an uncontrolled application of this ability to anticipate (which we will address in the chapter on Fear).

Past Situation: Traumas Create Patterns and Call for Healing

This type of emotional response can be the most confusing and troubling but is also one of the most valuable roles of emotion. You have a built-in self-healing system that is every bit as effective in healing mental and psychological trauma as the body is at repairing wounds. Wouldn't you like to know how your emotional immune system can repair injuries to your heart and self-esteem? The torture of your recurring emotions and self-defeating behavioral patterns is designed for your growth and strength—you will discover how to allow your Senses of the Soul to accomplish this.

Timeless Situation: The Human Condition Invites Existential Healing

The fourth and deepest level that emotions address lies in the very nature of human existence. Emotions' highest gift and ultimate purpose is to bring you awareness of your place in the Universe. The body is small, and a single life is fragile. It is intrinsically unstable and dangerous to be on Earth. So how is peace possible with so much to fear? Emotions bring Existential Healing; they help you come to terms with the trauma inherent to your human condition. When you work with Fear as an ally, it delivers you to Fearlessness. When you consciously allow Desire to work, it brings you to Desirelessness. Grieving can teach you that nothing is ever lost. And Depression can lead you to your true power.

In doing the work in this book, you will hear and say things that have been said by the great teachers and saints through all the ages. You will come to embody spiritual truths that are written in the holy books, not because you remember them—in fact, you may never have heard them before or maybe you don't consider yourself religious—but because emotions can put you in touch with that same source of universal truths. The experience of hearing the truth from within is wonderful; it has been called "seeing God" and is the origin of all religions and religious experience. But it is also so very practical. When you learn to live in your own found truth, you will enjoy the deepest pleasure life can offer. Far from esoteric, it is achieved in the same practical way that your Anger tells you how to avoid someone's attacks. It is this fourth role that makes it clear that your emotions are the Senses of the Soul.

Emotions Are Right, Even When They Are Wrong

How should you feel? How do you know whether your Anxiety is dealing with the past or the future or leading to a big profound truth? How do you trust your Anger and know whether it is valid or misplaced? Shouldn't you be feeling better by now? Shouldn't you be as happy as that friend who seems to have it all together?

Emotions are a form of guidance, so *all you have to know is what you are feeling*. Your sensory system knows what is happening and what you need. Your role is to participate and to cooperate by remaining sensitive, aware, conscious, and responsive. Yes, you may have some wires crossed after years of misuse, but the way to sort it all out is to make the big switch to validating the wisdom in emotions and to trust yourself once again.

Emotions are automatic. The appropriate emotion will arise and guide you to deal with what needs to be dealt with now. Just as your body makes thousands of adjustments to remain healthy under changing environmental conditions, your emotions respond as needed to help you adjust to life's challenges. Whatever you are feeling is what you should be feeling. The goal is not to feel any certain way—like happy—all the time. You think you want to feel good, happy, your best all the time, but the truth is, that gets boring. Actually, you enjoy the excitement and variety of changing emotions. Sometimes you even indulge in your drama like so much chocolate. Life is in constant flux, fair weather and foul. Your emotions are part of your ability to perceive those changes, handle them, and gain an ever-stronger equilibrium.

When you are aware and present, sensitive and strong, not stuck in the past but allowing the past to inform you, when you are not locked into a concept of what should be but are able to adapt to what is, then you can experience Anger when and for as long as needed to set things right. An enlightened master will become frightened or grieve when life calls for that emotion, but he will return to Peace promptly with no lasting residue. *What you are feeling is what you should be feeling.* The question is, are you dealing with it? By becoming responsive to Anger, you will be in control of it, just as a pilot works the levers of a jet with skill, using its power to guide it toward the destination. So too will you learn to control your emotions by being who you are, feeling what you feel, and allowing your emotions to exercise their innate wisdom.

The Reward: Feeling Good Is Your Base

When a challenge is met, you celebrate. When the work is done, you rest. When you clear up an issue that emotions are asking you to deal with, you feel better. That's the built-in reward system. Want to feel good? Deal with whatever doesn't feel good. Like so many unfinished projects on your desk, as you resolve the many past, present, and existential issues you face, you not only go back to feeling okay, you also advance in how deep and how high you can go. It really keeps getting better, because your natural state is one of clarity and peace. This will seem unlikely if you have been suffering a long time or if you have never really known profound and lasting serenity, but you can prove it to yourself in time. Emotions exist to regain and protect that innate experience; they monitor and report conditions and events that disturb your clarity so that a remedy can be made.

Want to feel good? Deal with whatever doesn't feel good.

For several millennia, we learned through "the school of hard knocks" (trial and error) and by depending on others for direction and guidance. The first method can be slow and painful, and the second is subject to abuse and human error. We are now shifting to a more evolved, reliable, and effective system in which all the answers are within us and are known to us, even before they are needed. It's called intuition, seeing the unseen, knowing the unknown. It's not mystical; it is a basic human faculty, and emotions are part of it. This shift takes us from a suffering-based learning process to a peace-and-enjoyment-oriented life. The job of teachers and educational systems now is to help everyone understand and use the equipment given them for their personal journey.

The goal of this work is no less than to help you understand your current consciousness, read the signs to the next steps and what is needed to get there, and figure out how to do it all for yourself from now on. You already have all of the equipment you need: your body, thoughts, emotions, soul, self-awareness, intuition, and creative imagination. Explore your self with new awareness, experiment with your inner guidance, and evaluate the results.

Self-Study: Build Rapport with Your Emotions

1 Spend at least 11 minutes or more in focused practice daily.

2 Use the See Clearly (page 41) technique first. It will bring clarity and will reawaken sensitivity, while also providing strength to handle strong or heavy emotions safely.

3 Once you feel clear and calm, allow feelings from recent events to arise. Use the SOS Method (page 42) to talk with the feelings. Listen to the answers—not in your head with thoughts but in your body with feelings.

4 Afterward, record any thoughts and feelings you had.

Ideas to Use: Principles of Emotional Liberation

We have within us a system of guidance and self-healing to handle and thrive in any situation that life gives us. This sensory system includes our five physical senses, the entire body as a sensory organ, our feelings and emotions, and our mind and its many facets, including our ability to interpret all these sensations. When these are all used consciously, we have intuition, often called our sixth sense. Emotions are an essential part of our sensory system.

This sensory guidance system protects us from harm and leads to ever-increasing well-being. It is available to all, but for most, it is not well used without correct modeling or training. But because it is our natural equipment, learning to use it is simple and safe.

Emotions are widely misunderstood and are often misused in two primary ways: by ignoring and repressing them or by reacting impulsively and acting under their direct control.

Correct use of emotions requires processing them through the intellect, with full awareness of their message, purpose, and intent, before taking action.

We will always have thoughts, and thoughts create feelings. Tens of thousands of both are generated by the mind each second. So let's get good at using them.

Mind and feelings are to serve you, your highest well-being, and your purpose. When you are under their control, life is a roller coaster. When they are your conscious control, life flows like a river.

Our sensory system takes care of us at four levels:

1 Immediate protection or need

2 Future protection or need

3 Dealing with past unmet needs or changing patterns and healing historical trauma

4 Healing our human condition and deep life lessons to produce profound Peace

Emotions are the Senses of the Soul. They are able to detect and correct how things are going for us in life as well as touch the highest realms of spirit.

Emotions Compared: The 7 Heavy Heroes and Their Gifts

The Emotion	Deals with	Its Limiting Belief (Consciousness) Is	You Learn Through	It Seeks	To Reach Its Gifts
Fear	Threat & Danger	Something's wrong Unsafe at any speed	Information & Action	Safety & Security	Peace & Bliss
Desire	Needs & Hungers	Want and don't want I gotta have it now	Attraction & Repulsion Scarcity & Excess	Contentment & Fulfillment	Joy & Serenity
Anger	Harm & Power	Who did what to whom Dog-eat-dog world Survival of the fittest	Weak & Abused or Forceful Abuser	Protection & Honor	Courage & Empowerment
Depression	Helplessness & Hopelessness	I don't know It's impossible I can't handle it	Effort & Giving up Will & Surrender	Rejuvenation & Resurrection	Willingness & Optimism
Grief	Loss & Change	I'm alone and incomplete I can't go on without it Go back to how it was	Attachment & Letting go	Completion & Wholeness	Love & Reverence
Guilt	Action & Reaction	I am wrong; they are right I am right; they are wrong Evil - Judgment - Punishment	Cause & Effect Taking Responsibility Forgiveness	Truth	Neutrality & Trust
Shame	Self-Image & Self-Worth	I am defective I am not enough	Belonging & Rejection Comparing & Competing Disgrace & Dignity	Acceptance	Compassion & Self-Love

➡ Each of the seven major emotions is specially equipped to *deal with* specific conditions in life. When an emotion dominates your consciousness, the world looks like the phrases in the third column. Each emotion helps you *learn through* the kinds of experiences in the fourth column. Each has its mission or intended outcome and its ultimate gifts, which are the higher emotions and states of consciousness—for example, Fear seeks your safety and security in order to reach its gifts of Peace and Bliss.

Chapter Three

Meet Your Emotions
Introducing the Seven Heavy Heroes

I grew up with stories of superheroes like Superman and The Flash. Each superhero has his or her own special powers, like strength, speed, or fire. It's common, with the greater evils all around, for these heroes to team up so all their powers can be used together, with each unique skill coming forward to save the day in a particular situation. Together the superheroes can take on and handle any challenge. Let's think of your various emotions in the same way, each with a special skill ideally suited for a particular type of situation. Together they have all the abilities you need to handle anything. But just like the heroes when they were young, you have to learn how your emotional powers work individually and together to take care of yourself and your world.

So far, I've shown you some new ways to understand and work with any emotion by looking at the common purpose that all emotions share. You practiced a simple process using careful awareness to get the essential information and solutions from any emotion. Now we will discover the special use of seven primary "difficult" emotions. Each of these Seven Heavy Heroes is the head of a family of feelings with many offspring or versions and variations that are forms of the main patron. Usually you feel a complex blend of several emotions that is confusing and even more difficult to respond to than a single one. The ability to distinguish each emotion when you encounter it in yourself and in others, and to then understand what it's trying to help you with, is an essential human skill that will bring you great benefits.

The ability to distinguish each emotion and understand what it's trying to help you with is an essential human skill.

The Seven Heavy Heroes

Fear brings safety, comfort, and fearlessness. It jumps fast for information and action during danger and change.

Desire leads to satisfaction, contentment, and empowered self-containment. Its hot sticky pull won't quit until you know how to take care of what you really need.

Anger is your intense protector and go-getter. Its hot strength teaches you how to use this power for the good of all.

Depression's strategy is to stop and give up so you can move on and win. Its dead dark energy forces you to relax, review, and renew until you surrender to your higher power.

Grief nurtures you to awaken and heal your heart. Its bittersweet longing dives deep within to find wholeness after any loss or change.

Shame drives you to accept yourself. You will hate or hide until you come to love all as perfect in its imperfection.

Guilt is an internal compass that uses mistakes to teach responsibility and integrity. This strict internal judge guides you to be true to your Self.

Each of your inner heroes can help you best in the situations it is made to handle. Just as sight works best to know color and touch and hearing works to help you get around a dark room, Anger is uniquely suited to protect you from harm, while Grief helps you recover from loss. Like your five physical senses, your emotional sensory system scans your situation and sends automatic reactions, called *instincts*. Our challenge is to use our human capacity to see the big picture and to act with the best long-term outcome in mind; this is the training you'll get in the pages that follow. With information and practice on the specific intent of each emotion, you can deal with those emotions intuitively, automatically, and highly effectively. In the chapters that follow, you will find a polite personal introduction to each major, so-called negative emotion. Together the Seven Heavy Heroes will give you a fluency and flexibility to understand what you are feeling, why you are feeling it, and what to do about it to feel better.

Emotions Reflect and Expand Your Consciousness

Let's start with a practical, working definition of Consciousness:

To be conscious means to be fully awake and mindful, to see reality more clearly, and to more fully understand all the consequences—short term and long term—of our actions. It means we have a greater awareness of our inner self, our external reality, and the impacts we have on the world. It also means having a greater commitment to the truth and to acting more responsibly according to what we know to be true.

> → John Mackey, cofounder of Whole Foods Market, *Conscious Capitalism*

Consciousness is a measure of awareness. There are degrees of awareness that extend from dead/none at all, through sleep and dreams and waking delusions (that of animals), to the vast range of human ignorance, to full transcendence beyond Self to Universal Consciousness. We are all somewhere on that scale, and each of us is gradually awakening as we live and learn. All history of living things can be seen as the progressive evolution of consciousness, and this evolution is occurring within you every day. As a child, your sphere of concerns was much smaller than it is today. You have moved on from many issues that were once huge and are now handled easily, but there are more complex problems that now confront and confound. As you learn and grow, your conscious capacity expands to again solve those challenges and move forward a little more. Awareness, put into action, can solve every problem. Higher consciousness brings more control, choice, freedom and happiness.

How do you grow in consciousness? Increase awareness. Your state of consciousness at any moment is the window through which you see and understand yourself and the world. You faithfully believe, defend, and promote your version of reality completely as a personal truth. But individual reality changes as consciousness grows; truth is revealed like the view through a slowly clearing fog. Although you may be aware of your pain, you may not be as clear on what is causing it or how to end it.

Emotions are a great part of your overall awareness. Knowing what you feel and why will help increase your awareness. Awakening to your emotions' sensations and messages is a way of awakening your consciousness. In fact, emotions accompany and reflect levels of awareness, or states of consciousness. My insecurity (Fear) shows a lack of awareness of my strengths. Unworthiness (Shame) means I can't see my value. Blaming (Anger) can only happen when my consciousness can't, at that moment, grasp my own role and responsibility to fix the problem. I may not want to live estranged from Love, but I can't yet see my way to accept and forgive. The clearer I am, the more able I am to handle life and live well. *Emotional awareness raises consciousness.*

Although emotions do reflect a temporary state of consciousness, please don't think of one as superior to another or a person as inferior for having any emotion. The most enlightened master will feel and use Sadness or Anger when necessary. But she won't let those feelings take over and use her. Instead, she will retain or regain clarity quickly. As Senses of the Soul, emotions continue their consciousness-raising work through all levels of awareness until you are a fully realized being. So there's no shame in Shame; it may simply be bringing you that last step to freedom. It's important to accept emotions and to overcome notions that they or we are worse/better, right/wrong than another feeling or person. The right emotion to be having is the one you are feeling. It is there for a specific purpose—to raise your awareness.

Each of the Seven Heavies has its own consciousness. This consciousness describes how the world looks when you are locked into and looking at everything through the filter of that emotion; it colors all that you see. In this state of consciousness, the emotion is in control and used only in its reactive or animal level. You will be obsessed on one or both sides of the emotion's polarities. For example, in Desire Consciousness, you are ruled by needs and are dealing constantly with having too little or too much Desire. This interlock is like a prison of the mind. But innate wisdom is always at work; there is a lesson, a particular piece of the awareness puzzle, that each limited state of consciousness is determined to unlock. Honest confrontation of your limitations through cooperation with your emotions will bring the prize. For a full introduction to emotions as levels of consciousness, see David R. Hawkins's *Power vs. Force* (Veritas, 2002) and *Transcending the Levels of Consciousness* (Veritas, 2006).

A Guided Tour of the Seven Emotions and Pride

This practice is essential when you are worried or upset and don't know what to do or when you feel like screaming, yelling, and misbehaving. When you are out of focus or emotional, give attention to the body's breath rate and water balance. Normally, you breathe 15 times a minute, but when you are able to rhythmically slow the breath to only 4 breaths per minute, you gain control over your mind. This control eliminates obnoxious behavior and promotes a calm mind, regardless of the state of affairs.

❶ *Begin with Getting Peaceful* (page xi). Tune in with the Adi Mantra and continue.

❷ *Listen Within.* This exercise can be done for 3–11 minutes any time you feel emotional or just want to sort things out. Before practicing this meditation, drink a glass of water. Place your arms across your chest and lock your hands under your armpits, palms open and against the body. Raise your shoulders up tightly against the earlobes, without cramping the neck muscles. Pull the chin back just slightly to lengthen the neck. Close your eyes. The breath will automatically become slow. After a few minutes, begin to follow the guided visualization that follows (or listen to the recorded version), staying in the same position throughout. Take a deeper breath between steps. Accept all thoughts and feelings that arise, even if different from what is suggested.

Drinking water, pulling the shoulders up to the ears, and tightly locking the entire upper area creates a solid brake that can be applied to the four sides of the brain.

❷ *Meet Your Emotions.*

a. Recall a memory of extreme embarrassment, where you wanted to run and hide or "just die." Let the thoughts and feelings flow and just watch them. Notice how you view yourself and how you feel about yourself.

b. Recall a memory of when you made some serious mistake and were perhaps caught or punished for it. Again, allow the thoughts, the physical sensations, and the emotions that arise. How is this feeling of Guilt different from the experience of Embarrassment? How are you seeing yourself now?

c.	Remember a time when you felt helpless, hopeless, depressed, not caring, or powerless. Accept and allow all those thoughts and feelings with all your senses and awareness. Compare this state of energy and consciousness, like a snapshot, with the two previous ones.

d.	Now recall an event of loss, sadness, or grief. Sit with these feelings for a few moments. As uncomfortable as you may be, do you sense greater energy available? Notice that as compared to Hopelessness, you now deeply care about the thing that you are mourning. With Grief, there is a much greater effort to cling to life.

e.	Remember an experience of anxiety and fear. Give yourself time to fully embellish the memory so that you feel your feelings clearly. This is not an enjoyable sensation, but feel how very alive your system is. Notice how you now care about something enough to preserve it.

f.	Now flash to some strong desire and craving—something you really love, want, or must have. Feel the rush of energy and allow it to flow; feel the life force. When your imagination is vivid enough, you will feel physical reactions in the body. The powerful motivating force of Desire can be intimidating and even troublesome, but can you sense that the raw energy is very enjoyable?

g.	Shift to a memory in which you really wanted something but couldn't have it. Let your frustration grow into Anger and follow it to any memory in which you were quite angry. Compare this level of energy with that of Desire, Fear, Grief, Hopelessness, Guilt, and Shame; do this briefly, as energetic snapshots. The feeling of power and anger gives you a lot to work with or to destroy with.

h.	Focus on the motivating force of you wanting to achieve, accomplish, and get something done. Follow a memory in which your efforts paid off nicely. You got what you wanted, you won, you excelled. See the various forms of reward, like praise, trophies, and other compensation. Now you've entered the state of Pride. It's an expansive feeling above all the rest. Go ahead and feel proud as a peacock, beautiful, bright, shiny. Enjoy feeling good about being you. Without leaving this feeling, can you quickly compare it with when you felt ashamed? Now quickly come back to the feeling of pride, using the memory of accomplishment, if necessary, and just see yourself on a pedestal, on a throne. Enjoy this for a moment.

i.	From this height, look down on all who are less than you in this area. You can feel even better by comparing yourself to them. Have you ever enjoyed seeing something lowly, like someone else's accident or illness or failure, and been relieved? Have you ever watched an actor doing despicable things in a film and felt grateful that you are better than that? Have you ever felt anger at another person who has more than you or is simply of a different race or belief system? Honestly view the positioning, both when you feel above and when you feel below the other person, their looks, or their accomplishments. Be honest as you see Praise and Scorn coming from you or others. Can you remember a time when someone or something made you feel elevated and great, only to later have events and opinions shift so that you were knocked off your throne and felt much worse about yourself? In all of this, you can see how very important it is to feel good about yourself, as well as the temporary nature of Pride and the price of comparing and competing.

j.   Now relax, breathe deep, and let everything go. Very slowly let your shoulders come down as you sense a feeling of relief. Come back to your grounding and your vastness and whatever else you do to create a peaceful state. Can you think of one quality, character trait, or positive attribute that you clearly know and trust about yourself? If that is elusive, what is it that people love about you or that you have heard someone appreciate about you more than once? It might be that you are caring or that you have good intentions or a good heart or that you try your best. (If you cannot admit even one, ask five people who have known you a long time.) When you have in mind something you value and do not question about yourself—which you know that no matter what or most of the time you can rely on—see yourself using that quality and the response that comes from others. Sit and allow yourself to feel this quality and feel good about yourself because of this quality that you know you are. Do you see that it cannot be taken away, that no one can successfully accuse you of not being it, that it is intrinsic to who you are? This is an example of an internally motivated pride; it is a stable basis for your self-esteem. Can you also see that you don't compare and compete (as much) with this, nor do you put down others, though you may be sorry that they don't value it as much? Feel the expansion and the freedom. "I am, I am!" Before you leave this expansive experience of your Self, which is the endgame lesson of pride, can you feel the presence of your soul? Can you feel that the truth of your being is more transparent and available to your human experience?

k.   Ask your soul this final question, "What is it you have wanted me to know about myself that I am now ready to hear?" You can ask for further clarification on the answer you hear or any other questions you wish. When you feel complete with this inquiry, be aware once more of your body and your human life sitting between Heaven and Earth. Know that this connection to clarity and spirit is always available to guide you.

To finish, take a few deep breaths and begin to move your fingers, toes and neck as you slowly open your eyes.

❹ *Capture Your Gains*. Immediately make some notes about all that you heard, including anything you might not have understood. No doubt some emotions were stronger than others. Look at the Emotions Compared chart (page 51). What emotion did you feel most intensely? What were the second and third strongest emotions that you felt? Make a few notes about the memories associated with each and anything else you have learned to refer back to as you continue your work with emotions. You may want to go to the chapter on your strongest emotion next after finishing this chapter. But first, read through "The Purpose of the Seven Heavy Heroes," especially for those primary emotions you identified, which are calling on you to help them do their work.

Ramanah's Strength of Feelings

It's hard to watch my husband of 40 years die. It took me a lot of work with my emotions to even accept that it is happening. So I had two fights going on. First was that this isn't or shouldn't be happening. Second, in that denial, I felt that I should be able to take care of him by myself. But when I hurt my back one more time while physically lifting him to the bathroom—simply unable to do it, feeling scared and angry amid my grief—I came to the limit of my ability. I could neither continue to do it all physically and emotionally nor ignore our reality. The denial became more painful than facing the situation of his inability to do anything for himself anymore and of my trying to keep things "normal."

I have always been quick to cry, and in my spiritual community, I am embarrassed to be so emotional. I felt a lot of intense feelings, but I couldn't make much sense of it all or of myself. This emotion work brought huge relief. First of all, I realized that I might not be bad, weak, or unspiritual for all my feelings. But most of all, I learned that those feelings could help me. I started doing that simple Listen Within practice for emotional balance, not just as a morning meditation, but every time I felt emotional—right then and there, when I was freaking out with Tom coughing uncontrollably on the toilet. With my hands under my arms and shoulders up, breathing, I would feel safer and more protected. The big breakthrough came when I asked the feelings what I/they needed. As clear as day, the emotions spoke back and said, "Get help with the heavy lifting." So I did. I told some friends I just couldn't do it all myself anymore. They are now helping, and we called hospice to get all that going, too. That was a huge switch to actually realize and honor my needs and to ask for help. It felt like the whole universe changed from a cold lonely place and opened up, giving me love. With that, I can handle anything.

The Higher Emotions: What about the Good Stuff?

People sometimes ask me, "You talk about all these hard emotions. What about the good ones?" Good question. First, if you look at the last two columns on the Emotions Compared chart (page 51), you'll see in the fifth column that each emotion has a job. Each emotion "seeks" some really nice things we all want more of, like safety, truth, and honor, so that we can experience the "gifts," or end results, like Peace, Trust, and Courage. So each "lower octave" emotion resonates with a "higher octave" emotion. No emotion is good or bad, though feelings certainly seem to make it so. These totally enjoyable higher emotions have no ill effects, though each has a unique contribution to the fulfillment of complete or universal consciousness.

Second, the Seven Heavies work a bit differently from the elevated emotions. Although we may always call intentionally on the power of the heavies for dramatic effect and to achieve a certain impact, we don't generally seek them out. They come unbidden and usually unwelcome when they are needed to deal with a problem and resolve a situation. The higher emotions are always there, like air; they are essential and present but unnoticed due to all the more tangible, stronger feelings. The higher emotions are felt when heavy emotions are finished clearing away anything that blocks us from enjoying life's subtler pleasures. So, dealing well with our dark feelings facilitates their work to bring us back to the light. The good stuff, like love and happiness, are our default feelings—they are always there when we are clear.

If you have felt bad for long enough, all of this will seem farfetched, but you *can* experience it whenever your mind is quiet enough—during times of relaxation, deep meditation, or sleep. Serenity, Joy, and Peace are very real experiences that are natural, normal, stable realities. They pervade the universe and are what you feel when there is nothing hindering their flow, when there is no disaster alarm ringing louder than these quiet truths. No matter how big the trauma or how long-standing the suffering, when things are cleared up, even for a moment, that background of happiness is felt.

Face it, neutrality is not nearly as exciting as Fear, and serenity is boring compared to hot Desire. Drama and commotion are games we have long lived with and that we may be reluctant to give up for Peace. Moreover, each emotion releases a distinct cocktail of glandular secretions, which the cells adapt to by increasing the number of receptor sites specific to that emotional "drink." Your cells literally develop an affinity for (or perhaps an addiction to) your predominant emotions; you come to feel a little itchy for that "normal" feeling of Anxiety, Anger, or Shame. But your body can similarly habituate to pleasant emotions. The more often you feel good, the more you will get used to it, and the more often it will naturally recur.

Every practice in this book is designed to leave you feeling better than when you began. When that happens, notice the sensations, pay attention to how you enjoy them, and remember the feeling. Just as it becomes easier to find a familiar place the more often you visit, once you feel any higher emotion, you can set it as a target destination, you can feel that way on command. This is another distinct way to use these emotions.

Religions and spiritual practices are a source of techniques designed to produce experiences like Neutrality, Love, and Joy through repeated practices that invoke those states of consciousness and their emotions. What gives ritual a bad name is when the act is done without the intention or result. If it elevates you, it is devotion; if it leaves you flat, it is ritual. But spirituality doesn't own the market—elevation can also be produced with your cat, a sunset, a flower, or a lover; any thought or thing can help you get into that desired state. So unlike with heavy emotions, which come as needed, you can go to the positive ones by choice. That is a skill worth developing, as time spent in any condition gives it stability. Every minute of insecurity or love gives it a firmer hold on your reality for you. Hence I'll mention again the importance of practice and experience.

Work This Book

As mentioned earlier in the book, to get the most results and benefits from this book, don't just read it—use it as a workbook. Along with information, you will always be given a way to experience the concepts directly for yourself through guided meditations and exercises. That is where the learning happens. The practice of my teachers, myself, and many students and clients helped to reveal everything you find here. Now it will be your personal experience to uncover your way, your truth, and your best life.

Note: If you jumped straight to this chapter, I strongly suggest that you go through Chapters 1 and 2 next. Once you understand the overall approach and the SOS Method, each of the next seven chapters that follows will guide you through the nuances of that emotion, as well as a customized version of the SOS Method. After that, you can work through each exercise in the Going Deeper sections for more help with the emotion you are feeling the most. But don't wait for a crisis. Peace time is a good time to prepare.

If you have a daily health routine of any kind, like yoga, running, or going to the gym, you know it takes time and commitment to get results. You also know that it is well worth the effort. Apply this same discipline to the practices in this book and weave them into your routine. (These practices best fit the model of a daily yoga and meditation practice.) Find at least 3 minutes a day, though 11 is better, and 31 minutes better yet. If you are new to or resistant to such discipline, I hope the inner exploration will be inviting and the results motivating enough for you to pursue the benefits.

Make a continuous study of and practice your way through every chapter. It will take at least one to four weeks to really get the experience and skills that each chapter has to offer.

Why not take a year? I promise your life will be better in ways you cannot now imagine. I can make this promise because I have observed it happen in those who are making a fuller study of this work. (Refer as well to How to Work with This Book, on page vii.)

The Purpose of the Seven Heavy Heroes

Use these summaries as a quick reference to clarify what you are feeling and why. This information is also provided at the start of each Seven Heavies chapter.

Fear, Anxiety, and Stress

When you are worried, confused, overwhelmed, anxious, scared, or panicky;
When you are threatened, in danger, or have been traumatized;
Or when you just want to create more security and stability in your life…
Fear is your friend, sounding the alarm and giving you the energy you need
To get information and take action until you feel safe, relaxed, and peaceful.
Fear ultimately opens your consciousness to realize there is nothing to fear.

Desire, Obsession, and Addiction

When you want something;
When you are hungry, needy, craving, or driven out of control;
When you feel insatiable and empty no matter what you get;
When you feel dead to desire and you live without pleasure;
Or when you want to fulfill the deepest longings of your heart and soul…
Desire pulls like gravity to feed your hungers until you are content and self-contained.
It brings the clarity to understand your needs and the tireless energy to satisfy them.
Desire leads to self-sufficiency, deep contentment, and ultimately the freedom of desire-lessness.

Anger, Frustration, and Power

When you are hurt, abused, or disrespected;
When it's unfair, something's wrong, and you can't take it anymore;
Or when you need more confidence to take action and get things done;
When you get irritated, frustrated, bothered, or fighting mad,
So you can get what you need and live comfortably with safety and honor…
Anger is your source of intense, hot energy to handle it all and make things right.
It will help you find your power and teach you how to use it for the greatest good.
Anger ultimately brings humility, which gives you access to your higher power.

Depression, Despair, and Apathy

When you are stuck or frustrated and you can't move forward or accomplish your purpose;
When you don't think you can, don't know how, can't find the power and the way;
When you desperately push harder or feel weak and give up;
When you need to stop everything and reevaluate…
Depression helps you lose interest and give up on what's not working, so you can awaken to new possibilities and approaches.
It breaks you free from attachments that no longer serve you.
Depression forces you to reevaluate your beliefs and approaches by taking away your energy and motivation to continue your old patterns.
Letting go of the old restores your energy and allows you to see life with new clarity.
Depression ultimately connects you to the Source of all power. It teaches you to let go and let the Universe do the work.

Grief and Sadness

When things change;
When something is lost or dies;
When you are heartbroken, sad, and lonely, pining for the past, longing for what you miss;
When the hopes and dreams you have set your heart on look like they won't happen;
Or when you need to get cozy and quiet to get in touch with your heart, to mend your wounds and care for yourself…
Grief and Sadness slow you down and bring a soft energy that allows you to look deep inside and feel what is most important; to know what you need to be complete and full; to move forward to getting it; to be able to adapt, change, and flow; to constantly renew and grow.
Grief ultimately opens your consciousness to love and reverence for all things that come and go.

Guilt

When you are unclear about your actions, ethics, and sense of Good and Evil;
Or when you want to learn about consequences, responsibility, and intended or unintended results…
Guilt helps you realize and rise to your highest caliber and conduct.
When you have violated a set of values or code of conduct, a painful pang of Guilt tries to stop you.
It asks you to check yourself—to reflect on the facts, recognize your truth, and correct with integrity.

Guilt returns your power to respond in your best interest. It sharpens your ability to sense the consequences of your actions, avoid mistakes and harm, or learn from them quickly. Guilt ultimately guides you to trust Truth—and that will set you free.

Shame

When you feel embarrassed, disgusted, ugly, or bad about some part of yourself;
When you are told or believe that you are different, defective, unwanted;
When you want to hide or die;
When you are abandoned, rejected, alone, and lost even to yourself;
When you've had enough and you want to rise, stand strong, and believe in yourself...
Shame shines a light on the shadows, those places where you don't live to your own standards and values.
It drives you to accept your worst, accept yourself as perfectly imperfect, and rise to your best.
When you live within your integrity, you feel comfortable in your skin.
Your identity is based on your Divinity. The ultimate lesson of Shame is unshakeable self-love.

Self-Study

Use Listen Within (page 57) as a daily practice or whenever you need it. Drink water, per the instructions.

Life Project

By going through the "tour" of seven emotions in the chapters that follow, you will become aware that some emotions are stronger than others. Reflect on which ones visit you most frequently these days. Has it always been so, or did others dominate at other times in your life? Can you correlate your life's circumstances and challenges through time to the emotions most present and to their intensity? Make a brief timeline or write a short personal history of your emotional life that matches events with emotions, their strength, and their frequency. Include all the happiness and love you experienced, too! On a timeline, you can have fun by creating a graph that tracks your relative emotional highs and lows through the years, along with key events. You are opening a study of a rich inner world—though it may have been quite painful at times, it is waiting to help you "get high."

Chapter Four

Fear
Use Anxiety to Create Peace

Fear brings safety, comfort, and fearlessness.
It jumps fast for information and action during danger and change.

The Purpose of Fear

When you are worried, confused, overwhelmed, anxious, scared, or panicky;
When you are threatened, in danger, or have been traumatized;
Or when you just want to create more security and stability in your life…
Fear is your friend, sounding the alarm and giving you the energy you need
To get information and take action until you feel safe, relaxed, and peaceful.
Fear ultimately opens your consciousness to realize there is nothing to fear.

Stress is a mess of wasted energy where health and happiness are lost. Harness your Fear to make it start working for you so it can deliver the Peace and Joy it is here to bring. This chapter takes you through a safe and supportive process to find your Strength and Courage.

Fear Is Your Friend

Desire is the emotion that fuels your positive drive to attain things, enjoy life, and advance your purpose. Its polarity is Fear, or the voice of your instinct to avoid harm and remain safe. It is primal and instinctual; it is from the animal urges in you that want you to survive. Fear's energy is quick, cold, sharp, and all about movement. Fear can activate itself in any number of physical forms: You get the butterflies, the shakes, the jitters, the willies, and the heebie-jeebies; you tremble, shiver, shudder, shake, fidget, squirm, pace. Or the action may all be in your head: Fear grips your thoughts with obsessions, compulsions, preoccupations, fixations, fluctuations. Your mind vacillates, wavers, fluctuates, hesitates. You have doubts, qualms, suspicions. I could go on and on, but you get it. These are all signs that you're experiencing Fear. The sheer volume of language we have to describe the many states and effects of Fear show how much time we humans have spent dealing with it. Fear is certainly Emotion Number One. All Stress—the great plague of our time—is Fear-based. So, if you feel it, be assured that you are not alone.

There is good reason behind all this Fear: You wouldn't be here without it. Think about how many millions of biological and environmental conditions must occur correctly and favorably each moment for you to be able to read this. Extreme temperatures, a car accident, a tiny bubble in your blood, or some random danger at your door can end your fragile life at any time. You would not have made it this far without an internal alarm to alert you when danger threatens. Fear is just that—it keeps constant watch over everything inside and out with one purpose: to keep you safe and secure. Every worry is an attempt to make things go well. If you befriend your Fear and use it well, you will have a greater chance at achieving that peace and ease you desire.

From Instinct to Intuition

Between all the real threats to your well-being and your Desire for happiness stands your very own early warning system. Fear is intended to sense danger before it strikes. Your animal instincts give you the ability to either fight or take flight. That's what you need in an immediate emergency. Your mind adds versatility, flexibility, and the ability to extend your sense of security into time—namely, the future. Safety is an immediate condition; security is a reasonable expectation that safety will continue. As fragile beings, we love that feeling—cozy, comfortable, taken care of—and this is all that your faithful Fear is after. As you've probably experienced, Fear can be relentless, until you are safe, that is.

A more sophisticated response to Fear than stress is intuition. Intuition isn't some great mystery; it's something we all share: the simple capacity to notice, pay attention, focus, and get more information. Alertness and intuitive knowing come first; Fear then supplies the energy to act on that knowing and to handle the situation until danger passes. Intuition is your personal radar to detect harm headed your way. It steers you away from injury to body, mind, heart, or soul, and it offers real solutions. Every species has built-in defenses—camouflage, a shell, speed, horns, or claws—to confront danger or avoid being hurt. But not you. You have only your self-sensory system: the ability to foresee and "sense" oncoming danger. It may come as a voice in the back of your head, as a tingly or queasy sensation, or as a nagging sort of push toward or away from something.

I have helped hundreds of people with situations in which they "don't know what to do," and I have helped clean up the damage that they didn't see coming. In all of these instances, I observed that they did hear that voice inside; they just didn't listen. They do know what to do, but they haven't learned to trust and act on that knowing. Just as understanding that emotions are Senses of the Soul changes the game by elevating what you expect from them, reframing Fear as Intuition will improve your ability to work with it consciously to get the results you want. Your work in this chapter is to pay close attention to the information always available from your internal security guard and to act according to that infallible wisdom—that is, to use your Intuition to attain relaxation.

> **Pay close attention to the information always available from your internal security guard, Fear, and act according to that infallible wisdom—that is, use your Intuition to attain relaxation.**

Fear Is a Change Agent

Have you ever been scared to commit to something you really wanted, scared stiff at the prospect of getting what you want, even paralyzed and unable to go after your dreams? A sinking ship is clearly unsafe, but what dangers lie in the dark waters? Similarly, although you may want out of a sinking relationship, something is better than nothing, right? You may stay in a dull, dead-end career for years rather than risk whatever unseen opportunity may lie in your future. The instinct to be safe has you cling to the known and to fear the unknown. Any change, whether you choose it or try to refuse it, is a move from the (safe) known into the (risky) unknown, and therefore it arouses Fear in some form. We are in times of huge change that is quick and constant, causing Anxiety and Stress to become the new normal for many of us. What's worse, it sometimes feels like change for the sake of change, without any clear reason. It can feel like we are running through rough terrain in pitch darkness—a scene from every horror movie. But Fear/Intuition can be your flashlight into that dark unknown ahead of you. With it, you can once again find solid footing. When used well, Fear kicks you out of your rut and moves you forward, so you can safely navigate change, growth, and expansion. Ironically—but as is true with all emotions—really feeling your Fear will make you less stressed, less fearful.

A Taste of Fear and Peace

❶ *Begin with Getting Peaceful* (page xi). Feel as safe and secure in this moment as you can. The more you have practiced Getting Peaceful, the easier it will come and the deeper it will be. This feeling is what Fear works to get you to.

a.   Recall an event that caused you anxiety. One may pop right up, or you might see several: sudden danger or long-lasting threats, you are lost, you don't know how to do something, you don't know what will happen or what people expect or what they will think about you or do to you. You might have been overwhelmed, confused, nervous, or outright frightened. If it is something that happened, feel the animal-instinctual reaction. If it is about what might happen, feel the urge to preserve something and avoid harm. Notice that you are dealing with some unknown. Check all of your bodily sensations: breath rate, heartbeat, tingling sensations. Notice the activity in your mind—are your thoughts racing, or has your mind gone blank? Notice the amount and type of energy in all of it. Although it may be uncomfortable, appreciate any increase in energy as more power available to you. Are your senses more awake and your mind alert, scanning for info, trying to figure things out? Refresh the memory to keep the experience strong, while also breathing deeply to remain present and in control. Trusting that all of this is here to serve you, get on top of the energy and use this power to observe. Decide that you can see and know everything, that you are bigger and smarter than this threat; you will prevail! What do you know that diminishes it? What can you do to avoid harm? Don't think; let the feelings do it for you; use the mind just to take notes. Using the power of your Fear, see exactly what must be done to handle this situation. Keep at it until you feel some relief, which indicates that you got the message Fear delivered.

b.   Now use the knowledge you have gained or imagine taking the action so you can see everything taken care of. See yourself with as much confidence, certainty, control, and stability as is there. Feel yourself calming down, being back in safety, and enjoying Peace. Do you feel a little more appreciative of Fear? Do you see its value? Do you see possibilities to use it better and the benefits to be had? Recall your attentiveness, readiness, and responsiveness, and see the benefits, the clarity, and the focus, which make you careful and cautious, effective, and strong.

c.   Now inhale deeply and hold for a moment. Then stretch your body, open your eyes, and make some notes about your experience.

Life through Fear-Colored Glasses

When Fear becomes a fixed viewpoint, the entire world is seen as a threat. Something is always wrong. Danger is expected and projected; reasons to fear are sought and found to confirm the belief. Suspicion, caution, prevention, and preemptive attacks are constant. Paranoia feeds on itself and becomes socially contagious and accepted as normal. Fear Consciousness weakens people such that they can be easily controlled by anyone offering safety. A fearful life is lived as a hunted animal; it's all about survival. Growth and expansion are limited or reversed; brief respite gained by distraction is the extent of available happiness. To what degree is this the operating truth in your mind? In the minds of people you know? In historical eras or in current culture? Gaining control of your own consciousness is the price of Peace.

Use Fear, Don't Abuse It: Our Excited Society

Fear can supply you with all the energy, enthusiasm, stamina, and joy you need to accomplish great things. It can give you the experience of your own effectiveness and help you reach excellence. Why do we so often live with less?

There's an old notion that idle hands (and minds) invite the "devil's work." This notion served the industrial revolution, but today, hyperactivity is the "devil's heyday." The itch and the twitch are the new face of the witch. Excitement, stimulation, passion, and intensity are the prized currency of our 24/7 world. It feels good to be "up," and we just can't get enough. We can choose from an unlimited number of drugs: caffeine or something stronger, ambition, or our countless, nameless fears. Excitement and Fear share the same physiology; they feel the same. Only a thought interprets the signals as desirable or not desirable. Theme park rides, thrillers, and horror movies—that is, Fear as entertainment— show how much we enjoy that thin line. Times of uncertainty and change, as well as our addiction to stimulation, propel us forward. In today's media-centric world, if you haven't checked your e-mail or followed the latest headlines within the past hour, you are out of it. This may be fun, but anything out of balance topples. These days, you might have to let yourself be "out of touch" or truly stretch yourself and take the risk of being a slacker to find your own pace. Face it—Peace is boring. Drama, trauma, and suffering are very exciting and can be habit forming.

GuruMeher's Story of Adrenaline Addiction

Ounce for ounce, adrenaline is one of the most powerful and addictive drugs you can get hooked on. I saw this in my own life when I recognized that I was a workaholic. Adrenaline was my drug of choice; ambition, excitement, drive, and fear were my ever-available dealers. It's uncool to give an alcoholic a drink, but people are happy to load you with projects to feed your adrenaline habit. It was all so exciting: I worked 75 or more hours a week at a job, I had a full two-hour daily exercise and spiritual practice, plus teaching yoga, community leadership, family responsibilities, and my own natural enthusiasm for everything in the world. What a fun ride—until the heart palpitations started. I was so busy at the time, that my whole day was one big swirl. Then I'd be sitting at my desk, and suddenly my heart would start to flutter. I am very committed to my health, and it was obvious that I needed to slow down. At that point, I had to ask myself, "Who am I without all that drive?" I had been creating a constant state of urgency in an endless effort to prove to myself I was adequate and deserving. My heart was sending a message that this was unsustainable, but the thought of not running heroically at top speed felt like certain annihilation. "Don't take away the one way I have to feel worthy!" Exhausted, I had to turn and face these fears. It was awful to feel that fear of inadequacy that was the engine of all my activity. To my surprise, however, I didn't die! I could handle that awful feeling. Then an amazing thing happened—I began to relax, deeply, and the price for that was just being willing to face my darkest fear. It felt bad, but it was so much easier than all that desperation. I saw that my ransom was to start saying no to more projects and commitments. I thought I would die of shame the first time I said no to someone who wanted me to do something. I felt like I was saying, "I can't handle that," which was my worst fear. But I lived through it and was amazed how one "no" saved me from several extra hours of weekly work for the next 5 years. That was power! It took many years to lighten my load to a level that I could manage well. But I found that doing fewer things and more of what I wanted to do meant I could handle those things much better. I could handle things—just not everything. I am a recovered workaholic, and it's an addiction that is no joke. I still work a lot. It's 6:30 a.m., and I have been writing for hours, I have a full day, and I teach all weekend. The difference is that I enjoy everything and do it without desperation or urgency; my self-esteem is not on the line. I can stop and goof off with equal satisfaction. My thanks go to all those who didn't leave when I was too busy to be present. If only I had been able to stop sooner and listen within to find the source of my Fear rather than trying to outrun it.

But the Peace at the end of that long lesson was worth it. I hope my experience can save you some time spent suffering. The work you are doing for yourself will be so worth it, too, no matter what your current situation or internal emotional climate may be. Are you committed to your own recovery? If so, work with your Fear and follow it's truth.

Lighten Your Load

Being too busy, living in overwhelm, and taking on too much, even if for the best reasons, are treated by your nervous system the same as living under attack. You may have made these choices consciously, but your body doesn't perceive it that way. People often think they have no choice but to live this way—that is, until the doctor gives them the bad news and an ultimatum. But you can make choices to change your circumstances; you can prioritize and then eliminate some responsibilities and energy commitments to free up your time and bring your life into greater balance. Challenge and sacrifice can achieve great things, but it's also possible to ignore the consequences until a lot of damage has been done. In our culture, it can be an act of Courage to make these unpopular, "selfish" choices, but it's worth it in the end. You, your family, and your community will thank you.

Conscious Recovery from Modern Life

Ideally, when something causes an adrenaline spike, you act quickly, and the danger passes. Your system then works to recover a relaxed metabolism that is energetically economical and sustainable. But when the shock is intense enough or the stressor smaller but repeated often enough, you can get stuck in high gear, always on the defense. This constant state of alert and defense depletes your energy and fatigues your nervous and glandular systems, affecting your ability to respond. The reality remains: whatever danger was there continues—Fear continues, fatigue increases, and the cycle escalates. As exciting as a busy modern lifestyle might be, your system treats it like nonstop danger. When you perceive the danger as constant and relentless, you remain agitated, shaky, and anxious; effective response deteriorates, and healthy, self-sustaining behavior starts falling apart. Recovery requires better conditions. It's a lot to ask yourself to become calm if you live in a whirlwind. Is your life arranged such that Peace is accessible? Reducing self-created and avoidable stressors is a start.

Release Fear from the Body

The sympathetic nervous system is like your car's accelerator. However, in today's world, it is wired to be constantly on and ready to jump at a moment's notice. It takes a strong, activated parasympathetic nervous system—your brakes—to maintain equilibrium and not go out of control. Another way to respond to long-term Stress is to create an outlet for this fight-or-flight mechanism. Releasing Stress through both physical activities and relaxation techniques is a necessity. Find a way to sweat every day. Do something you enjoy! Get out and get going. But be sure you balance stimulation with relaxation. I see people out power walking with their earphones on, and they look anything but relaxed or vitalized. The ideal is stimulating exercise followed by deep relaxation, which is the makeup of every Kundalini yoga class. Other options are walking in nature, spending time in beautiful and peaceful environments, listening to uplifting music, taking hot baths, getting a massage, eating a relaxing meal with calming foods and supportive friends, meditating, laughing, having fun, enjoying vacations. Whatever it is, do what inspires you. Find out which activities truly work for you by becoming aware of your immediate response, the aftereffects, and the long-term results. And then put them in your schedule!

Be Compassionate—to Yourself!

Unrelenting stimulation and ignoring what's going on are both unsustainable. Even if you ignore the situation, you'll be exhausted while still being under tremendous pressure. Eventually, a messy adjustment will be forced upon you as nature seeks to create balance in your life. It can come through an eruption, such as the destruction of a relationship or a career falling apart, or through a withdrawal into Grief and Apathy. Or your body may take over through exhaustion or illness, forcing you to rest. The compassionate, though sometimes scary, thing to do is to be conscious. Don't allow fate to determine the outcome; tune in and participate in the change. The idea of facing your Fears may be intimidating; so don't face them. Just try sitting still with them; it can even look like hiding under the covers.

Create a rapport with your Fears; start a conversation about what's happening, what's going on; share honestly how you feel. Build Trust in that relationship with yourself.

Just be still and be real with yourself. Create a rapport with your Fears; start a conversation about what's happening, what's going on; share honestly how you feel. Build Trust in that relationship with yourself. Maybe you need some compassionate nurturing, some caring encouragement, or the acknowledgment and confidence that *you* are on your own side, at last. Having others in your life give you these things helps, but only to mirror how it's done. If you can't bless yourself, you will never feel your own worth or experience your own value.

In addition to nurturing and believing in yourself, you need a second type of energy and support that can derive from Fear—strengthening and energy building, which can occur when you get yourself out of bed, take a cold shower, exercise, get to work, and feel the joy of vitality in action. Throughout this book, you will find that every idea and practice represents either nurturing and relaxing *or* strengthening and energy building, or sometimes both at the same time. Be aware of the different flavors these two opposite approaches generate, and notice that together, they create balance. You need both, but you should also begin to discover and discern which you need most at any given time: a firmer hand to get you moving or a kindhearted encouragement.

Knowing what you need and taking care of yourself accordingly seems simple enough, but then why aren't we all satisfied? I propose that it is the only way out of your suffering. Whether the issues interrupting your Peace call for minor adjustments or a major overhaul, you have an innate ability to self-repair, sort of like your immune system. Emotions are there to help remove what's bugging you, but they need your cooperation. In time, you will learn to believe in and trust your emotions; your Fear and your Intuition will become your faithful servants, and you will have solid faith in yourself. That is all the safety you need, and it produces a sweet powerful life. Whatever your story so far, that relationship of Faith and Trust that comes from knowing someone deeply and truly can be built with yourself by going inside and working things out. Let's do that now.

Breaking Fear by Facing Fear

❶ *Begin with Getting Peaceful (page xi). Tune in with the Adi Mantra and continue.*

❷ *Create a Safe Space.*

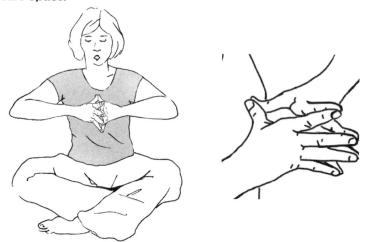

a. Raise your arms with elbows bent until your hands meet at the level of the heart in front of your chest. Your forearms make a straight line parallel to the ground. Spread the fingers of both hands. Touch the fingertips and thumb tips of opposite hands together. Create enough pressure to join the first segments of each finger. The thumbs are stretched back and point toward the torso. The fingers are bent slightly due to the pressure. The palms are separated. Fix your eyes at the tip of the nose.

b. Create the following breathing pattern:
   - Inhale smoothly and deeply through the nose
   - Exhale through the rounded lips in 8 equal emphatic strokes.
   - On each stroke of the exhale, pull the navel back sharply.

c. When you first start this practice, continue the breath for 3 minutes. As you gain strength, build the practice slowly to 11 minutes and longer.

d. To finish, inhale deeply, hold the breath for 10–30 seconds, and exhale. Inhale again and shake the hands. Relax.

e. From this place of stillness, continue into the following self-guided visualization.

❸ ***The SOS Method for Fear.*** Allow Fear to serve its purpose in you by helping it do its job. We'll use the SOS Method for working with your emotions, as introduced in Chapter 2 (page 42). This method combines the nurturing element of compassionate listening balanced with solution-oriented action required to create your own safety.

a. ***Stop and Listen.*** Let your shoulders drop, take a deep breath, be centered in yourself, and look clearly at your current experience. Slow down and let the feelings flow. It's safe to feel; the feelings won't hurt you. They are here to help. Continue breathing and feeling until you feel stable, until you feel that you can handle the feelings. At this point, the feelings will back off a bit, because they have achieved their first purpose—to get your attention. Sometimes stopping and acknowledging is enough. But when your Fear demands more of you, be willing to go further.

b. ***Find the Source.*** Ask your feelings, "What's really going on here? What's the threat? Where is the danger? What is it you want to be happening to me instead? What do you want for me?" Have Fear point you from the harm to the relief it seeks. See it all clearly. Go deeper, using each answer as the next question. Get to the bottom line.

c. ***Ask for Solutions.*** Know that you know everything and that all you need to know is right there. The Fear will be less now, because you are paying such fine attention. Don't stop; stay with the feelings; don't go into thoughts, opinions, and analysis just yet. Ask your feelings for their solution. Make it about what you can do right now. Although this may be a long-held anxiety, the present moment is the only time you can make a difference. "What is it that would make me feel safe, right now? Are larger, longer-term actions and changes in attitude needed?" Don't stop asking questions until you see it all, feeling each answer. Then use the mind to remember all that you have learned.

d. ***Take Action.*** Use Fear and its gift—the desire for Peace—to act! Let the mind figure out the details, but be sure to keep the mind obedient to the instructions from this higher source of knowing. Actions may take courage and time to carry through. Fear will be there to remind you to get it taken care of.

❹ ***Capture Your Gains.*** Make notes of anything you realized in this practice. How can you use this information to create more safety and peace for yourself?

How Fear Functions: The Fear-to-Peace Cycle

Let's assume that calm clarity and freedom from unwanted Stress is your normal baseline experience. You leave that experience only when something threatens you and disturbs that Peace. Your body, mind, and soul rush in to restore the natural order of harmony. Fear arises to take you through the problem to resolution. That pathway contains a sequence of steps, each of which is required to return to "all clear" and peacefulness. When Anxiety lingers, it is a signal that the cycle from Fear to Peace has been interrupted. A return of tranquility may be gained by understanding and completing the remaining steps. Here is the sequence:

We'll walk through the steps using an analogy from my youth. When I was a kid, we used to get thrills down on the railroad tracks, and believe me, those trains are huge, loud, and rightfully Fear inducing. So, imagine you are peacefully sitting on the tracks, enjoying the day. (It's an analogy, okay? So, what is your "train," or your threat?) The danger: You hear the whistle blow in the distance and the engine rumbling your way. Fear arises to save the day; its initial intensity depends on many factors, such as your history with trains, how close the train is, your ability to get away, and so forth. If Alertness fails because you are distracted or dull, tired, unable to feel, you won't know about the train. Alertness helps you pay better attention; you use it to gather information: "Why am I scared?" If you don't identify what is happening or the consequences, you may feel the Fear but not know why it is there. When you are confused, overwhelmed, and don't know what to do, you will do nothing, or you will squirm but not get out of the way. When you identify the problem—the train is coming, and it will kill me if I don't move—you must find a solution. The solution? Get off the tracks! But how? When? Go where? It seems so obvious, but do you see that if any of these steps is not completed, the train will continue to get closer, the danger will become greater, Fear will increase? Fear may even escalate into confusion and paralysis. Even if you comprehend it all but don't respond (you don't take any action, can't face it, won't deal with it), there is no remedy. Fear will keep ringing the alarm as the danger continues to increase (as the train bears down on you); Fear will correctly scream louder, perhaps furthering the paralysis. Taking the right action in time to reach the solution has to happen. And when it does, the train goes by, the danger passes, and you are safe. Ahh! When you recognize that the danger is indeed over, you take the time to calm the nerves and recover physically. You then learn from this experience how to avoid that danger altogether in the future. Go enjoy the day.

Fear is not the problem; the train is. But Fear persists until it has completed every step. When any part of your recovery process fails, you remain in escalating Anxiety. Your awareness of the steps and your conscious participation are all it takes to complete the cycle and rest in peace. You can discover any weak links by carefully observing yourself in the process.

Follow the Flow of Fear

Now try the cycle using your own real-life situation. Choose any fear-related situation to use with the cycle to see why past situations have not been resolved and to solve current ones. Read each step; then close your eyes to allow the feelings of Fear to take you into and through that one process. Start with the earliest time you first realized you were no longer peaceful; something made you uneasy. Walk through the memory one step at a time: Remember feeling the Anxiety? Did you pay close attention? Did you gather information, see the problem, find the solution, act, and recover? Check off each step that you completed. For any step that is not yet complete, do it right now and then move on. Any of these steps could take some time, especially in an ongoing and long-standing situation. Here are the steps with some prompts that may help.

- **You feel Calm:** If this part of the sequence is rare for you, then you need some major repair. I suggest that you use this chapter as part of a long-term recovery project that you practice daily in order to rest and restore.

- **There comes a Threat:** Whether it is slight or life-threatening, you will only know it when...

- **You feel Fear:** Learn to let Fear talk to you; it's here to help. Identify beliefs and habits that block Fear.

- **You're more Alert:** Watch how Fear wants to awaken your mind and prepare your body to act. You can't respond if fatigue, checking out, distractions, confusion, drugs, or apathy have dulled and fogged your mental alertness. Recover your clarity so that...

- **You can seek more Information:** Use all your senses, reason, and intuition to see and understand everything about the threat. This will automatically lead you to...

- **Identify the Problem:** This step is essential for persistent and vague Anxiety. Even the source of danger, and thus your Fear, is totally obvious—go deeper. What exactly is the danger, and what is it threatening? Be specific. Is it your body, reputation, future prospects? Your ability or willingness to clearly name the exact problem may be a little rusty from disuse, habits of victimization, avoidance, and suffering. But face it all honestly within yourself; it is safe to do so. If needed, get some coaching to reanimate your ability to see what's really wrong.

- **You look for a Solution:** Don't use the mind yet. Instead, ask the feelings what they require to be satisfied. Test solutions by imagining them happening and checking for the relief you feel.

- **You choose a Response:** The miracle cure won't work unless you use it. This part of the sequence begins the empowered move toward taking care of yourself. It is the first step in really dealing with it; it's a commitment. "It won't work," "That has never worked," "I can't," and other such thoughts may come to stop you. Don't let the mind shoot it all down prematurely. Even if you have no idea yet how to respond, just stand with whatever you have seen so far. If it is revealed in that clear neutral space, then that means you have heard the voice of your soul. You can feel very certain while allowing time for the mind to figure out the logistics later.

- **What you learned Handles it, or you take Action, or you Decide to act later:** It all comes down to this part of the sequence. Sometimes the clarity handles it, because you see that everything is or will be okay. Realization is the solution. When action is required, you may be able to do it immediately, or you may commit to and plan the right time to act. Whichever you choose, you will feel better already. But if you fail to follow through, your faithful Fear will remind (nag) you until it is done.

- **The Threat is Handled:** Ahh, the problem is handled; the danger is gone.

- **Safety is Obtained:** Your reward for a job well done.

- **Fear retreats:** "At ease," the sentry is told. Emotions work in the moment and are ready when needed. Fear stands down until needed again.

- **Peace and Calm return:** Relax and enjoy. But don't get bored and go start trouble. Learn to love serenity more than stimulation.

Going Deeper: Solutions to Modern Forms of Fear

Now go further to handle Fear in its various roles and time frames: immediate safety, anticipating the future, haunting memories of dangers passed, and timeless existential security.

- **A Present Threat:** Fear handles an immediate danger or shows the need to create safety.

- **A Future Threat or Need:** Imagining, planning, and preventing Fear to create security

- **A Past Threat:** Healing wounds and restoring Trust from past traumas that create patterns of pain

- **The Existential Threats:** Resolving the danger of the human condition

The vital role that Fear plays in your survival has created a huge variety of forms and special functions to best handle the many challenges you face. As with every emotion, Fear's intensity varies to match the degree of danger, how immediate it is, and whether it is in front of you or in your imagination or memory. In an ideal world, the fear you experience is appropriate to the level of the threat. However, most of us have learned to live in a constant state of high alert. Modern life generates so many repeated stressors that our sensory system begins to shut down, and we live in a timeless sense of threat. What follows is an outline of how Fear acts within the four modes of time: immediate, future, past, or existential (or beyond time). We start with a look at Fear in its most common and modern form, which we categorize as immediate, because that's how our body is responding to it: as if danger were ever-present. Recovery requires conscious, effective communication with Fear in order to achieve the safety that Fear seeks. Once Stress has become habitual, long-term strategies are necessary to restore Resilience. The Resources section on page 327 contains additional techniques for quick relief that, when practiced regularly, will help bring you back to Peace as your normal experience.

Fear and Safety: Dealing with Immediate Threat

This is your most primal form of Fear, and it is the reason you're still here. Unlike the long-term Anxiety that's experienced as immediate, this form of Fear is actually useful to you. Learning to listen and respond to it quickly and efficiently can mean the difference between life and death, or at least health and stress-related illness.

Fear addresses an immediate threat with animal instinct and gives you instant energy to either flee or fight. Fear uses strong reactions and quick responses to get you out of harm's way. When your body jumps from a sudden pain or noise, that's your automatic response mechanism; there's no time to think and no need to. Heroes say they acted in the moment without any thought at all. This role of Fear is hardwired into your body to take care of you. When you are constantly anxious or fatigued from Stress, however, you lose the ability to respond accurately and immediately. So, first, you need to get out of immediate harm's way, and then you have to work with the body to restore your Strength and Resilience. The burning house analogy works well here: First, get out of the house; then put the fire out. Later you can learn how to prevent fire so you can sleep more easily. Don't live in a burning house and wonder why you can't relax!

Living Under Attack

Situation. I often work with people living with high levels of Anxiety that seem dysfunctional and irrational. They don't know why or how to stop it. But Fear is *right* even when it's wrong. So the first thing to check for is danger. I often find that for these people, Fear really is working correctly—they are in significant danger. A battered woman is a clear example, though there are many less extreme but common situations—living with emotional abuse, digs, and degradations that may be subtle and socially acceptable but under which it is impossible and inappropriate to be calm. Economic hardship, job harassment, unsafe living conditions, unattended health issues—anything you are ignoring or avoiding needs to be examined as a very real source of Fear. If you have grown accustomed to the situation, you may not even recognize it as the source.

Solution. In these situations, there is no simple solution. There is only a clear message: Get out, deal with it, and take care of yourself now! Trying to be blissful when blind to the fact that you are in battle is unnecessary and dangerous, especially when you could get off the field. Don't suffer; get to safety. And yet the reality is that most people living in chronic abuse environments don't have the strength or resilience to act. That's why it's so important to cultivate these skills when you're *not* in danger, so that you can learn to recognize it and avoid it *before* you enter a life-threatening situation.

Here is a practice to bring alertness to your protective ability. As you do it, feel that you are here for yourself, ready and able to defend and lead yourself to safety.

I Can Handle It

This posture induces openness and fearlessness. The sounds SA-TA-NA-MA are regenerative. *Sa* is Infinity. *Ta* is Life. *Na* is Death. *Ma* is Rebirth/Transformation. These sounds describe the cycle of life. They open Intuition and stimulate the pituitary to make you calm and fearless. See Resources for research on the many benefits of Sa-Ta-Na-Ma.

❶ *Begin with Getting Peaceful (page xi). Tune in with the Adi Mantra and continue.*

❷ *Steady Warrior.* Close your eyes and relax your arms along the sides of your torso. Press the elbows to the sides and lift your forearms up until they are parallel to the ground and the hands are in front of the body with palms up. Separate the hands about 3 feet from each other so the forearms form an angle of about 120 degrees. Bring the fingers of each hand together so all 5 fingertips touch and point up. The arm position should feel very relaxed. Remove any tension from the shoulders and neck. Mentally focus at the top of the nose where the eyebrows meet. Regulate the breath precisely: Deeply inhale and then completely exhale. Suspend the breath out for 16 regular beats. Then quickly inhale and exhale again and hold the exhale out. Continue this
cycle. As you hold the breath out, concentrate at the brow point with a mental mantra. Pulse these sounds: SA-TA-NA-MA—SA-TA-NA-MA—SA-TA-NA-MA—SA-TA-NA-MA. The sounds regulate the time of the breath so it is the same on each cycle. Continue the meditation for 11–31 minutes. Finish with a few deep breaths and some light stretching. *Note:* By holding the breath out, you intentionally create a small "emergency" that excites your survival instincts and fear. The hand posture and mentally repeated sounds create a conscious counterbalance that puts you consciously in control of Fear. That's all you need to use Fear wisely and to handle any real-life challenge.

Fear and the Future

Whereas Fear's first role relies on our animal instincts, its second role is very human; it uses our cognitive mental abilities to extend safety as far into the future as possible to create security, stability, and longevity. Whenever there is enough time and space between danger and the need for action to think and make choices about how to handle it, your mind can assist intuition to enhance the outcome. The mind makes Fear less automatic and more versatile. This more complex role opens us up to greater dysfunction as well as greater opportunity. In fact, the most common and bothersome experience for most people is that, like most everyone reading this book, they enjoy the vast majority of their lives in relatively safe environments, free of immediate threats to life and limb. So why is Anxiety so common and so chronic?

A Tool that Can Play You for a Fool

The mind gives you the fantastic ability to visualize and foresee the future, so you can prepare, plan, and save up for a rainy day. That vivid, creative imagination, however, can also get carried away and work against you. The mind that can imagine and anticipate a future threat can also fabricate millions of them. A stick becomes a snake, and a deadline feels like impending doom—death even. Nothing seems safe. You can't tell friend from foe, stimulation from stress; your mind sees everything as a threat. On the other hand, fantasy can also shield you from real danger. The entire science of yoga identifies this aspect of the mind as the source of all suffering: you believe whatever you think. Because every thought has the potential to create a feeling, however, you can control your feelings by controlling your thoughts. A better thought gives you a better feeling.

Thoughts Create Your Reality

Here are several approaches to help control Fear with your mind. Unreal fears are only sustained by thoughts. *Thoughts create your reality.*

Situation. The mind churns intensely with unruly and haunting thoughts. It's out of control, and you are overwhelmed and ineffective.

Solution: Self-soothing. Don't believe everything you think! Self-criticism and negative reinforcement are common habits. I find that most people don't even realize they're doing it. Just listen some time to your own thoughts when you are stressed out. When a client of mine, who's a preschool teacher, began to actually hear all the harsh criticism she had been giving herself for 25 years—"You are so dumb, you can't do that, no one likes you"—she was shocked. "I would never talk to my students that way; it is so mean and would really stunt their abilities." She now understands why she had been so stuck and unable to move toward her dreams; this realization shed light on why she always felt so bad about herself.

To self-soothe, you first acknowledge the event and then choose thoughts that make you feel (even a little bit) better. First, *acknowledge the event.* When something hard happens, mentally or verbally acknowledge that it's happening. Encourage yourself during the challenge: "It's okay, you've done this before. I've got your back." When it is over, say to yourself, "That was really awful, but it's over now. I'm okay. I am fine." If it's a reoccurring stressor, tell yourself: "That wasn't as bad as last time. I did just fine. I will handle that even better next time. That was scary, but I am fine now." Take the time to rehearse how you would handle it better. Walk through it step by step—all the way to the end. Then use the thoughts that make you feel better. The trick is to keep trying thoughts until you find one you truly believe; you will know it by the instant relief you feel, however slight. Here are situations and suggestions to try on. Only you can find what works for you; but I, and many others, can tell you that it will work if you keep at it.

- *Write your own script.* At any moment, there are a million facts about how bad life is and a million other reasons to be hopeful. Write out those truths that make you feel strong and safe. Affirm them by reading them often. It works best when they are statements that you believe or that represent the possible—something within your reach. You can't B.S. yourself; make it real. This may come hard to you if you've spent years berating yourself; it's a new language, but you will get it because it feels *so* much better. If you don't support yourself, who will?

- *Commit to equal time.* Make a deal with yourself to give equal time to positive thoughts. For every negative, demoting, and disempowering thought, you must say a supportive, encouraging, promoting one—it's only fair. Counter each negative with a positive that you truly believe. Try gratitude for anything: it works every time.

Situation: The source of Fear is unclear or unresolvable. Most modern fear is either undifferentiated Anxiety arising out of nonurgent, non-life-threatening situations or Anxiety focused on a future event that cannot be solved until it arrives. Here are some examples: living in a hectic city, being late for something while stuck in traffic, feeling worried about whether you will keep your job, being nervous about a big interview, anticipating a performance, speaking in public, getting ready for a big date or a big exam, managing your monthly budget and paying bills, getting sick, travelling, growing old, finding love. These may not have a solution at all, or at least not one that can be acted on right away, so what do you do? When there may be no danger at all, but you feel uneasy that bad things *might* happen, what can you do?

Solution: Make Fear talk. If your mind hassles you under the influence of Fear, it's only fair that it give you the conditions it needs to get you back to peace and ease. Emotions are road signs pointing away from a dangerous curve and over to the safe side. Every warning has some positive intent. When you have vague or churning worries, make them work for you to find the positive; don't just let your mind complain! Negotiate the terms for Peace. What brings up this type of Fear for you?

Bring up an issue you have worried about—preferably one that reoccurs—and apply this *modification* of the SOS Method (page 42, 75, and Resources).

❶ Stop and Feel. When you feel anxious and unsettled, get as still and clear as possible. Use the Create a Safe Space breath (page 76) or any other breathing practice. Some people need to have a focus, like knitting or walking, to settle down. See Techniques to Bring Peace in the Resources section for more ideas. Let go of any resistance to the physical and emotional feelings; let them flow.

❷ Name the Threat. What threat is Fear trying to prevent from happening? What is the problem you foresee? What will be the result if that happens?

❸ Ask for Solutions. What does your Fear prefer (or demand) to happen? Find the positive of the negative that Fear detects and wants to protect. Every "negative" feeling is a warning directing you to a desired positive. "FIRE!" points to your innate desire for "no fire," for safety and security. Listen beyond your Fears to the positives they point to.

❹ Realize and Relax. Many times, just knowing something is all that Fear requires. You will feel greatly relieved simply by understanding the problem. Realizing you are actually just fine may be all that's needed, with no action required. But don't stop here! If action is needed, Fear will return until you handle it.

❺ Take Action. From the information you discover, do all that you can. Find another route, call the airline, get whatever help is available. Deal with the situation within your control until it is as good as you can make it. That is Fear's endgame.

Fear, for a Favorable Future

I realized I had distanced myself from my emotions, as well as from others in social situations who are emotional. I have been uncomfortable with emotions, my own or anyone's, and I am always controlling myself not to feel or express—all out of fear. Now I speak to my fears every day. I let them know, "I've got this! I will never let you down!" When I pay attention to the needs of my fear, all of a sudden, I am not fearful of my future. The problem I was having with my hips since last summer went away soon after I began confirming the trust in the process of the universe I'm feeling. I'm stepping into the future with ease and joy. My next task is to be fully present, to feel and express myself without fear in each moment.

→ *Paula K.*

Situation: Obsessive thoughts. The danger is out there, possibly. There may be nothing to be done about it now, but you may waste a lot of energy and generate a lot of Anxiety with your mind's creative what-if fantasies. Use this to your advantage by being mentally prepared. For example, the woman next to me at the airline check-in counter was told that she may be checking in too late to make her flight. She immediately went white and said, "Oh my God, I am having a heart attack. I have to be there on time to... ." She began breathing fast and shallow, saying how dire it all was. I felt her pain as she went over and over how bad it all would be if she were late. Fear could have helped her solve this possible threat, but she was stuck in "What if?"

Solution: Worst-case/best-case scenarios. When your mind gets stuck on a problem that it can't really solve now, it will churn, causing a great deal of Stress. Imagining all the bad that might happen is the mind's attempt to deal with the future. By answering the what-if's with solutions so you are ready if and when the time comes, however, you allow Fear to do its job. "The worst case is I miss the plane. Then what? I have to catch the next one. What will that involve? I will miss a meeting, but I can call and notify them. I may lose face or lose their business, but I can apologize and make it up to them. I could lose my job. Then what? I could end up out on the street. I could die!" You may not need to go that far, but pain and death are the endgame of your every worst case. Any of these thoughts may actually begin to bring relief. Missing a plane is not so bad compared to death.

Use your mind's creativity to take advantage of every threat by turning it into an opportunity. Isn't that a better use of your mind and time than fruitless worry? When s*** does happen, and it will, entertain the "best case." Take your mind's worst fear as a given. Accept the painful thought that you might lose the job, the plane, the friend, or whatever you fear. Just try it on. Then solve it. "What would I do in that worst case to make the best of it?" The power of the mind to reach into the past and future, to move as fast as light, can be controlled to innovate and improve, to rise from the ashes. When the mind is like a zealous dog jumping up and nipping at you, throw a ball for it to chase. When you give it a specific problem to solve, it becomes gainfully engaged in what it does best—that is, strategizing to take care of you. Then Fear can subside. As often as a protective thought arises, match it with a reassuring possibility—a positive thought—even if you have to do that every 2 seconds. Wishful thinking won't do it; you will be relieved only by your own truly believed thoughts. Keep trying until you feel the relief. Remember, your Fear wants safety; use the mind to create safe scenarios given any bad situation. Like a good parent, Fear just wants to know you will be okay!

Fear cannot insure your future safety, and it does not require that safety in order to leave you alone. It is satisfied knowing that you are aware and able to handle whatever comes. This exercise gives your mind both a plan and the assurance that you are ready to take care when necessary. Once you trust in yourself, that you can and will do your best as things unfold, you can move out from under the shadow of what might happen.

Situation: Overwhelmed and paralyzed. Sometimes you may feel that you don't know what to do, you can't handle it, it's impossible. You feel small, and the world, the situation, the challenge, the forces against you seem large. But this is all a fabrication of your mind, a debilitating belief; it's a lie. The universe is designed such that you are always a match to the environments. Your survival and success are always accessible. But when you *feel* weak, you act poorly or not at all, and you lose. Your belief becomes validated.

Solution: It's all about voltage! Get the current flowing to jumpstart your heart's capacity for courage and action. A simple physical and mental adjustment can revive your effectiveness. In the Ready to Respond activity, you first use the Steady Warrior, which brings the right balance of strength and clarity under fire. It returns your power and confidence within a challenge to bring you into control. It strengthens your capacity to act consciously, respond alertly, and be steady. With this clear head, you can be Ready to Respond!

Ready to Respond

❶ Begin with Getting Peaceful (page xi). Tune in with the Adi Mantra and continue.

❷ Steady Warrior. Practice the Steady Warrior (page 83) for 3–11 minutes.

❸ Modified SOS Method. Sit silently as you use the modified SOS Method as applied to the situations described in this section.

a. **Stop and Feel.** Get comfortable. Breathe slowly and deeply for a few minutes while focusing on your sensations, without staying fixed on any one. Feel grounded and safe, and then feel vast and connected. See and feel your daily life and your present situation. Can you feel or see evidence of Fear in healthy and repressed forms? Can you see yourself ignoring, discounting, or distracting yourself from the Fear messages? Allow them to rise and settle into the feelings; just let them be felt.

b. **Name the Threat.** Once you have some stability in the feelings, ask them what is threatening you. What specifically is threatened—your body, income, dignity? Suppose the feared thing happens. Ask what will be bad about that, what will happen then. Make your Fears clearly spell out all the downside results it wants you to avoid.

c. **Ask for Solutions.** Ask what Fear wants from you, what you need to know, what it wants you to do. Can you begin to hear or feel solutions? Ask, "What needs to happen for you, my Fear, to be satisfied, to relax again? What will maintain my peace and calm well-being?"

d. **Realize and Relax.** The mere thought of these questions brings relief. Write the answers down without question or rejection, without knowing how you could do them. Your soul has spoken, and you'll want to record its truth.

e. **Take Action.** You'll feel relief, but if action is called for and you don't act, Fear will return until you do act to remedy the situation.

Enjoy the results of greater ease. Relax and let the peace in!

Jillian's Calm within the Storm

I have been feeling a lot of fear about my Dad being so ill and feeling afraid that he might die soon. The guided meditations helped me a lot. First I had a very physical reaction. I felt very cold, and for a short time, I couldn't catch my breath and kept crying. As I experienced this and let it wash over me as you suggested, the intensity lessened, and a feeling of calmness came at the end. I have felt less anxious about his illness and more centered since then.

Fears from the Past

Remember, Fear just wants Peace for you. In the present, we showed how Fear can get stuck in your body, but you can release it. In the future, we demonstrated how Fear works in your mind and how you can take conscious control, using the mind to serve Fear's preventative purpose. In relationship to the past, Fear gets stuck in your subconscious, where it can haunt you with memories of every past threat, crisis, and injury.

The subconscious is a huge secret vault containing impressions of everything you've seen, felt, or imagined. Fear uses this vault as a reference library to perform a "background check" on current events and to gather information to keep you safe. Here is an example of your subconscious: "This man you are talking to seems nice enough, but it was a man who hurt you when you were 6, and another broke your heart at 16, and that mean boss you had last year was also a man, and here are 327 horror stories involving men, so be on guard with this guy." You have a powerful capacity to learn from the past in order to keep you from any similar harm now or in the future; however, even though the subconscious is vast and powerfully influential, it is not smart. It is a primitive recorder of events; it doesn't interpret them. Without the conscious assimilation of a memory into your current reality, you remain stuck in subconscious patterns and fears. Only the conscious mind, controlled by the frontal lobe, can sort out the valuable lessons of the past and apply them to your advantage today. Until memories are processed consciously so that the past and present are distinct and serving each other, your Fears will be hypervigilant. You will feel constantly and irrationally unsafe and unable to handle things, which makes you avoid the things you want and need to do.

Until memories are processed consciously so that the past and present are distinct and serving each other, your Fears will be hypervigilant. You will feel constantly and irrationally unsafe and unable to handle things.

We all have a collection of events and issues we haven't dealt with. Some are like chores on your to-do list that you haven't gotten to yet, but they aren't that urgent (though they will become urgent given enough time—the noise your car's been making, the pain in your tooth that you haven't made time to look into yet). Others are like e-mails piling up in your inbox—some marked urgent—that you are dreading and avoiding because you know they will be uncomfortable or will involve issues yet to be resolved. Some are events you could not or did not deal with at the time; things that didn't feel right but that you didn't know what to do with at the time. And there are millions of small insults or threats and bothers that you didn't notice at the time. These are all clamoring to be addressed, and they will remain there until you take time to read the mail and get up to date with what's going on. The SOS Method can help you break the pattern. However, with long-held, unresolved Fears, sometimes we have to go deeper.

Rebuilding Trust

When you were a child, you had nowhere near the ability to take care of yourself that you now have. You were much more vulnerable to danger, and you depended on "the big people," your caregivers, to provide safety. Any memory, *even from yesterday*, is from the perspective of the earlier, less capable, less secure you. When you use memory to gather more information about how dangerous something happening now might be, you don't get just the facts; you also get all the fears and anxieties of that earlier version of yourself, all compounded with your positive mind's unique ability to expand on those anxieties. Danger is always gauged by how big the threat is compared with your ability to handle it. When you get scared today by a situation reminiscent of something you faced at a more vulnerable time, you regress; that person with that consciousness from that time period takes over. Your subconscious doesn't know you are older and wiser now; only your conscious self can intervene.

Unresolved Issues Overload the System

When too many things remain unresolved, you stop listening and become overwhelmed and confused. Unaddressed fears can be like listening to a crowd of people all yelling at you at the same time. All of the noise and clamor just becomes an echo chamber. You may need to take the time to let them all speak so they are satisfied, so they can unload their frustration of trying to protect you. Then they can quiet down so you can have a productive discourse. Just like with your e-mail, you first sort out the junk so you can identify the real task, figure out what's really important, and then make it more manageable. Start addressing items one by one until you are current and everything is taken care of—until *you* are taken care of.

Clear Old Fear

It's not that your Fear isn't working; it's that you are not listening or acting. Here's an amazing practice to focus some quality time on your protective thoughts and feelings to relieve the pressure. Listen to your protective Fear, dump past memories that aren't serving you any longer, clear any strong feelings you've been avoiding, and offload the toxic buildup of unheard and unheeded fears from the past. When all the old "unread mail" is cleared out, you will be able to distinguish current messages from old and now unreal ones. Apply yourself fully to this conscious confrontation!

❶ *Begin with Getting Peaceful (page xi). Tune in with the Adi Mantra and continue.*

❷ *Dump Anxiety.*

a. Sit straight in an easy cross-legged pose. Make a cup of your hands with both palms facing up and the right hand resting on top of the left hand. The fingers will cross over each other. Put this open cup at the level of the Heart Center. Elbows are relaxed at the sides. Keep your eyes are slightly open, looking down toward the hands. Inhale deeply in a long steady stroke through the nose. Exhale in a focused stream through rounded lips. Feel the breath go over the hands. *Let any thought or desire that is negative or persistently distracting come into your mind as you breathe. Breathe the thought and feeling in and exhale it out with the breath.*

b. After 11–31 minutes, exhale completely and suspend the breath out as you pull in the navel. Concentrate on each vertebra of the spine until you can feel your spine all the way to the base, as stiff as a rod. Then inhale powerfully, exhale completely, and repeat the concentration. Repeat this final breath 3–5 times. Then relax completely.

❸ *Capture Your Gains.* What happened during this meditation for you? What did you learn? You will know whether you need to do this daily for a few days or even up to 40 days. Most people feel relieved immediately afterward. When you feel noticeably better most of the time, it means you are coming into real time with your awareness of

Danger. Fear can now address the present more effectively, as it is unclouded by the past. Fear is so instinctual, and your protective mind is so capable. Whenever I have worked with highly anxious people who are not taking care of themselves well, I find that the equipment is all working, but they are either not hearing or not responding to the messages that are there for them. This exercise will help you clear the past and reset the present for a more effective and fear-free future.

Christina's Breakthrough

Christina is a bright and powerful woman in her 40s. She's never been in a long-term relationship, though she has always wanted to be. She remembers being 5 years old and crawling up on her beloved grandfather's lap. But this day he was drunk. For some reason, which she still doesn't understand, he yelled at her and slapped her so hard she flew across the room and hit the wall. Since that day, she has avoided getting close to a man. Physical contact and dating are okay, but when the emotional depth she felt for her grandfather arises, her 5-year-old mind takes over, still firmly entrenched with the protective belief she adopted that fateful day. That 5-year-old consciousness doesn't have the power, the verbal skills, or the protective boundaries that she has today. Instead, the survival directive of her 5-year old subconscious finds a clever way to end the relationship and the threat, while her current consciousness is sad it didn't work out.

I had Christina meditatively relive this painful episode from so long ago while also holding an awareness of her present mature, capable adult Self. She said and did things to create safety and positive outcomes that she couldn't do at age 5, but that she might do if it had happened today. She imagined not climbing up into his lap in the first place. On another run through, she got up and slapped the living hell out of him. Standing over his shaken body, she said in no uncertain terms that he would never ever do that to her or anyone again. A third solution was to love and nurture herself, assuring herself that though she is small now, she will grow into a powerful woman who deserves love and support, and that she will be able to apply all she has learned over the years about men and know how to be treated well. Each of those solutions, when used in appropriate ways, helped her feel safe with men today. Once she had the tools, she tested them in real situations, and they always worked! Once there was confidence in her ability to be in love and to be safe, it began to happen. When you trust you to take care of you, you can relax and be happy.

Using Fear to Heal the Past

To satisfy Fear and create Peace, you must guide the mind away from the impossible task of changing the past and of using the event to create safety now and in the future. You can heal painful memories through an empowered confrontation of the past. Your consciousness is capable of creating internal and external conditions that make you safe from that ever happening to you again. You will become complete, healed, and whole. But confidence comes with practice. Remember, a wound is healed when its lessons leave us wiser and stronger.

Replay and Roleplay

❶ *Begin with Getting Peaceful (page xi). Tune in with the Adi Mantra and continue.*

❷ *Paranoia Flush.*

a.

b.

a.   Sit in a meditative, yogic posture. Stick
      out your tongue—not all the way; just relax the tongue. Use the diaphragm
      to strongly inhale through the mouth over the relaxed tongue. Feel afraid
      as you breathe heavily from the diaphragm. This heavy, deep breath from
      the diaphragm is called Paranoia Breath. Continue breathing in this way for
      1½–3 minutes.

      Feel afraid! Breathe heavily from the diaphragm. If you do this breath about
      20 times a day, you shall never have nightmares. If you practice this breath,
      two things will never hurt you. One is hysteria; the other is paranoia. You
      usually only do this yogic breath in a natural emergency, but I am asking
      you to do it in a conscious emergency. I want it to be done by the pull of the
      diaphragm. When paranoia hits you, hit it with this breath. This is the time to
      really let yourself feel Fear!

b.   Open your mouth and begin a strong diaphragmatic breath, pulsing at about
      2 complete breaths per second through a rounded mouth. Breathe very
      quickly and forcefully for 30 seconds. Regain your confidence and recover
      your strength now.

c.   Bring your ring finger and thumb together on each hand. Keep the other three fingers straight and open and stiff. Circle the hands around each other in front of the chest. Only the fingers move over each other; the wrist remains straight as the entire forearms participate. Move as fast as you can for 4 minutes. To end, inhale deeply, close your eyes, and interlock the hands palm to palm, with the fingers holding the back of the other hand at the center of the chest. From this place of stillness, continue into the self-guided visualization.

❸ *Save Your Self.*

a.   Choose an incident from the past that disturbed you. Replay it a few times and just allow the feelings and thoughts that arise.

b.   From your current perspective, which is older and wiser than even yesterday's consciousness, use your information to gather all the fears associated with the incident. Explore how much you did or didn't see the danger coming. Don't judge. Just observe, as a curious scientist would, in full awareness of all the data, including feelings. Just replay the tape as you watch and learn.

c.   Rewrite the scene based on what you have seen and learned. How would you like it to go? How would you experience it differently now? What could you have been aware of and acted on earlier? See the movie now, maintaining an awareness of all you have learned since then in order to handle it better. Try several different outcomes, from the outrageous and fantastic to the practical. Creatively explore all the possibilities and see them play out just as you wish. Assume the role of your strongest, wisest, most skillful Self and let that guide you to several ideal outcomes. This "rehearsal" can open a new pattern of behavior.

d.   Record the best practical possibilities to come from this exercise.

e.   Experiment with these practical possibilities—find easy situations first and then try new behaviors. These new behaviors will become available to you the next time something more intense occurs. Keep using this same process as soon as possible after an emotional or fearful event to remain conscious and aware of new perceived threats.

❹ *Capture Your Gains.* Write down what happened in your meditation. If you did not find a safe and satisfying resolution to the story, it may take more time. If you weren't able to translate those solutions into current-day possibilities, some coaching may help you see the connection. Athletes do this exercise after a game—they replay the tape to learn and improve. The idea is that your consciousness always knows what you need; it always knows how to handle things. When you use your current awareness and intelligence to solve an earlier problem, you learn a valuable lesson that can work in all similar situations, present and future. Replay, then Foreplay, then Roleplay. Keep trying out and trying on your new moves until you can handle anything and everything.

Lisa Gives Her Fear a Lickin'

I have lived with plenty of fear, but I really understood what is must be like to live in high anxiety when Lisa said, "You know that feeling of standing on the edge of a very high cliff? I feel that all the time." Here is her story of how she found some relief.

"I have always felt unsafe with and bullied by my father, from earliest memory to today as an adult. I recalled a specific memory of fear—being a small child in a rowboat with my dad. I was so frightened out in the water. Instead of understanding he got really mad at me. He kept trying to convince me it was safe, and he just got more upset as I kept crying. He then angrily threw both oars in the water to show me how safe we were. I went into panic and can now see how hurt and unloved I felt on top of feeling unsafe. This memory instantly dropped me right into my familiar everyday fear. But from my current viewpoint of safety, I could feel something new: Anger! I was pissed! I think it was there even then, and it has been hiding under my sweet smile every day since. Feeling grounded and in a safe emotional place before engaging the memory helped me to not be intimidated by this strong emotion.

"When I imagined an alternate ending from the perspective of an adult, when I imagined what I would do differently today, I instantly heard my soul laugh, and a great image appeared in my head. I saw myself on the boat with my dad, but this time I was all grown up. Mentally, I picked up one of the paddles and hit him with it! 'Take that,' my soul said. 'That's what you get for scaring a little kid; now row me back to shore!'

"Today, when I am feeling powerless in a situation at work or in my personal life—which happens all the time—I close my eyes for a moment and mentally pick up a paddle and whack the person who is acting like a bully. I always feel much better afterward. That feeling of power is helping me to have the strength to stand up for myself more, to speak up and say what I need to say."

The Human Condition: Fear's Soul Role

The highest function of Fear is to make you look at life's biggest questions, resolve your Fears at the deepest level, and come to terms with the human condition of impermanence. Call it existential healing. Facing Fear—or rather working with it—will bring you to the source of all safety. Death is the mother of all fears. When death and all impermanence are embraced, security comes from allowing and enjoying things to be as they are. When this happens, no harm can touch you; there is nothing wrong—no matter what. It all appears as Love. This is the highest state of consciousness. It is not created or sustained by beliefs; rather, it is grounded in direct experience, the foundation of true spirituality. It is nice to think and say that God will take care of you, but the litmus test comes in a crisis.

> **The highest function of Fear is to make you look at life's biggest questions, resolve your Fears at the deepest level, and come to terms with the human condition of impermanence.**

Fear Leads to Fearlessness

At every level, Fear is acting to protect something and to bring safety. Like all emotions, it serves the greater process of evolution, as well as individual human progress. It first helps the animal survive; it then pushes you further to extend security and thereby increase serenity. In its ultimate role, Fear helps expand your consciousness beyond the limitations of the body and this particular lifespan so you can experience yourself as something much greater.

Try to fathom the currently known universe: billions of galaxies created from nothingness billions of years ago. On our 4.5-billion-year-young Earth, there are about 9 million different species and 7 billion people, all of them continually coming and going, changing forms long before and after you have borrowed this tiny collection of atoms and breathed your allotted number of breaths that you call "my body, my life." From this grand perspective, our individual identities are no more than a passing drop of mist. Once these facts are accepted, what might at first appear to be an existential crisis becomes entirely liberating— you are part of it all, and that's not small. Seen impersonally, the atoms and energies you use are not yours; instead, they belong to life itself. In this consciousness, there is no longer anything to protect; so Fear is no longer needed! Safety is in the very structure of things. Matter and energy cannot be destroyed; they just change forms. It is attachment to the form that generates what we call Fear. Release the attachment, and you release the Fear.

I'm not saying that mere words will take you beyond all worries. But many souls have reached a state of consciousness and then left clues that became systems and religions for others to be able to reach and enjoy that same consciousness. Fearlessness may seem a spiritual artifice to one who is currently living in terror, but it is the endgame of working with your Fear. The question is, how do you get there?

First, you must deal with what's right in front of you. The Senses of the Soul will always lead you to the business at hand. Through action, you grow toward recovering your Trust in yourself and then on to Trust in all there is. Expand your perspective, think vast, relate to infinity, and wrap your head around timelessness. This is why we invented God! That belief gives us a handy way of imagining and relating to these qualities. Then, "in His image," we make the leap of seeing ourselves as having these same attributes. Highly effective spiritual and meditative techniques have had more "clinical trials" over thousands of years than any modern methods of handling stress and mental or emotional trouble. In my experience, there is nothing better than "spirituality" to accomplish the goal of Fearlessness. But whether it's through spirituality, science, nature, or love, you must reach beyond yourself and your human limitations. The results will be deep levels of "peace that passes all understanding", which is undisturbed by circumstance. This is the status of saints, and we are all equipped to reach it.

Empty your mind of all thoughts.
Let your heart be at peace.
Watch the turmoil of beings,
but contemplate their return.

Each separate being in the universe
returns to the common source.
Returning to the source is serenity.

If you don't realize the source,
you stumble in confusion and sorrow.
When you realize where you come from,
you naturally become tolerant,
disinterested, amused,
kindhearted as a grandmother,
dignified as a king.
Immersed in the wonder of the Tao,
you can deal with whatever life brings you,
and when death comes, you are ready.

→ **Tao Te Ching: Twenty-Two, Lao Tsu**

Fear Means You Have Forgotten

At its deepest level, Fear reveals our priorities: we are wrapped up in earthly things and have, in that moment of Fear, forgotten the bigger picture. The vastness of the universe shows us that we are the deathless nature of our spirit. Fear can be a reminder to open our awareness to all-that-is, beyond the moment. Expanding the consciousness or point of view is an antidote to the natural fear of death. When the spiritual practice of remembering God with every breath is achieved, there is truly nothing to fear. Saints and noble warriors who achieve this state are remembered as heroes and saviors. Described various ways in the different traditions, this state has been called "Trust in God," "dead while alive," "heaven on earth," "Fearlessness," and "conquering death." Healthy Fear still operates, even for those of the saintly persuasion, but it functions from a place that is deep and unmovable, a foundation that never loses touch with Love. This reality is available to us all. This is our destination and our destiny. As you work with your Fear, be open to this level of consciousness, and it will begin to transform even the most intractable fears.

A Stress Litmus Test

Albert Einstein said, "The most important decision we make is whether we believe we live in a friendly or hostile universe." At any moment, we make a choice to think, feel, and believe that something is going to go wrong or that all is well. The first choice is the source of all your Stress, whereas choosing the latter produces Peace. The difference in the stress levels that go with these two beliefs is like day and night. How friendly or hostile you experience your world depends a lot on your history: trauma creates a protective fearful stance, whereas loving environments create Trust. It would be so nice to relax, believe that we'll be all right, and trust in God—but we don't.

However, you are not confined to past or present conditions. Both types of experiences—Heaven and Hell—are always available. Regardless of circumstances, your perception of them is yours alone. This is not wishful thinking; rather, "There is nothing either good or bad, but thinking makes it so," (William Shakespeare).

Moving From Fear to Trust

Insecurity and Trust are mental habits based on your life's experiences. Thoughts and habits can both be changed. Trust can be attained with focus and repetition. Here's a practical approach to moving from Fear to Trust using thoughts to change your consciousness.

Fact: We are vulnerable and subject to pain and death. How we confront that vulnerability is a choice. There are two states of consciousness from which we see the world and from which we base all other beliefs and actions:

- **Deprived:** "Something's wrong. There's not enough. Help me!"

or

- **Provided for:** "I'm okay. It's going to be fine. All is well. I am loved. Things will work out."

Check out this fact for yourself: First, dwell upon the thought, "I am deprived." Observe how you feel; get in touch with the sensations in your body. Now think, "I am provided for." Notice the change. Get familiar with these two beliefs and how they show up in your mind and in your body. Fear, Anxiety, and all other Stress result from deprived thoughts. So when you feel those emotions, you know that your consciousness has narrowed. Having recognized that, find your way back to feeling provided for. Every negative, fearful thought carries with it the opposite reality, and you have the power to generate that thought, too.

"Deprived" Thought	"Provided for" Thought
I can't do it.	Well, I guess I have made it this far okay.
It won't work.	It worked out before.
I'm scared.	What's the worst that can happen?
They hate me.	But Mom loves me.
Mom abandoned me.	But I'm safe and taking care of myself now.
I might lose my job.	I'll find a better one.
He left me.	I deserve someone better.

Deprived No More

This practice opens the Heart Center and the feelings of the positive Self. It is a gesture of happiness. It has a great history and is said to have been practiced by many great and wise spiritual leaders, including Buddha and Christ. The hand mudra has become a symbol for blessing and prosperity.

❶ *Begin with Getting Peaceful (page xi). Tune in with the Adi Mantra and continue.*

❷ *All Is Well.*

a. Sit with an erect spine. Curl the ring finger and little finger into each palm. Bend the thumbs over the top those fingers to lock them into place. Keep the first two fingers straight. Bring the arms so the elbows are by the sides and the hands are by the shoulders, with the ring and little fingers of each hand pointing straight up. Bring the forearms and hands forward to an angle 30 degrees from the vertical. Press the shoulders and elbows back firmly but comfortably. The palms face forward.

b. Close the eyelids. Roll the eyes up gently and concentrate at the Brow Point—at the top of the nose, where the eyebrows would meet. Create a steady, slow, deep, complete breath. Mentally pulse rhythmically from the Brow Point out to Infinity the sounds Sa-Ta-Na-Ma. Practice for 11–62 minutes.

c. To end the mediation, inhale deeply and exhale 3 times. Then open and close the fists several times. Relax in silence. From this place of stillness, continue into the self-guided visualization.

❸ *Guide Yourself into Provided.* Sit still and work with your Deprived and Provided thoughts (page 102). Think of a common, Stress-oriented conversation that goes on in your head and respond to each deprived thought with an all-is-well thought. Because these positive thoughts feel so much better, in time you will choose them. Choices become habits. These two types of thoughts and the distinct emotional states they produce need not be dependent on circumstances. We often operate as if "something out there" will make us feel safe, and if we have enough positive evidence, we'll someday begin to trust God. In this way, we make ourselves fragile and subject to and dependent on the whims of changing conditions. But there is far greater power in self-determination and the attitude that "all is well" no matter what. The truth is, there are rich, beautiful people who feel lacking, and there are fully contented homeless people. So begin by not believing everything you think. Rather approach this as a game that you can win once you find a way to truly feel that all is well.

❹ *Capture Your Gains: Scarcity to Abundance.* Did you experience your ability to make the switch from deprivation to abundance instantly from within? Thoughts, feelings, and peace shift instantly. Can you tell the difference between the two beliefs and when you are having each? What percentage of your thoughts each day are deprived versus provided for? Check in as frequently as you can during the day to see which belief rules. When "something's wrong," practice switching to something that is also true. You'll know it by a feeling of relief. When this becomes your habit, your consciousness will have risen beyond Fear into Fearlessness.

> Don't go out and become a victim, Go inside and become a master.
>
> ⤳ Yogi Bhajan

When you search outside for help, answers, or salvation, you are a beggar. When you look inside for what you need, you are the master of your domain.

Becoming Limitless

Whenever we transcend the perpetual back-and-forth of duality to reach unity, we find rest, stability, and peace. One of the great threatening polarities is "all or nothing." We can't handle everything, but its opposite—nothingness, emptiness, the void—means annihilation Neither can be avoided, but Fear serves to resolve the conflict by unifying the two. Whenever you face a Fear, you stare into possible harm and the end of something. Every time you close your eyes, whether to meditate, sleep, or die, you face that darkness.

Getting to the Zero Point: An Oasis Within

Scary at first, each form of emptiness brings rest and relief. Nonexistence becomes comfortable and then enjoyable. You discover that there in the nothing lies everything. It's one of the truly grand paradoxes, and to experience it is transformative and liberating. With no limitation, you expand infinitely but without burden, because it brings nothingness in its wake. I invite you to discover for yourself how becoming zero fills and satisfies. I hope this exercise helps you experience it for yourself.

❶ Begin with Getting Peaceful (page 105).

❷ Fearless Heart. Either close your eyes or look straight ahead with your eyes one-tenth open. Place the left hand on the center of your chest, with the palm flat against the chest and the fingers parallel to the ground, pointing to the right. Touch the tip of the right index finger with the tip of the right thumb. Raise the right hand up to the right side, as if giving a pledge. The palm faces forward, and the three smaller fingers not in the "OK" position point up. The elbow is relaxed near the side, with the forearm perpendicular to the ground. Concentrate on the flow of the breath. Regulate each bit of the breath consciously. Inhale slowly and deeply through both nostrils. Then suspend the breath in as you raise the chest. Retain the breath as long as possible. Then exhale smoothly, gradually, and completely. When the breath is totally out, lock the breath out for as long as possible. Continue this pattern of long, deep breathing for 3–31 minutes. Inhale and exhale strongly 3 times. Relax silently. From this place of stillness, continue into the self-guided visualization.

❸ Go to Zero.

a.   See the cloud of thoughts and memories, the push of Fear and the pull of Desire, the subconscious stew that drives you to go, go, go; running a mad race, trying to be someone, to do, do, do and deal with everything. Me, me, me. Take it to the limit of all effort, commotion, and chaos. Full, full of everything. Take it to the peak of totality.

b.   Now explode in a big bang that clears away everything. Nothing but black, restful emptiness is left. Be weightless, empty, free. See nothingness. No thoughts, just pure consciousness, as you take in the experience of pure existence with no urge at all. Peace, ultimate rest. All is complete. Perfection.

c.   Enjoy this state as long as you like, then inhale deeply and stretch to come back to activity.

In the Getting to the Zero Point exercise (as in other similar exercises), holding the breath excites the primitive urge to survive, which arouses emotional force that is designed to take action. This force is met with signals from your conscious command center—the neocortex—saying that everything is fine and you have it under control. The struggle for control is engaged, giving you a controlled opportunity to train both parts of the brain to listen to *you!* This training will serve to keep you cool in times of crisis and to reach an elevated state of Peace and Bliss when all is calm—which was the Soul's goal for you all along!

To be all and nothing, alpha and omega, is the endgame of human experience. It is described in as many ways as there are beings who have experienced it. It is an ability to rise above the pressures of time and circumstance and see that everything is taken care of and as it should be. This liberated state of consciousness is available to everyone. It may take training and practice, but it is so worthwhile. In that emptiness, you will find everything.

> Soul receives from soul that knowledge, therefore not by book nor from tongue.
> If knowledge of mysteries come after emptiness of mind, that is illumination of heart.
>
> → *Rumi*

The Gifts of Fear: Security, Intuition, Peace, and Bliss

As we've talked about throughout this chapter, Fear brings great gifts if you will but cooperate and cultivate them all. It starts with awareness, an alertness to whatever threatens your peace. It gets practical with action to create safety. It extends security through intuition to avoid problems before they start. It teaches self-defense lessons from past dangers. And it shines a light on every dark corner of the universe so there is no place of danger, no reason to fear; you become limitless in scope and peace.

Through the full range of human issues—from the daily concerns of your body to the handling of your affairs to the concerns of your soul—Fear will guide you to take care of it all. Be real and deal with things one at a time as they are intuitively brought to your attention. No matter how huge the problem or how many the threats that have accumulated to rob your peace of mind or to wear down your health, remember this: "When the time is on you, start, and the pressure will be off." In other words, do something. This is the fourth step in our SOS method—take action to solve the threat! (The first the steps ensure that you are taking effective action.) Babies learn to self-soothe, and so must you. The ability to calm yourself must be practiced, strengthened, and put to use. You must create peace for yourself on a regular basis to maintain health and happiness. Stimulation is the norm and comes easily nowadays. Relaxation is a learned skill that you must prioritize; your well-being requires it. Simply said: practice Peace.

Self-Study: Practicing Healthy Fear

To get the kind of result you want, it is essential that you practice working with your emotions daily. When your Fears achieve their purpose by creating safety and well-being, *you won't feel fearful!* Improve your relationship to Fear and diminish its control over you. Work with it as the ally it is meant to be. Here is a suggested daily practice.

40-Day Anxiety Detox

Take 6 weeks to focus on Fear and increase Peace.

Practice consistently. Choose a topic from the chapter that speaks to your situation. Do the related exercise every day. During or immediately after the exercise, talk to your Fear using a version of the SOS Method. You can use the recordings, guide yourself using the text, or follow your own creative script.

Projects for Growth

- **See the blocks to your peace.** Use your Senses of the Soul sessions to create a list of all the situations that disturb you. Under each source of Fear, list a solution. Go back again and again, using the SOS Method to clarify and expand these lists. Maybe there is just one main issue to deal with. Intuition, through feelings, will show you what's important.

- **Make a firm commitment to your growth.** Use a mixture of focus and effort, balanced with patience, compassion, and nurturing.

- **Put ideas and actions to work.** Move to obey these messages every day. Some solutions amount to remembering new truths to replace old thought habits. Some actions are small, to be taken daily. Some are huge and take time just to muster your Courage. Get support to make the big changes. Roleplay the big scary steps in your mind, write what you plan to say, rehearse with a friend. But do what Soul says is the price of freedom. Record brief notes of your realizations, intentions, actions, and results. Note changes in your awareness and feelings.

Chapter Five

Desire
Cravings Guide You to Contentment

Desire leads to satisfaction, contentment, and empowered self-containment.
Its hot sticky pull won't quit until you know how to take care of what you really
need.

The Purpose of Desire

When you want something;
When you are hungry, needy, craving, or driven out of control;
When you feel insatiable and empty no matter what you get;
When you feel dead to desire and you live without pleasure;
Or when you want to fulfill the deepest longings of your heart and soul...
Desire pulls like gravity to feed your hungers until you are content and self-contained
It brings the clarity to understand your needs and the tireless energy to satisfy them.
Desire leads to self-sufficiency, deep contentment, and ultimately the freedom of
desirelessness.

Don't go around hungry. Spend time getting really clear about what drives you, what you
really want, and how to create a habit of satisfaction and contentment.

Desire: The Engine that Drives Every Other Emotion

You may not think of Desire as an emotion at all, but you know it well. It's an emptiness in the belly, a warmth in the heart, or a burning in the groin. Your pulse, thoughts, and drive grow from mild to wild the longer you go without the object of your Desire. You think you can't live without it, so you push and obsess, or you give up and go cold. The mother of all emotions, Desire gives rise to all the others. You emerge from the womb with the life force prevailing above all things, like grass pushing through asphalt toward the sun. Although that universal power is unstoppable, your individual body is fragile. A million external conditions and internal processes must come together in order for you to survive. And even if all of those conditions were met in the womb, you are still born vulnerable—needing care, yearning to be fed and held, safe and warm. Each day there are myriad things you need in order to stay alive, plus a whole lot more to be happy. So you have a special built-in sensor called Desire, which helps you perceive what you need and gives you the energy to get it.

The mother of all emotions, Desire gives rise to all the others.

Desire can get complicated, but you'll know it by its magnetic pull. Desire is an itch that craves to be scratched. You are "attracted" to something that promises enjoyment, pleasure, or advancement. You imagine gratification, a sort of temporary peace gifted by obtaining the object of your desire. Growing stronger with anticipation, Desire becomes impatient and gets more intense the closer you get, eventually becoming hard to stop—all of which helps you fulfill your desire. That same push can also drive you to regret. For with attraction comes Desire's equally active other half, Aversion. With equal-but-opposite energy, Aversion pushes away whatever you don't like or don't want. This push-and-pull ranges in flavor and intensity in direct response to the importance and urgency of your constant and countless needs. It's all meant to serve you, so you can survive physically, thrive psychologically, and expand spiritually.

Desire may be difficult to distinguish from other emotions because it so quickly joins forces with others, such as Fear or Anger, which bring their own strategies, energies, and skills to the prime directive of "gotta have it now." Desire works with your positive mind to acquire and expand.

The Three Functional Minds

A "meeting of the minds" is difficult; there's even conflict within your own head, but that's because you have three minds or mental functions. Each has its own purpose and generates its own type of thoughts and feelings.

Your *Protective Mind* is primal and urgent, for its job is your survival. It looks for danger and reacts to pain, seeking security. Also called Negative Mind, since it looks for problems in order to avoid them, it calls on Fear as its emotional ally for energy and intuition. Both are so dedicated, they take over the other two minds when threats are not handled.

Your *Positive Mind* has the job to acquire things for you, so Desire is its ally. It experiments and enjoys, invents and creates. When it takes over, Desire is misused for protection, and you can get lost in fantasy and drown in excess. Without the balance of the Protective Mind, obsession and addiction "feel" safe but create danger.

Your *Neutral Mind* is the wise judge, without which the other two minds forever debate the pros and cons of anything. Also called Meditative Mind, it gives you access to the bigger picture, can see the effect of things on your long-range goals, and guides you beyond short-term success or failure to ultimate fulfillment. It is your ability to see beyond negative fears and positive desires. The peace and clarity you feel after doing the sometimes-intense practices in this book is the experience and action of the Neutral Mind, which is invoked so you can see what is really happening.

Each of us has a unique blend of strengths and challenges with these three mental functions. Understanding them helps us better work with their allies— our emotions. Meditation strengthens the Meditative Mind, which then gives us access to the "higher" emotions.

Fear is the emotional agent of your Negative Mind, which works to protect you. Together, they work to drive most of human behavior. The thought of not getting what you need or the idea of a possible loss of something you already have brings Fear, which then fans the flame of Desire into cravings, compulsions, addictions, and irrational and self-destructive behaviors and control–victim syndromes. In this heady stew of compulsion, the purity of the desire and the simple satisfaction of that desire get mixed with pain, which is then confused with suffering. The simple pleasure we began seeking is now experienced as Guilt and Shame. This cycle can keep us enmeshed in Desire for lifetimes.

The frustration of unfulfilled "must haves" invokes the power of Anger so you can conquer obstacles and go get them. Long-term lack creates a loss of hope, and as such, some will resort to Apathy as their "Plan B." You might descend into Sadness and regret over the loss of opportunity or of needs previously satisfied. Desires fulfilled or unfulfilled can blend with Guilt or bring on Shame. The ability to distinguish emotions separately, as we will chapter by chapter, is essential to responding to them appropriately so they can help you. Every emotion reveals an underlying desire—for relief, for peace, to fulfill that emotion's purpose. Learn to distinguish this urge at the center of every action.

A Conscious Encounter with Desire

Close your eyes after reading each phrase that follows and create that feeling within yourself. Identify someone or something, either from memory or expectation, that generates each level of attraction.

Slight preference	*Strong yearning*	*Burning passion*
Sweet inkling	*Determined wanting*	*Overpowering demand*
Appealing interest	*Pleading necessity*	*Insatiable lust*
Wishful longing	*Strong craving*	*Ravaging addiction*

In the same way, now sample the other side with a feeling and object to match the level of intensity.

Displeasure	*Revulsion*	*Detesting*
Dislike	*Disgust*	*Abhorrence*
Aversion	*Loathing*	*Hate*

Do you notice the strong physical sensations that make the emotion very real? Was either attraction or aversion stronger or more familiar for you? Was there a certain range of intensity that was more familiar or habitual to you? These stronger feelings reveal where you spend more of your time emotionally. Could you detect other emotions present and distinguish them from the Desire? Anger, Guilt, and Shame commonly accompany repulsion, whereas Fear and Sadness may pair up with attraction. All combinations are possible.

Desire (and its opposite) has obvious advantages. It's the evolutionary push that drives life up from the seas, out of the mud and into the trees and onward toward the skies. It is that same drive that compels us to improve ourselves and pursue our dreams. Every great story from human history and literature is about desires pursued, won, or lost. In your own history, every move right up until you reading this book now is motivated by that infinite energy source—Desire. It holds the power to build and destroy health, wealth, careers, and empires. Fearing Desire, in ourselves and others, we have created countless ways to control it, regulate it, and punish it. But Desire has never been stopped. It expresses itself in infinite ways, in every moment, in everything.

Can Abuse It, Can't Lose It

Desire is the source of so much of our emotion—and commotion. Therefore, it's no wonder that classical yoga names nonattachment (or freedom from desire) and meditation (or regular practice to control the mind) as the most important tools to gain self-mastery. Great masters enjoy a freedom from the constant seeking of pleasure and fleeing from pain that drive most of us. They have desire, but it is for things as they are. When there is no striving for or resistance to things, life flows; peace is possible under any condition. We have observed the deep joy of those who, throughout time, seem content with little. The ascetic traditions are often attempts to find peace through nonattachment—that is, through having no possessions and little care or concern for the body. "If I don't have it, then I must not want it," right? But most attempts to control yourself or others through denial often fail, because the intense energy of Desire comes roaring back. In contrast to asceticism, our government, church, parents, and culture (namely, marketing and advertising) are doing everything they can to control our desires for their own ends. Desire is a powerful thing, and there is a lot of well-deserved but misplaced demonization and fear about it. But it is just pure energy that is there to help you get what you need. Where it takes you depends on how you use it.

Here are some examples of misused Desire: The animal in you jumps toward immediate gratification with no regard for the consequences: You eat what tastes good, with no thought of tomorrow; you have sex when you feel the urge, no matter what damage may result; you attack in a "crime of passion," without regard for either the other person or the punishment. Repression of desire—that is, pretending it doesn't exist or ignoring or distracting from the signals—fails like a dam in a mighty river with no overflow; it eventually breaks. Prohibition, our war on drugs and pornography, a thousand fad diets, religious celibacy, the notion of self-regulated financial institutions, gun laws—none has stopped addiction, lust, gluttony, greed, or violence. So what will work? Our approach in this book is not to control Desire but to let Desire do its job. This is the middle way. Between unbridled expression and stifled suppression lies the ability to clearly discern our real needs. Maturity and the desire for real, mutual satisfaction allow us to let go of fantasy and immature wants and needs, and even to postpone immediate gratification, if necessary, in favor of long-term contentment.

Desire Consciousness

When Desire dominates your consciousness, you will be needy, always hungry, ever on the hunt, lustful, insatiable, obsessive, addictive; you will never get enough. Trapped by the idea of what you have or don't have and who has more and who has less, you become a slave to the polarity of too much or too little, of satisfaction or dissatisfaction—overfed or starving, austere or indulgent, lustful or prudish. Your life becomes a seemingly endless cycle of pursuing and getting and having, not to mention always asking the question,

"How much?" Instead of judging this natural polarity, look at it as an experiment: Your consciousness is playing with the edges of what you need and how much you need by experiencing every side and size. In Desire Consciousness, there is no containment and no contentment; but beneath it all the while is the Soul's Desire for you to experience complete fulfillment.

When Desire dominates your consciousness, you will be needy, always hungry, ever on the hunt, lustful, insatiable, obsessive, addictive; you will never get enough.

Everyone needs the ability to harness and use Desire's force to take greater care of him- or herself—to thrive rather than subsist, to enjoy rather than just indulge, and to attain an enduring happiness through the fulfillment of the deepest needs that sustain the human spirit. This may seem a distant goal in the midst of your millions of ever-changing needs, but in the end, quenching that fire is not so difficult. It requires communication with your inner depths and your greater heights, which emotion can facilitate. When you know what you really need and get good at obtaining it, you are never weak, needy, dependent, manipulative, scheming, vengeful, or blaming. True fulfillment—physically, mentally, emotionally, and spiritually—is the foundation of your greatest strength and peace. Now let's use our tool, the SOS Method, to create the foundation for our own fulfillment, which is what Desire seeks.

Guiding Desire

❶ Begin with Getting Peaceful (page xi). Tune in with the Adi Mantra and continue.

❷ Cool the Fire. Roll your tongue into a "U," with the tip of the tongue just outside of the lips. Inhale deeply through the rolled tongue; then exhale through the nose. The tongue and mouth relax and close as you exhale. Repeat and continue for 3–11 minutes. Finish with a few deep breaths through the nose. Relax.

❸ The SOS Method for Desire. In the stillness during or after the Cool the Fire exercise, follow this self-guided visualization:

a.   **Stop and Listen.** Sit still with closed eyes, breathing slowly and deeply as you become calm. Bring up a memory of wanting something very much before you got it. Vividly relive the memory and let yourself feel Desire flow freely through you, without resistance. It is safe to feel this. Is there a bodily sensation? Where? Does it feel good, safe, or is it uncomfortable? Do you feel other emotions: Fear, Frustration, Sadness, or Guilt? Let all of the emotions rise and be felt. Now let the other emotions go; curiously and fearlessly feel the need as a pure energy, without judgment.

b.   **Find the Source.** Ask your Desire what it wants from you or for you. Ask why it's important or what is underlying that want or need. Does it feel desperate, like you will die without it, or is it more like a passionate craving of pleasure? Then ask, "Why is this so important? Will I be all right without it? Can it wait? Will getting it take care of me?" Once you sort that out, try it on—imagine getting, having, or doing the thing. How do you feel? If it satisfies, enjoy and proceed to the next step. If it leaves you wanting, look again. Let the feelings lead you. Don't let past memories come in; don't think about what was before. Instead, get the current update of what is wanted now. Continue with this step until there is relief, a feeling of satisfaction. Is there satisfaction or more peace? Can you allow that to be—to sit and enjoy the lack of desire? Or is doing so unfamiliar or uncomfortable? Are you still itchy?

c.   **Ask for Solutions.** Ask Desire for its solution. Are the objects of your desire available to you? Shift your focus from not having them to the joy of wanting them. Longing for something is a good feeling; it contains its own enjoyment. Can you just enjoy the energy of Desire? It is a fuel you can use, not only to try to get an immediate thing but also to be redirected to any other, perhaps more important, goal. Ask: "Is there a next best thing—something within my control that is easier to get but also satisfying?" Continue until you see a real solution. When you imagine getting that, do you feel contained for now?

d. **Take Action.** Is the object of your Desire still needed? Do you need to do something, or can it be handled within yourself? If you got information on what you need and how to do it, write it out, step by step, and then use the power of Desire, its own energy, to take action and do it!

❹ **Capture Your Gains.** Write down what you learned. Did you have immediate needs, future needs, or needs just out of past memory and habit? Were the desires you examined real and currently relevant, or were they driven from memory? Did you find new or truer needs? If so, are you able to take care of them? Why have you not given their satisfaction to yourself yet? Are you deserving? Worthy? Capable? Do you trust yourself with it? Is it safe to have it? Are you willing to be satisfied?

Going Deeper: Four Roles of Desire

The four time frames in which you feel Desire are (1) need it now, (2) insatiable future, (3) old flames, and (4) the Soul's needs. By developing your ability to care for yourself at all four levels, you can attain health and happiness. Your own needs vary widely, from urgent bodily functions to subtle spiritual longings, with a million various needs in between. At every level of your existence, Desire serves the same purpose: to take you from needy to fulfilled. Let's start by understanding human needs.

What Drives You?

> Once you have enough basics to maintain the body, everything else you do is driven by something that depends not on anything or anyone; rather, it is the product of thought and feeling.

Abraham Maslow studied human motivation in the 1950s and listed needs in a hierarchy in which each need becomes important when previous levels are well met. You can survive quite a while on your last meal, but hunger *will* return. After survival, knowing that your next meal will be there when needed addresses the second level of need—security, which is survival extended into the future. As basic as it is, this second of eight levels of ever subtler needs is metaphysical; it is a thought and a feeling, not an actual thing. The next level of need is belonging and love, followed by competence and esteem, all of which are essential to security for you as a social animal. Beyond these come your needs for understanding, beauty, self-actualization, and transcendence—or living for something beyond yourself. The astounding conclusion is that once you have enough basics to maintain the body, everything else you do is driven by something that depends not on anything or anyone; rather, it is the product of thought and feeling. If you can afford to be reading this, you are now in a position to fulfill yourself by internal means.

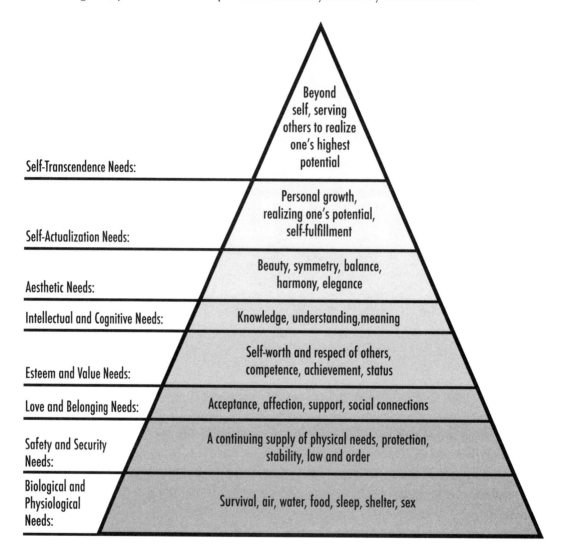

Self-Transcendence Needs: Beyond self, serving others to realize one's highest potential

Self-Actualization Needs: Personal growth, realizing one's potential, self-fulfillment

Aesthetic Needs: Beauty, symmetry, balance, harmony, elegance

Intellectual and Cognitive Needs: Knowledge, understanding, meaning

Esteem and Value Needs: Self-worth and respect of others, competence, achievement, status

Love and Belonging Needs: Acceptance, affection, support, social connections

Safety and Security Needs: A continuing supply of physical needs, protection, stability, law and order

Biological and Physiological Needs: Survival, air, water, food, sleep, shelter, sex

I Need It Now!

Strong, immediate needs are based on survival and have an impulsive, animalistic urgency. The power behind this form of Desire can be overwhelming and frightening, completely unreasonable in its demands. The object of Desire is pursued for instant gratification, with no thought for the impact on others or any long-term outcomes. There's no thought of anyone or anything other than what you want and must have. Anything that gets in the way only concerns you as an obstacle to overcome, not as something of any consequence in and of itself. The cleanup comes later. Although there is nothing evil about any of this—animals are innocent in their fight for survival—as humans, damages are definitely accrued, and the price must be paid.

Experience Your Instinctual Desire to Survive

In this safe and controlled experiment, you can call up Desire by simply withholding your most immediate need—your breath!

❶ Begin with Getting Peaceful (page xi).

    a.   Sit calmly and relax with a few deep breaths.

    b.   After a deep inhale, exhale completely and lock the breath out with your tongue at the roof of your mouth. Sit and observe your thoughts and feelings as the clock ticks. At first you are fine, no problem. Soon your focus on breath escalates from interest through want, need, craving, and then to fear. If you can hold out long enough, you may begin to bargain, plead, or get angry and mean or weak and helpless. Hold back the breath. Feel that Desire for breath, for life. You can see it all in 1 minute.

    c.   Now feed your need for air! Watch your changes and feel the relief when that need is met—the satisfaction, the gratitude, the return to peace.

    d.   Repeat the previous two steps 5 more times. Try to lengthen each suspension of the breath further into your fear zone.

❷ Capture Your Gains. Do you accept your vulnerability—that you have needs? Your needs don't make you weak unless you fail to deal with them in a balanced way. Do you feel how poised and ready your feelings are to alert you to and solve your immediate needs? It's your energy to use as you wish. When you use it in service of your need, you will feel satisfaction. Write a few lines describing what you saw about yourself, your desire, its power, and its usefulness.

While the Experience Your Instinctual Desire to Survive exercise shows how Desire brings energy to an emergency, other needs, like sex, recognition, and love, are often cluttered with judgments. We don't feel bad about the basic need for air, so why do we place judgments on our other needs? Air (the object of Desire) is not the problem, and your need for it is not a weakness. This need simply exists and is to be filled. Our needs usually underlie all our other emotions. When you are emotional, can't get it together, and maybe don't even know why you're upset, there is most likely an unmet need behind it. When you feel scared, cranky, or weak, try the When Your Are Upset exercise to reveal the source of your suffering.

When You Are Upset: Hear the Cry, Feed the Need

❶ *Begin with Getting Peaceful (page xi).*

a.　Go within and hear the cry: allow the mind to complain, gripe, and rant about whatever is bothering you. Loosen up and let it all flow. Get dramatic and exaggerate if it helps to get you going. No one is listening but you. Keep going and allow yourself to have a fit, a pity party, or any kind of tantrum. Is it all in the present, or is it an earlier time? Notice all you can about the situation. Can you recognize the need when it first arises, before you get upset?

b.　Let it all out. As you rant, cry, and complain, hear yourself explaining all that you want. What's the candy that will make the baby stop crying? Name the pacifier; have anything you want.

c.　Imagine yourself getting whatever it is you were crying out for. Hungrily "devour" whatever it is. Enjoy it with every sense and sentiment. Feel how a desire satisfied brings calmness. Are you content for the moment? Will something else stand in for your "hunger," or do you need that one thing?

d.　Act from the information. Now go get what you want. Do you think it is impossible to do so? You'll be amazed at how a second choice or something "close to what I want" will satisfy. You may crave Italian food, but Chinese can also take care of your hunger if you will let it.

❷ *Capture Your Gains.* Relax. Mentally step back your perspective from the details and take in the entire story. Realize that you named a need, something you want. Did you ever get it? Did you get the exact thing you needed, or did something else make you feel better temporarily, with the real need remaining? How long will the satisfaction last? Just knowing what you need will ease you a bit, but Desire will eventually require fulfillment. When will you be cranky again? Can you prevent it next time by acting earlier?

The When You Are Upset approach will handle a surprising number of problems. However, you may have beliefs and patterns that stop you from getting what you need—such as a habit of scarcity, honor in poverty, righteous suffering, desires seen as evil, feeling spoiled and indulgent, demonizing wealth or ease, guilty pleasures, noble sacrifices, feeling undeserving. Any of these thoughts will leave you hungry when you could just as easily eat!

Ravi's Sweet Love

My earliest memory of desire was when I was 4 years old. I was sent away to live with a foster family. I don't remember being scared or lonely, but I recall becoming obsessed with sugar. I remember designing the perfect candy-only diet. I could go on a candy fast. I couldn't wait to grow up so I could eat as many Twinkies as I wanted. I remember thinking how happy that would make me. The desire steadily grew and became my addiction. When I would see movies about drug addicts, I would think, "Wow, that's me, but with sugar!" I tried many ways to stop, both complete abstinence and full indulgence. I used many therapies to address it, but nothing worked. I finally just accepted that it would always be a burden on my back. As I started my work with GuruMeher and SOS, I learned to listen to that craving feeling and began to understand what role sugar played for me. Eating sweets was my way of completely nurturing and loving myself; it was something I could actually control. Trying to give it up meant that I had to give up the one thing I could count on. With this awareness, I started the slow journey of listening to myself more carefully—understanding, forgiving my perceived weaknesses, and learning other ways to cope. It's a daily process to stay aware of it all, but I have created a good space for myself of feeling loved in a balanced way. I can desire something sweet, I can listen to why the desire is coming at this particular time, and I now have many options to respond to that desire. Sometimes it's something sweet; sometimes it's getting a hug from my loved ones; sometimes it's just acknowledging the emotion, the need, and moving on. Learning that the sweetness of love comes in many forms has been the sweetest gift of all.

The Insatiable Future

In Dante's *Purgatory,* the gluttons' punishment was to be forever chained just out of reach of tables of luscious food, craving but not satisfied. I have felt that living hell, even when eating all I can stuff in. Rather than a punishment (and obsession is hell!), let's compassionately find what will satisfy. Physical needs are endless: I eat today and am hungry again tomorrow. But most needs are less urgent than the breath, heartbeat, or even your sweet tooth.

Your mind's ability to imagine the future allows you to anticipate needs so as to better fulfill them. That is a great advantage. But imagination can certainly depart from reality and motivate weird and self-destructive behavior. It's a problem when that wish, whim, or fantasy begins to seem as real and urgent to you as your truly vital needs. You lose touch with reality: you eat when not hungry, chase what harms you, want what you already have or can never have. When the source of Desire and its solution are distorted, things can go very badly: Health and Happiness are cut off from their direct connection to needs and Desire ends up working overtime to compensate. This can create insatiability and addiction. In the end, you seem to be putting water on the fire, but it keeps raging.

Mindfulness, or being present, and increased self-awareness are fundamental to breaking this cycle. But when the mind, in its capacity to go beyond time and space, perceives a need, it is very difficult to distinguish real needs from projected, future needs, especially when those needs recur again and again. For example, you feel hungry and eat, but your hunger returns, and you need to eat again. Hunger can be temporarily satisfied; however, by its nature, it is interminably insatiable. Needs that are higher up on the Maslow Scale have a longer cycle; you can even live without love, but not happily. These nonphysical needs can also become sources of perpetual hunger, leading you to pursue them as an obsession, with satisfaction never reached. Your heart and soul know what you need. Do you?

Putting Water on the Fire

You have natural needs that should and can be met. In fact, we all have a million ongoing conditions to satisfy in order to live and thrive. We are all equally needful, so being "needy" means you don't know what you need or can't get what you need. But you are self-contained: you have the need, the sense to detect it, and the energy to get it. These are learnable skills you may not have fully developed yet. Neither you nor the need is the problem; you can get better at taking care of yourself.

We are all equally needful, so being being "needy" means you don't know what you need or can't get what you need. But these are learnable skills.

Strong, self-secure people have this same basic "neediness;" they are just better able to get their needs met and thus enjoy more satisfaction. I remember the first time my son could navigate food (a banana) into his mouth by himself, a basic skill we all learn. But there may be many less urgent needs we did not develop. It's the simple skills of identifying needs accurately and then learning how to take care of yourself by getting them that are essential for success in any area of life. You must know where the fire is coming from, use the right "quencher" (water works, but not gas), and then still make sure you hit the fire with it. Mistakes are easy to make and lead to what appears to be an unquenchable fire.

Examine your own behavior when you are under pressure. Can you identify the immediate need that's driving it all? How effective is your approach to getting that need met? How do you react when you don't get it how and when you want? Do you shut down? Do you blame others? Are your efforts bringing satisfaction and more energy, or are they bringing more stress and draining you? If you are busy but not effective, identify any such behavior. What is the water (satisfaction) to your flame (real need), and how will it reach the flame?

For example, "When my boss talks about business being slow, I get scared and withdrawn; then I go home and overeat, which only makes me feel more out of control. I realize I need to take direct action: I need to discuss these fears with friends, ask the boss directly about my position, get a realistic view of my finances with a job-loss backup plan, start a serious savings plan, get more education for career upgrade opportunities, or look around for other, more secure work." After you see more clearly what you need, use this process to identify and cultivate the necessary skills you need so that you are no longer needy!

Old Flames, Still Smoldering

Continuing the fire analogy, we all have smoldering hotspots from our past that flare up and continue to cause damage. When you feel small, your needs can look huge and beyond your ability to fulfill—especially when you are young, more fragile, and dependent. If your needs aren't met or you are uncertain of ever having them met in the future, this can create long-term insecurity. That early trauma can create a defensive "black hole," which feels like perpetual hunger, no matter how full you may one day be.

Chronic Neediness: No Amount of Love Will Make Me Feel Loved

It's doubtful that anyone reading this is living at the edge of survival. Your fears and frustrations come from subtler, less-pressing desires, which are all subjective; they depend on what you think and feel.

> You are very insecure. And you hoard things. You live by the richness that is outside of you. You don't live by your inner richness. If the richness inside you is balanced by the richness outside, then you are okay. But if the richness outside is more and inside is less, you are corrupt.
>
> → *Yogi Bhajan, July 25, 1996*

Memories of great pleasures and the pain of unfulfilled Desires leave deep imprints meant to help us get more of the good stuff. These memories can tempt and hypnotize until the Desire becomes its own reality; the here-and-now is ignored, while the imagined object of Desire is all that matters. Soon that constant wanting is as good as it gets; the constant pursuit of the dream takes the place of satisfaction. Your identity becomes caught in the web and consumed; the Desire narrowly defines you and limits your freedom to go elsewhere. Being trapped this way brings secondary responders: nostalgia, procrastination, regrets, detachment, and depression. The Clear the Cobwebs of Past Desires practice will help you be present and thus drop past temptations. It will help you let go of things that do not concern or serve you now. You can then learn from your current sensations what you need right now.

Clear the Cobwebs of Past Desires

Drop past intrigues and enticements so you can Be Here Now! Be clear, see all, enjoy, but don't get caught. The guided meditation is designed to help you see your current needs and focus your efforts there.

❶ Begin with Getting Peaceful (page xi). Tune in with the Adi Mantra and continue.

❷ Let It Go, Let It Flow. Look at the tip of your nose. This pulls the optic nerve to create pressure on the pituitary gland, creating alertness in the brain. Don't strain your eye muscles; instead, relax and expect a little discomfort until you get used to it. Touch each fingertip on one hand with its corresponding finger tip on the other hand, then spread the fingers on each hand apart so no finger touches its neighbor, forming a

"teepee." Place your hands in front of your torso at the level of the solar plexus with the wrists straight so the fingers extend forward and the thumbs point up. Inhale deeply through your nose. Hold your breath as you mentally chant "Sa-Ta-Na-Ma" once, slowly. Then exhale through a rounded mouth by segmenting the breath in eight equal strokes. The exhale is not from the tip of your lips; instead, it comes from the middle of your mouth and is generated from a strong pull at the navel. By the eighth exhale, your lungs are empty; squeeze your navel all the way back toward your spine. Continue for 11 minutes. With practice, slowly increase the time to 31 minutes.

❸ The SOS Method for Desire. Be present and drop all traces of past—what you liked and hated, what you got and didn't get. Just see clearly that you are here now, and you are doing just fine. In this moment, all of your desires are already being fulfilled.

    a.   **Stop and Listen.** Meditatively recall all that you have felt, seen, and learned in the previous exercises of this chapter. Allow all the feelings of need to flow and be felt.

    b.   **Find the Source.** Ask the feelings what deeper need is driving them. Look beneath the object, person, or situation. What will you get out of it? "I want to be appreciated." "I need to be nurtured, to feel safe, to feel deserving, to feel loved." What will it mean to you or about you—that you are loveable, worthy, good? Keep asking the question until you hit the deepest level. Your deepest needs are often great timeless truths, like Freedom, Joy, Love. Accept whatever you feel, which may include Sadness, Relief, or Fear at identifying your deepest need.

c. ***Ask for Solutions***. Just as you have done with more surface-level physical needs, ask these vast noble desires how you can fulfill them. These are the needs that won't accept substitution—Chinese food instead of Italian won't work here. This is more like vitamin A can't fill in for vitamin C. However, there are many ways to get vitamin C, just as there are infinite sources of Love and Joy. These deeper needs are with you forever; they demand attention, but do so very quietly. They can't be understood when there's too much noise and confusion in the pursuit of a million physical things. But when they lie hidden, long unfulfilled and smoldering, you take that discomfort as normal, you develop a habit of hunger, you get used to pursuing but never reaching satisfaction. That becomes the game. Therefore, you still need to consciously take care of it.

d. ***Take Action.*** Once identified, these deep burning needs can easily be satisfied. The stuff that quenches them is not bought, sold, or in limited supply. It's simply a matter of accurately identifying and creatively satisfying. The habit of feeling dissatisfied can be changed with practice by consciously "letting it in," or allowing your deepest needs to be quenched.

❹ ***Capture Your Gains.*** Write about what you learned of your most essential needs and what you can do to take care of them to fulfill your true Desires.

Belonging, Self-Esteem, Love, Beauty, and Fulfillment are supported by events, but they are not manufactured somewhere out of you. They are internally generated. That realization may come easily, or it may seem impossible; it all depends on your history of experience, which becomes habit, the source of your belief system, essentially your "reality." The good news is that all of your deeper Desires are more than able to be fulfilled, if your beliefs and habits will but let them in.

The Soul's Needs: Answer to the Human Condition

The ultimate way to heal the trauma of "needing" is to discover that you have the ability to take care of your deepest needs yourself, completely and forever. At this point, you've likely touched an existential truth, a state of the Soul that the mind and your everyday self have forgotten. Now you are healing at the highest level—knowing and living your Soul's truth is the only way to quench the many endless thirsts. When you know the mother of all your needs, there are countless ways to become satisfied. The more universal and subtler the need, the less dependent you are on physical circumstance, and the more able you are to feed it yourself. Your deepest needs are always within your power to fulfill.

Your deepest needs are always within your power to fulfill.

If I discover that chocolate makes me feel loved and nurtured or that alcohol makes me feel safe or empowered, even though I may not have access to chocolate or alcohol right now (and even though satisfying my need at that level may even harm me), I can pursue healthy options that will take care of those very real needs. I may not get my father to like me or even speak kindly to me, but I do have many other ways to feel valuable, respected, connected, or worthy—whatever my need may be.

When you believe that your happiness depends on that one special person doing or saying just the right thing, good luck! But when you identify a deep need for love and can deliver that love to yourself, then you are free and fulfilled. When you can feel that love in every breath you take, when you can stop right now and feel love in and around you at every moment, then you are healed. Imagine a relationship between two fulfilled people—not a lot of hurt and blame are exchanged. But when the mind is attached to particulars, when it assigns specialness to things and sets up limited conditions, it does so all in an effort to have control, to feel safe. Soul feels the essence of things, sees what's most important, and is unattached to temporary details or to how an experience comes about. This perspective gives you unlimited access to what you really need. You can freely ask for what you need and know that you will be provided for; or, more likely, you can meditate on thoughts and feelings that self-fulfill and know that you have no need at all. All of your Soul's conditions for happiness preexist within yourself. It has been said in many ways by all of the Great Ones throughout the ages: "The Kingdom of God is within you."

Listening to the Soul's Needs

This exercise guides you through a process while you are breathing. This beautiful experience can help you hear the deepest longings of your heart, the mandate of your Soul. Your mind can fulfill everything it can conceive when it is focused and clear of other distracting thoughts and attachments. There is no limit to your mind's creativity. The best way to practice this is on an empty stomach with only liquids taken during the day.

❶ *Begin with Getting Peaceful (page xi). Tune in with the Adi Mantra and continue.*

❷ *Quench the Longing.* Sit in a comfortable upright posture. Stretch your spine straight and become very still. Close your eyes and relax the back of your hands on your knees, with the index finger touching the tip of the thumb.

a. Drink the breath in a single, deep, long sip through your pursed lips. Close the mouth and exhale through the nose, slowly and completely. Continue this breathing for 7–15 minutes. You are cooling and soothing yourself. This is a good way to start working with the intensity of Desire. A Desire is either fulfilled or thwarted, and your experience with it is very subjective. If it is thwarted, it creates frustration. That is why you cool off to start, with no particular thought. Instead, dwell upon the sipping, the crucial need you have for air; deeply satisfy that need with that long sip, drinking in that life-giving, need-satisfying air. Protective Fear is always ready to jump in when Desires are present; it is ready in case you don't get what you need or want. Frustration (Anger) is equally ready to fight for the need. In this exercise, however, you are getting all the air you want. Feel the satisfaction and the power, the capacity to get what you need, and let these give you a deep feeling of safety and peace.

b. Sip the air in through the lips again, but before exhaling, hold in your breath comfortably. As you hold the breath in, meditate on zero. Think in this way: "All is zero; I am zero; each thought is zero; my pain is zero; that problem is zero; that illness is zero." Meditate on all negative, emotional, mental, and physical conditions and situations. As each thing crosses your mind, bring it to a zero single point of light—a small, insignificant nonfact. If you notice positive things, allow them without zeroing. Exhale through the nose long and deep. Then repeat. Continue to breathe in this comfortable rhythm for 7–11 minutes. Search for things you are frustrated, mad, scared, or troubled about in any way. As you hold the breath, shrink the thought and feeling; make it all insignificant, make it disappear. Keep trying with whatever you bring up. Find desires, obsessions, addictions, things you can't live without, things that have been satisfying, things that you can't get enough of, things that are unquenchable or unattainable. You may find Fear and Frustration closely related. Things you fear and desire have a great power over you and make you feel small, incomplete, and powerless. Meditatively shrink each thought, feeling, and scenario to little or nothing. Like a teeter-totter, as it shrinks, you expand; you have victory and regain your proper place of power over the things that serve you. Let any positive, powerful, peaceful, all-is-well thoughts remain with you so you can enjoy them.

c.   Think of the thought you need the most. What quality or condition do you most desire for your complete happiness and growth? Summarize that thing in a single word like Wealth, Health, Relationship, Guidance, Knowledge, Luck, and so on. It must be one word. Lock on that word and thought. Visualize facets of it. Inhale and hold the breath as you beam the thought in a continuous stream. Lock onto it. Relax the breath as needed. Continue in this manner for 5–15 minutes. Focus on any of the desires that come to mind. Look to the deeper need underlying it. If the physical desire is food or a lover, a job or sex, feel the deeper need that this "thing" is trying to bring to your experience—security, safety, connection, support, love, freedom, empowerment. Every desire, no matter how mundane or twisted, is the agent of a Soul-level longing for a universally recognized experience that, amazingly, is always and everywhere available to us by direct thought and feeling. So, while holding the breath, as you identify and directly feed that need, you are feeding your soul. You feel better immediately; you feel stronger and more peaceful. With practice, you develop Saibhang, a self-contained, always-complete status, undisturbed by loss and gain. Hence, all Desires lead us to Desirelessness, or the very essence of ourselves. Keep practicing.

d.   To end, inhale as you move your shoulders, arms, and spine. Then stretch your arms up, spread your fingers, and breathe deeply a few times.

Use Desire to Serve Your Soul

Life's road is long, and the lessons are many. We are all working things out and learning by working through challenges. Whichever face of Desire you are dealing with right now is exactly what your Soul wants you to learn. There is no issue that is higher or lower than the next; yours is the right one to be working on, and all will lead eventually to Peace. Desire's lessons guide you toward contentment and fulfillment. Yes, your body has needs;

but if you are a slave to those needs, there is no peace. Your Soul's goal is for you to feel complete, capable of getting what you need, trusting that you will be provided for, and knowing that what comes to you is somehow just right. You are no longer a beggar; instead, you are rich with all you need to be content. You become self-contained. You desire only what is. In that state, you are free, and no one can control you because they have nothing to hold over you. You have no lack, no fear.

> **Your Soul's goal is for you to feel complete, capable of getting what you need, trusting that you will be provided for, and knowing that what comes to you is somehow just right.**

Life is not meant to be lived the way we live. It has to be fulfilled in itself. It has to have contentment. There is no substitute for contentment. There is no price for contentment. There is no kingdom that can buy contentment. There is no soul that can destroy contentment. There is no tragedy that can totally beat it out of us. A man who is content, he is king of kings, he is the God of Gods, and he is the God... There is no king who can be a king without contentment. It is a Catch-22. Once you are content, everything will come to you. When you are discontent, everything will go away from you.

→ *Yogi Bhajan, November 8, 1989*

Joy and Serenity: Desire's Ultimate Desire

Desire holds precise and subtle information about exactly what you need, including how much, when, and even why you need it. Without this self-knowledge, as well as the energy and ability to take care of yourself, you are weaker, crankier, angrier, and more afraid. Or you can become endlessly absorbed in satisfying desires. Our culture even supports this self-centered approach to life and happiness. However, progress is only made when you get good at satisfying one level of need and then graduate, or move on to, the next level, as described in Maslow's Scale (page 118). Look at the scale again. You'll see that the first needs are purely physical, and each succeeding level is less physical, less visible. Needs become internal, mental, emotional, or spiritual. There is ample evidence that attempts to be religious as a strategy to ignore or compensate for unfulfilled needs create imbalance, hypocrisy, and suffering in the name of God. The most rapid and reliable spiritual progress comes instead by taking care of each human need as it is brought to your attention so you can learn to fulfill it and then move on.

As Senses of the Soul, emotions guide you directly to what needs to be dealt with for your greater good. Historically, emotions—and Desire, in particular—have been seen and used as the enemy of spirituality. But as we've observed in this chapter, they are essential tools for higher development. When you take care of your human needs really well, you become calm. When you recognize your deeper needs, you become fulfilled. When you recognize the Soul and feed it, you become Desireless—that is, free to have and not have. All needs come from the Soul—serving the body first, then honoring the sense of self, and finally leading to full realization of the exalted nature of the Soul and its material incarnation. When you learn to deeply quench your Soul, you appear to be Desireless. When there is no hunger left, Joy and Serenity are the ultimate gifts of Desire.

> The highest desire is to become desireless.
>
> → *Yogi Bhajan, July 19, 1981*

Self-Study

1 What are your most important and useful discoveries about Desire? How can you apply what you know? What further work can you do now?

2 Choose the practice that had the most impact on you. Continue it daily for 40 days. Use the SOS Method for Desire (page 116) and simple self-awareness to be present to actual physical and emotional needs rather to those from memory, imagination, or fantasy.

3 Work for lasting change in how you see the present, future, or past. Change your habits and resolve within yourself to fully quench your fires of Desire. You have all the power you need to fulfill your deepest desires.

Ideas to Use

- Although seeking satisfaction from things is natural, it creates a habit of going outside for your happiness. This results in the belief that you are limited and dependent, which makes you fragile and your happiness uncertain. You then try to control everything to ensure your position, but then you become controlled by the possessions. To make things more precarious, the ego assigns specialness to a thing—"My thing!"—so that it appears to be your one-and-only, irreplaceable source of support. You cling harder, feel smaller, and see nothing else. Soul, which is defined by your ability to see all and everything, can rescue you from this situation.

- Emotions are motivating. Desire is an emotion and a state of consciousness that identifies what you need physically, mentally, and spiritually to survive and then thrive. You can use Desire to identify needs very specifically: what, when, how, and why.

- Your needs exist on a continuum. The higher needs will not fulfill the lower, and the lower will not fulfill the higher. Until needs are identified and addressed, Desire seems insatiable. But when you are in touch with your deepest needs, satisfaction is very near.

- Skillfully knowing and taking care of your progressively subtle needs leads to deeper experiences of Contentment and eventually to Desirelessness. Needs lead to Soul.

Life Projects

- Cultivate a consciousness of contentment. Let go of wanting; instead, consciously develop a habit of satisfaction and contentment. Caution: It can be boring! Contentment is rather a quieter pleasure than being on the hunt. It involves owning your own personal power and using it wisely. Choice, decision, and commitment become the means to take care of yourself. This is part of growing up and is a hallmark of spiritual maturity.

- Progress from having to have things the way you want them to accepting things as they are. Develop resilience, patience, and trust in yourself and the universe. Enjoy the feeling of Desire without having to act on it every time. This is the great longing that the poets of countless traditions write about.

- Realize that satisfaction is internal and can't be manifested externally with more stuff. This shift takes work and requires honesty, humility, responsibility, and surrender.

- Stop putting conditions on your own happiness. Use this affirmation: "All that I want to experience is immediately accessible and within my control."

- Practice simply enjoying what is, rather than preferring what could be. Begin to practice no preferences, no judgments. Allow yourself to silence the ongoing commentary about what you like and don't like. When you enjoy what is, including pleasure and pain alike, you become free of striving, and pleasure is found in everything. Shift from resisting what is to accepting and allowing what is.

- Try gratitude! It is instant self-created satisfaction. You cannot simultaneously feel gratitude and lacking.

Chapter Six

Anger
Find and Refine Your Power

Anger is your intense protector and go-getter.
Its hot strength teaches you how to use this power for the good of all.

The Purpose of Anger

When you are hurt, abused, or disrespected;
When it's unfair, something's wrong, and you can't take it anymore;
Or when you need more confidence to take action and get things done;
When you get irritated, frustrated, bothered, or fighting mad,
So you can get what you need, live comfortably with safety and honor…
Anger is your source of intense, hot energy to handle it all and make things right.
It will help you find your power and teach you how to use it for the greatest good.
Anger ultimately brings humility, which gives you access to your higher power.

Your Anger is your power. Discover how great life is when you channel Anger to protect you and gracefully create a comfortable life for yourself and those you care for. Whether you need to let off steam or get your fire ignited, this chapter will help you channel the heat you need to thrive.

Playing with Fire

Do you want to get rid of your Anger? You may want to think twice, because without Anger, you'd be dead! Anger is the fire that digests your food and powers each cell of your body. It's the great motivator; it's both the energy to protect yourself and the confidence to get what you need. It's the power that builds relationships, businesses, and empires, as well as the force that destroys them. Fear is thrilling; Desire, enticing; but Anger is intoxicating because of the power it brings. And Anger is Power; think of both as forms of fire. They heat things up, make them move, and leave everything they touch changed. They aren't good or bad; it just depends on how you use them: Cook your food or burn it, warm your house or burn it down, create love or betray it. When you learn to use Anger to protect yourself, you will become more comfortable. When you use it to serve others, you will be happy. And when you learn to enjoy the greater play of power and allow it to work through and around you, there will be Peace in your Soul. If enough of us reach that consciousness, there will be Peace on this planet.

When you learn to use Anger to protect yourself, you will become more comfortable. When you use it to serve others, you will be happy.

Recognizing the Many Faces of Anger

Anger is more than a big, mean monster. You have, at times, experienced Anger in the form you enjoy and need most: smooth, effective action to handle what needs to be done. You don't think of it as Anger, but as Strength. Intentional action and achievement are like nice controlled flames. When you hit an obstacle, the heat rises to match the situation. You take your efforts to a higher gear; you push harder or go longer until it's done. If that doesn't get you what you want, however, you start to feel irritated and frustrated. But if you can channel that into clearer thinking or more decisive action, you might just win and relax.

However, the extra energy may also throw you off and become counterproductive. If you blow off some steam in the wrong way, it makes things worse. Now you are mad; you feel flushed, sweaty, and hot; your heart is pounding; you become loud and intense, going after anything in your way. Your fire may even burn out of control—furious and full of rage. Or maybe you internalize your Anger, send it under cover and go cold, shut down and "stew" silently. Still, the pressure to create change is faithful and finds its way—sometimes in passive-aggression, self-hatred, or self-sabotage. Either way, damage piles up, compounding the problem. The fire feeds on itself, with no stopping, until everything is consumed: career, health, relationships, hope—all destroyed. Perhaps you've experienced this intense Anger before, or maybe you've seen it on the faces or in the words and body language of others. Your primal instincts can detect Anger in others to the exact degree of risk such Anger implies. You can read Anger between the lines by following very subtle clues and changes in behavior. Other familiar forms of Anger are sarcasm, complaining, blaming, resentment, grudges, manipulations—the list is long. Which forms are most familiar to you in yourself and in others?

> There are a lot of sad things in life, but the saddest of all is when you do not recognize your anger, and you do not deal with it.
>
> → *Yogi Bhajan*

Anger Consciousness

The consciousness of Anger sees everything in terms of ego: Does it benefit me? If not, then Anger names it "enemy." Anger is animal-driven, defensive, and easily excited into confrontation over ownership and rights. It seeks stimulation to keep pumped up and is always ready to attack at the slightest provocation. This constant vigilance against someone taking what is "mine" seeks and finds validation for its beliefs, as well as ample justification to use force. Might is always right, and the bully always makes the rules. Anger generates energy and a reassuring feeling of power that serves as a safety mechanism. It is always on the hunt, comparing and competing, looking for trouble—sometimes as the "bad" guy and sometimes for the "good." Either way, more Anger is always the solution.

Anger Isn't Good or Bad—It Just Depends on How You Use It

When you don't get what you want, Anger cleverly escalates from bothered to rage to match the size of the obstacle until its purpose is achieved. Anger has received a bad reputation from all the damage that occurs in this process. But your Anger is not the problem; no more than your stove is to blame for burning your dinner. As with any form of power, the outcome depends on how it is used. When Anger is used reflexively, without your careful guidance, you may cause harm rather than prevent it. The goal in our work with Anger is to be skillful in applying its power. Although the many abuses of Anger are enough to have us fear it and want no part of it, the image of a disciplined ninja fighting only to defend and restore peace and honor can serve as an inspiration to harness the wild beast within and put it to good use. Used well, Anger brings just the right amount of energy to handle any situation. Think of it as your guardian angel, taking care of you, sending you the energy necessary for you to get what you need to live well. So don't be afraid of your own power; when you claim it, you'll be safe. When your use of Anger is refined, balanced, and wise, you will instinctively use the right level of energy to get the job done; you will get what you need without generating a lot of collateral damage. Simply put, when Anger is used well, it arises in response to harm, supplying the energy to take care of yourself and others.

Anger Is an Ally to Other Emotions

Emotions work together in your sensory system, just like different parts of your body do. Each emotion has its own function that does its part to make the whole system function. In Chapters 4 and 5, we learned of two primal forces: the negative polarity of Fear and the positive polarity of Desire. One protects you, and the other motivates you to get what you need. Anger is the driving force that carries both of those emotions into action. Fear warns you to get out of the way before harm comes; but if you are hurt, Anger provides the energy to fight. Desire craves things and builds potential energy, which must be converted into action—kinetic energy—before anything can be accomplished. When you don't get what you want, frustration increases the energy available—all the way to rage, if need be—to make it happen. Anger is the emotion that helps you "protect and go get." Anger can serve to pull you out of Depression and gets you back into action; it's Anger that demands you stand up for yourself in Shame, take responsibility in Guilt, and find the will to live on in Grief.

Understanding the chakras, or the body's energy centers, is also helpful in appreciating Anger's role. The urge to survive in the First Chakra awakens Desire in the Second Chakra. When sufficiently charged up, the even greater energy in the Third Chakra is stimulated, giving you the power to take action and fulfill your desires. We share these same urges with every animal, and much of our daily behavior—feeding, mating, self-promotion—is simply this. But when your energies are guided by the Fourth Chakra, consideration for the greater good is added to the equation; this is the beginning of true humanity, the start of fulfillment beyond mere gratification. Energy from the Fifth, Sixth, and Seventh Chakras make possible the healing and higher awareness you need to resolve the pain of the past and the crises of now—that ever-present "human condition." Although not specifically stated, every exercise in this book activates and utilizes some combination of these energies, which, like the emotions, work together fluidly to handle anything.

Both yoga and the martial arts teach that anger and power originate in the Third Chakra and are essentially the same energy. As we continue, we'll use the word *anger* in a positive way. In order to help improve our relationship with Anger. I will use the words *anger* and *power* interchangeably to mean personal power and the capacity to protect, take care of, and accomplish. It is useful to distinguish *Power,* or Anger channeled productively, from *Force,* which is the less conscious and less powerful form of the same energy. This is brilliantly explained, along with a thorough examination of the relationship between emotions and consciousness, by Dr. David R. Hawkins in *Power vs. Force* (Veritas, 2002) and *Transcending the Levels of Consciousness* (Veritas, 2006).

Personal Protection

This practice conquers the state of self-animosity and gives you the ability to be in total support of yourself.

❶ *Begin with Getting Peaceful (page xi). Tune in with the Adi Mantra and continue.*

❷ *Power to Protect.*

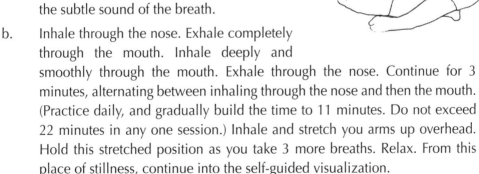

a. Relax your arms at your sides and raise your forearms up and in toward the chest at the heart level. Draw your hands into fists, with your thumbs pointing straight up toward the sky. Press your fists together so that your thumbs and fists are touching, with palms facing each other. This meditation requires that you hold your upper torso straight, without rocking back and forth. Fix your eyes at the tip of your nose, as you follow the subtle sound of the breath.

b. Inhale through the nose. Exhale completely through the mouth. Inhale deeply and smoothly through the mouth. Exhale through the nose. Continue for 3 minutes, alternating between inhaling through the nose and then the mouth. (Practice daily, and gradually build the time to 11 minutes. Do not exceed 22 minutes in any one session.) Inhale and stretch you arms up overhead. Hold this stretched position as you take 3 more breaths. Relax. From this place of stillness, continue into the self-guided visualization.

❸ *The SOS Method for Anger.* Take a few minutes to center and relax. Cultivate safety.

a. *Stop and Listen.* Is there anyone or anything that is bothering, irritating, or frustrating you? Explore what happened. Who said (or didn't say) or did (or didn't do) something to you? Let the thoughts bring up lots of feelings. Feel all the sensations in your body; allow them to flow as you observe it all.

b. *Find the Source.* Ask and listen for a response—not in thought, but in feeling: "What has hurt me? What do I need that I'm not getting? What needs protecting?" Use each answer as the next question to go deeper. "What exactly was hurt: my body, feelings, self-esteem, heart? Or was it someone else who was harmed?" Get to the core issue, while validating all levels.

c.   **Ask for Solutions.** Ask the feeling to give you its solutions. What would take care of this? What would make you feel better or satisfy you (your Anger)? Don't think about how or if it's possible. Don't think at all yet. (Mind will solve all the logistics later.) Let your feelings tell you what they want, and accept that as truth for the moment. One way is to ask your feelings how you want to feel. Identify that and sit with that feeling.

d.   **Take Action.** Let the mind help you figure out how to implement whatever solutions were presented to you. Do it, get it, protect it. Use the faithful energy of Anger to make it happen. You will feel relief and, therefore, less Anger just knowing what to do. You will feel much better when you do it.

Finish with a few deep breaths and some light stretching.

❹ **Capture Your Gains.** Immediately make a few notes to capture any information and instructions that you found during this exercise. Remember that emotions are not satisfied until their mission is complete. So if action was called for, take care of it.

Going Deeper: The Journey of Power

Power—you know you want it. You want to thrive. The urge to live, grow, increase, extend, and flourish pervades this expanding Universe. You feel it every time you are hungry, want a raise, feel envious, try to find a faster way to get somewhere; when you compare, compete, get excited, go shopping, save and invest money, drink coffee—it's all about energy. Nothing moves without fuel. When energy is transferred to do work, that is called *power*. Your ability to use resources in exchange for results is your power. It is natural that we all want more power; life is expansive, and we are wired to want to live larger.

Human history is the story of the discovery and the use and misuse of power—the discovery of fire, the conquering of land, innovation in weapons, finding oil and gold, or access to information and influence. Each of our lives is a story of the personal discovery of power, a continuous experiment that includes contrasts of having and not having, using and misusing. You've had the experience of being powerless, the thrill of getting what you want, the rush of beating others in a game, and the remorse of hurting someone. "Do I have power, and how do I use it to protect my interests to get what I need?" That is a question driving your trial-and-error journey. It is a road that leads to understanding the extent and limits of your personal power. You are both far greater than you imagine and humbly smaller before the power of the Universe.

Anger plays a key role in your story; it is your personal fuel source on this journey; it is your teacher. Anger is the fire in your belly that digests your food, that gets you out of bed, that compels you to go out to conquer the day. You need Anger's heat and light. Don't get rid of Anger; without it you are dead. Instead, learn to use it. We have all been hurt, and we've all harmed; we've played the victim and the victimizer. We try both sides—too hot and too cold—until we get it just right. We learn by contrasting experiences. You might take advantage of others without feeling you've done anything wrong, but when you are betrayed, you suddenly see it: "That hurts. It's not right!" You may strike back against the wrongdoer, who then, in turn, seeks revenge. Used this way, Anger spreads until nothing and no one is left untouched.

Anger can also be used to help, protect, build, and serve the well-being of all. In this huge, timeless learning cycle, the best thing we can each do to diminish suffering is to learn to control our own power. There are four contrasting forms of Anger through which we experiment with power.

The best thing we can each do to diminish suffering is to learn to control our own power.

Understanding and working consciously with your Anger through each of these life lessons will bring you out of intimidation and weakness, past causing destruction and harm, to reach true empowerment, courage, and heroic giving for the good of all. Take this experiential tour through the four lessons of power.

The Four Lessons of Power

Anger and power are interconnected. When our anger is unaddressed or out of our control, we are left in a powerless position. When we address and learn to express our anger in a balanced way, we increase our power and effectiveness.

The four lessons of power anger teaches are:

> **Suppressed Anger: No Power**
> **Expressed Anger: Animal Power**
> **Addressed Anger: Human Power**
> **Finessed Anger: Higher Power**

The First Lesson of Power
Suppressed Anger: No Power

> *This form of power is power-less. With it you become a doormat, helpless and begging for what you need.*

The first lesson in power is the experience of feeling and believing that you have no power. In actuality, you are completely taken care of—you came into being, grew in utero, and now breathe with no effort on your own part. But you forget that and feel that it is all up to you. You then struggle for survival. It may take a lifetime of spiritual training for you to once again relax and dwell in ease and gratitude and to receive life in all its abundance. To let life take care of you is the endgame of human experience, and Anger is your teacher and taskmaster.

The Powerless Path

Powerlessness begins with an experience of frailty and insecurity: "Will I be fed when I need it? Will I be okay?" You are born with an urgency for air, warmth, food, and protection. The power in your lungs protects immediately by grabbing that first breath, taking care of your most urgent need. Then, if you've been traumatized by birth, you wail on your first exhale—that powerful sound, which cannot be stopped or ignored, declares, "I am here, and I need stuff! Bring it on or face my wrath!" Anger thus begins its Soul-sent purpose to protect you and to go get things for you. Crying is initially your strongest use of Anger power. Each time that fearful-needy-angry sound brings the nurturing you need, it reinforces the idea that power is good, and healthy, supportive environments will refine your effectiveness at using that power.

But if Mom is tired, sick, not getting what she needs, or drunk, your cries go unanswered, and your use of Anger changes. If your efforts don't seem to work, life becomes a dangerous and frightening prospect. Because it's impossible to live without power, you instinctively cope with one of two types of strategies. In the first coping strategy, you push ever stronger with Anger until you get some response, even if it is a slap. This path leads to the troublemaking wild child, gangster, raging alcoholic, and repeat offender. The other coping strategy is to believe that power doesn't work for you. Instead, you get passive, quiet, and wait; you are at the mercy of greater forces for whatever may come to save you. When "the powers that be" in control of your environment come down hard on you when you rebel, assert, or even ask for what's right and fair, they push you further into your aggressive or submissive tendencies. Whichever coping strategy you adopt is reinforced by daily experience to form an enduring reality—your sense of self, what you can do and expect to get, how well you can take care of yourself. Your beliefs about your power in relation to your world are thus created by how the people, culture, and times you live in use or abuse power.

When your role models of power are abusive and your assertiveness is slammed down, you may feel safer without power, accepting all kinds of abuse as normal and the price of your existence. You are like a tiny creature in the jungle, hiding from the ever-threatening cruelty all around. People mistreat and abuse you or dismiss and ignore you. It's difficult or impossible to get what you need; you have no rights and no voice. This is called *Doormat Consciousness*—people can walk all over you, trample your rights, and rub their dirt on you, and you have to take it. No choice, no voice, no ability to stop it.

Living with Suppressed Anger

Because life without protection and action is impossible, you develop creative coping mechanisms for a life lived without it. You depend on the fickle kindness of others, taking whatever they dish out; you use sex, beauty, cuteness, intelligence, or hard work as the currency you exchange for what you need; you take care of others and act the martyr, the giver, with no right to receive or take care of yourself. The battered woman is the extreme example of this last strategy; perfectionists, people-pleasers, and shame-based humble do-gooders are the healthier and more socially acceptable versions.

Here are some signs that your Anger and Power are blocked: Anger is scary, and Power seems a bad thing when used by you or others. You suffer, lose out, get left out or left behind, complain but don't solve, resent but don't act, bitch, or become apathetic so that nothing improves. You seek sympathy for your weakness and suffering, and you suffer more to attract more sympathy. You can't say what's bothering you; you think people are mean; you think that if people really cared, they would just know and do what you need. Life is unfair and impossible; you don't deserve anything; what you need is out of reach. You feel small and weak.

Situation: You can't say what you want and need to say. Anger gives you the energy to say what you need to say in order to take care of yourself. So when you block that energy, that urge, and those words, you don't get what you want, and whatever is hurting you continues. After a while, you have trouble even knowing what you want. You urgently need to tap into Anger's lifesaving fuel and put it to use protecting you.

Solution: Give your Anger a voice. Somewhere along the line, you got the idea that you don't have or can't use your power. Start by getting real in a way that will hurt no one. In the safe and sacred space within yourself, let off some steam with The Sacred Tantrum exercise. Doing so will connect you with what's bugging you, will let you feel your Power, and will help you begin to take better care of yourself.

The Sacred Tantrum

❶ Begin with Getting Peaceful (page xi). Sit in a private place at a time when no one can hear you. **Tune in with the Adi Mantra and continue.**

❷ Handle Yourself. Do the exercise series Handle Yourself in the Resources (page 329). This simple set of exercises, which can be done in 15 minutes or less, is powerfully effective in helping you turn on your personal power. Then follow the guided meditation.

❸ Use Your Senses.

a.   Declare yourself in a safe and sacred space where you can allow your anger to come forth in a way that won't hurt you or anyone else. Know that your intention is to access your anger in order to protect, nurture, and learn about yourself.

b.   See before you a panorama of experiences in which you have been bothered by something but were told (or thought it better) to keep your mouth shut. You wanted to say something and planned it out, but then you couldn't. Instead, you forced a strained smile, when you really wanted to scream; you complained about someone but did nothing; you obsessed about asking for a raise or a date but didn't; you suffered in silence. Allow the feelings to flow through you as you observe the emotions. Feel the urge to speak. Feel the urge to separate from the feelings that warn you not to speak. Feel the feeling that arises from not doing so. These may be three distinct sensations. Can you realize why you chose not to speak? Was it a thought, a feeling, something you were once told, or a previous consequence?

c.   In your head, start complaining about it all. At any time, you can speak aloud; you can even freely switch back and forth from inner and outer self-talk. Grumble, whine, groan, nag, knock down, blame, and attack. Complain to yourself, any person, God, or the whole world—whatever works for you. Get out every past, present, and future problem, including what you don't like, what's wrong, what they did, what's not fair, and what you think and want to do about it. Build some momentum to become as angry as you like. Let it get as loud and intense as it will. It won't hurt anyone. Get it out where you can hear it all. Feel the power flowing. Is there something you like about the energy? Go as long as you like; you'll know when you are finished and ready to relax quietly again. Send thanks for the experience and to every person and event mentioned.

d.   Be aware of your feelings now. Think about the main situations you focused on. Is there a common refrain in your complaints? Notice the main issues and patterns in your life.

④ Self-Assessment. How does it feel to know you have the power to speak and protect? Don't act on what you saw; instead, spend 10 minutes writing what you found out. Finish your writing with a list of unfinished business—things you need to take care of. Repeat this exercise daily until it is boring. Each time, refine what you need to say or do for yourself to finally be safe. Speak your mind on paper until you are ready to speak up. If you have some big, tough things that need to be dealt with and said, write a letter first. Run it by a friend to see if you need a reality check. Only then do you send the letter and speak up! It's hardest the first time, but once you get used to how good it feels to say and have things right, it will become habit. Work to deal with things when annoyances are small. Respond when things first bug you. See it all as your Soul wanting you to be comfortable here on Earth. See page 157 for an introduction to Boundaries, which is a skill you can learn that uses your choice and your voice to take better care of yourself.

The costs of living without power are high in terms of real harm and unrealized potential for happiness and success. On the plus side, if you are still alive, congratulations! It worked! Your defective, backward adaptation to harsh environments was the best you could do when it all began long ago. Even if there wasn't abuse, you have faced times when the forces against you seemed too great to confront. Sometimes it can be wise to retreat and live to fight another day when your chances are better. The problem with *permanent* retreat, however, is that it doesn't get you anywhere. With permanent retreat, you always have a reason not to speak up when something's wrong, not to ask for a raise after three years, to suffer silently when he doesn't call, to hope he'll know how much he hurt you. When you don't take the chance to live your dream or to initiate a conversation with an interesting person, then you believe "it" to be bigger and beyond you. In the Sacred Tantrum, however, you learned about power by feeling *less* of it.

Living with Concealed Anger

Energy cannot be created or destroyed. It simply changes from one form to another—this is physical law. Thus, Anger's energy doesn't disappear when suppressed, because your Soul would never leave you stranded like that. Instead, Anger goes somewhere inside you, patiently building a reserve and looking for an outlet. If you don't use it, the problem remains or gets worse. More Anger comes, and pressure builds within. Like a loyal ninja, it will find some way to fight, to break through whatever is stopping it from taking care of things.

If you think it's not okay to feel Anger, then that Anger will look for a form of expression that you *will* allow. Resistance is one form of disguised aggression. Noncooperation is an invisible form—mentally "sticking it to the man" behind the scenes; watching something fall and fail without doing anything about it; letting someone suffer without saying anything; feeling smug satisfaction from destruction all around that you can't be accused of causing—these are all weak forms of power. For you, the second best to getting what you want is others not getting it either. Passive aggression is a creative, but ineffective, attempt not to remedy but to at least get even with a source of harm. Cleverly not saying or doing something creates a problem, while you can rightly say, "I didn't do anything!" Sabotage, hidden interference, and subtle damage that build and show up over time are other impotent uses of power that arise from the illusion that you have less power than you need.

More active expressions of Anger that are often used with silent sabotage are mental and verbal complaining. You run through all the things that are bad and wrong, which makes it seem like you are doing something. This may feel satisfying, but it is more like revenge than real accomplishment. Some of that blather will be blaming. Rather than taking responsibility and fixing, you list who did what, as if that will make it better or make someone else fix it. But any energy spent blaming or complaining is not being used to solve. You can complain *or* resolve, but never both in the same moment. However, when treated consciously, as in the Sacred Tantrum (page 142) and Eliminate Inner Anger (page 146), complaining consciously can be the beginning of action and resolution.

When you find healthy, effective forms in which to express your Anger and Power, these concealed and ineffective behaviors won't be needed anymore and will stop.

Living with Inner Anger

If you are in the way, blocking your own protective Anger, then you become a problem, a source of harm to yourself. Anger seeks protection from any hurt. It first goes after the outside problem, but part of the energy is wasted by your resistance of that first effort. In this case, some Anger turns back at you to break down your resistance so the problem can be solved. This confused mixture of suppressed and inwardly expressed anger is an exhausting, fruitless, and very damaging inner attack that may become normal to you and visible to others only indirectly. Emotions don't quit until their purpose is achieved, but you don't know where to direct the energy of those emotions. When you keep all this undirected power bottled up inside, you become like spoiled wine; you go sour inside—physically or mentally. Something eventually explodes. Subtly and mildly at first, and more aggressively in time; like a cancer, it turns on you. It slowly destroys the host. This is Inner Anger.

Inner Anger is the basis of inferiority and superiority complexes, manipulations and lying. All skin diseases and misbehavior. Miscalculation, destruction of business success, and destruction of relationships. Inner Anger blocks you from having a relationship with yourself.

→ *Yogi Bhajan, 1993*

Inner Anger is tragic and unnatural. What should be the most loving, supportive relationship possible becomes a lonely internal battle. You are your own worst enemy. That's quite some misdirected Anger! Healing requires the energy to be accessed and directed to benefit you. Your innate self-healing power can make peace and repair the damage. You have to move back into the abandoned home of your Soul and take charge to get things in order.

Eliminate Inner Anger

This practice helps relieve latent anger stored internally that is unused or misdirected. Burn it all away so you can rebuild it all fresh and clean.

❶ Begin with Getting Peaceful (page xi). Tune in with the Adi Mantra and continue.

❷ Controlled Demolition.

a.   Sit with a straight and erect spine, with your lower back pushed forward as if you were sitting "at attention." Keep your eyes closed throughout this part of the exercise. Make fists of both hands. The starting posture is with your forearms parallel to the ground at the elbow level. Move the left fist with force toward the center of your chest, near the Heart Center; at the same time, move the right fist with force toward the center of the chest under the left fist. Stop your hands abruptly in front of your chest, without touching the chest and without touching each other. Your elbows are out to your sides, and your arms move in and out while the elbows remain at the level of the fists. The movement is more like a hard-hitting motion using full strength. With each hard-hitting motion, chant the sound "Hud" loudly and with force from the navel. Repeat the action rapidly at a rate of about once every 2 seconds for a total of 6½ minutes.

Do this exercise with great intensity, calling up all the Anger and Power you have. Feel every block and self-directed attack. Let the strong pull at your navel guard you. Match the blow and repel it with the power of your sound and solar plexus, just like a martial artist's "ki-ai." Exert and stop the blow at the same time. Get hot. Imagine fire, bombs, and volcanoes destroying every wrong thing. During the exercise, or at the end, your Anger may subside and leave you feeling powerful.

To end this part of the meditation, inhale through the nose and make your hands and arms tight near the chest, like an iron rod, making the body stiff. Exhale powerfully through the mouth, like an explosion. Then repeat the inhale, tensing, followed by a powerful exhale. Repeat this 2 more times.

b. Place both hands over your Heart Center, touching the chest with your left palm, and the right palm touching the back of the left hand. Close your eyes.

Talk to that feeling of Anger or Power. Ask questions to get to the very bottom of what is bugging you or what has hurt you. Keep at it; you'll know you're done when you find your core issue. You will feel a great shift. Remain with the feelings, but not yet with thoughts, as you ask for solutions. "What will make all of this right again? How must I live in my power? What actions will honor me?" Feel a new balance of power arise that can serve and protect your precious self. In the calm after that storm, ask what the Anger is trying to do, what it wants to accomplish, and what would cool it off. Is the original issue over? If so, then the Anger isn't needed now. Or is there business to take care of to make things right? All the answers are there. Learn what you can and follow through with whatever you hear is needed.

c. Let yourself feel very protected, safe, and peaceful. Let all thoughts go now. Go into a state of "nonexistence." Feel and imagine "nonexistence," a state of no thoughts. Nothing to do, get, or protect; nothingness. Continue this for an additional 8 minutes. Then relax. Finish with a few deep breaths and some light stretching. Then lie down and rest as long as you like.

❸ *Capture Your Gains.* When you revive yourself later, write about your experience and what you now know. How can this experience change you and how you operate?

The Second Lesson of Power
Expressed Anger: Animal Power

With Expressed Anger, you are intense, like a raging bull or a bully using instinctive reaction as force to selfishly defend, fight, take, conquer, and get what you want. You are learning about Power by having, using, and abusing it.

Whenever Anger is not suppressed, its protective power naturally flows when you need it. It is instinctually ready, in partnership with Fear, to bring the energy you need to take care of yourself. In raw form, it is an instinctive reaction to selfishly defend possessions and territory; to fight, take, conquer, and get what we want. You are safer when Anger/Power is naturally available and not repressed. But when "brute" force acts with no thought of consequences, it's called "the law of the jungle."

> As long as a person is engaged with this passion and impulse, he is an animal. Whether you look human or not doesn't make a difference. It has to be understood.
>
> → *Yogi Bhajan, July 30, 1996*

When emotions rule without conscious guidance, crimes of passion, relationship-damaging tantrums, and long-regretted harm are the norm. The history of "civilization" has so far been written primarily by the most brutal, who conquer by force and who rule by intimidation and oppression. Anger-fueled passions build and destroy families, companies, and empires. Abused Anger lays waste to people and the planet. The cleanup takes a long time and is usually done by others. Future generations step on the land mines, drink the toxins, and inherit the emotional fallout. You can stop and actually feel the generations of pillage, rape, betrayal, and murder that you inherited in some form, in some dosage. Everyone has a family story with skeletons of neglect, physical, verbal, and psychological abuses that haunt and harm today—what your father did to you as a result of what his mother did to him. Relationships become battlegrounds of reactive revenge of past deeds. The very force given to us to get what we need pushes love and support farther away.

Once you experience power and control, it feels good to get what you need, to be safe and respected, especially when compared with being exploited and abused. The shift restores hope, builds courage, and raises self-esteem. Some will be grateful and satisfied; some, having been on the receiving end of abuse, will have learned to live in peace with their power. Others will test the limits of their newfound command, seek retribution for their previous suffering, or just see what they can do. Power, and all that comes with it, is very enjoyable. Like any other pleasure, however, it can become intoxicating; we call it "drunk with power." There is a tendency to want more and more of it until you become

Power, and all that comes with it, is very enjoyable. Like any other pleasure, however, it can become intoxicating.

the new oppressor. Each of us will, at some time, play both roles many times—victim and victimizer—to compare and contrast the experiences of power in a great quest to understand what works best. And so the cycle continues, throughout time, with this drama playing out everywhere in nations and in the humblest of households.

What was the power play in your home as a child? Who had it, and who didn't? How did the power holders use it? Kindly and consistently, or abusively and erratically? How did those without power cope? Where do you stand with this power dynamic now? At home? At work? In your community?

Active and Radioactive Anger

Intense raw Anger causes lots of damage, like a wildfire burning through homes, land, and lives. Its intensity makes it difficult to control. When not consciously directed at safety and solution, it does damage and leaves you worse off. A bull in a china shop just wants to walk outside, but it doesn't know how; each crash of broken finery incites wilder wreckage.

The intensity of rage is sometimes needed to protect us from great harm or to handle an intense crisis. Suppressors and victims will, at times, lose control of the mounting pressure to protect themselves. When the harm is so great or cumulative, or when the response is long overdue, when Anger is finally expressed, it's like a bomb. Energy meant to protect pours out in an unfocused and usually destructive way. The very thing, person, comfort, or love desired is destroyed or pushed farther out of reach. Anger will increase again and burn hotter to be misused again. The cycle continues throughout history.

But with power comes responsibility. Just when it is most difficult, great care and skill are required to guide Anger to its benefits. Consciousness and awareness must be used in order to advance Anger's objectives of well-being, rather than incurring its lasting damage. The skillful use of Anger can be used to plan for, protect from, and prevent harm. Just as fire can warm your home or destroy it, this Sense of the Soul can be controlled. Just the right amount of Anger for the job at hand can protect and serve all your needs.

Rachel Rattles Her Cage

Rachel's dad was abusive when she was young. Now, her boss is mean and condescending. She lives alone and loves coming home from work to her long-time companion, Pete the parrot. However, she's often annoyed by his loud squawking and the mess he makes on the floor under his cage. Rachel's most recent of a long list of fiery relationships just ended with the biggest of their frequent fights. Soon after that, when Pete got out of control, she would hit the cage while screaming at the big bird. Immediately afterward she would feel bad and be confused by her outbursts, since Pete's behavior was nothing new. This reaction has been happening more often, and she always regrets it afterward. After working with her Anger, she figured out that she was mad at her boss, her dad, and pretty much all men. It took time to get the courage to talk to her boss and demand better treatment and respectful communication. Soon after, her outbursts stopped; she's now working on using the same skills with boyfriends. Soon she wants to heal the old wounds with her now-deceased father.

Situation: Sir Mad-a-Lot. Are you frequently angry, easily bothered, often irritable, or constantly frustrated? Do you have occasional raging tantrums or frequent outbursts? If your reactions are much greater than is appropriate, you most likely leave yourself and others feeling wasted and confused about what happened and why. You may not know what you are mad about, because in this situation, the expresser (you) is not a victim like the repressor is. Instead, you use Anger to push everything and everyone away in order to be left "safe," but alone. You may use force to obtain love, or at least obedience. You often attract repressors who cower in the shadow of your might and who accept the high price of intimidation in order to be near all that power and to feel a conflicted protection.

Solution: Remedies for rage. If you are in relationship with an angry person (mate, boss, child, neighbor), you may be a repressor who takes whatever that person dishes out. In this situation, your work is to find your power and use it to set healthy boundaries. If you are the frequent Anger expresser, however, your Anger is frustrated and working overtime to heal a wound, resolve a source of pain, and get something you desperately need. Think back to how Desire seemed insatiable when the need and your effort to quench it weren't a match (see Chapter 5). Just so, when your Anger is misdirected at something that cannot restore the exact protection and honor you need, it will rage on, doing damage in all the wrong places. It wants to build something, but it only destroys. Ironically, you have to go soft to solve it; yet it's hard to let down your guard and open up when you are wounded and waging war. But the exhausted respite that comes after any big exertion—a long race, a tantrum, or passionate lovemaking—is a moment of peace that can be used as a moment of neutrality and clarity to find out what is really going on. Once you know what is going on, you can consciously guide your Anger to achieve the purpose it has been trying so hard to reach. The Your Might Is All Right practice will give you such an opportunity, even if you don't think you have an Anger problem. This exercise will help you master the fire within and redirect it from useless destruction to a source of power that can warm and brighten your life.

Your Might Is All Right

During this exercise, access Anger. You are not hitting yourself; instead, you are stimulating your ribs to release dormant or misused energy. You are embodying a positive use of power for your own benefit, like a strong massage. Shift your relationship to Anger and see it as raw power you need in order to be safe and happy.

❶ *Begin with Getting Peaceful (page xi). Tune in with the Adi Mantra and continue.*

❷ *Handle Your Heat.*

a.   Bend your elbows down along your sides. Extend your forearms straight up, so your hands are in front of each shoulder, with palms facing one another and about an 18-inch space in between your hands. Point your fingers toward the ceiling. Bend the ring and little fingers into your palm and hold them down with your thumb. Spread your index and middle fingers into a "V." Make sure you keep these two fingers spread wide throughout this exercise.

b.   Lift your elbows up and out to the sides, so that your bent arms are parallel to the ground. With a forceful motion, bring your elbows down and into the body, slapping against the seventh rib with full force. This movement will cause your shoulders and body to vibrate. Do this in a strong, rhythmic, dancing motion to a beat of one repetition per second. Some uplifting music can help you keep going. Let your head and shoulders move with the music. Your eyes may be open or closed. Your breathing should come to a Breath of Fire, a rapid and even diaphragmatic breath through the nose.

c. Continue for 23½ minutes. Then inhale deeply, stretch your arms up tightly overhead, and lift your body to the extent you stretch your spine. Hold your breath and this position tightly for 15 seconds. Exhale and relax.

❸ *The SOS Method for Expressed Anger.* Sit and rest, with your eyes closed, remaining still and focused as you go through this version of the SOS Method.

a. *Stop and Feel.* Feel the energy and emotions; let them flow. Feel the perfectly balanced feeling of great energy that is peaceful, that has the potential to serve you, and that is under your command. Enjoy having it but not using it right now. Feel how confident you are to be safe and get what you need. See the possibility of the good this energy can do.

b. *Find the Source.* Let the power under your control bring you a sense of safety, hope, and relief. Take a self-compassionate and nurturing stance as you go into your heart and look for the wounds. What happened? Who hurt you? Go deep until you see all the sources of pain and urges to protect or to get something. Compare those answers with visions of all your angry actions. Can you see why those actions didn't work?

c. *Seek Solutions.* What do you need? Get to the bottom of your need. Let your heart tell you. Peacefully see the attitudes and actions that will satisfy you. Nurture, ask for love, learn to give and get love, reach out rather than isolate, use power from the heart rather than the teeth of the shark. Your power includes finding win-win solutions. A healthy, respectful argument can reach a resolution.

d. *Take Action.* Imagine yourself doing what you see and the effect it has. You will know by the relief you feel if it is right. It will create lasting peace, rather than short-term gain with some later cost. Be amazed that you have the power to take care of yourself in a way that does no harm.

e. *Relax and Realize.* When you have all the information and relief you need at this time, come out of the meditation and relax.

❹ *Capture Your Gains.* Make some notes about what you learned. Commit to trying the things your Anger has shown you.

We learn by trial and error about what works best with power. Being out of control is part of the comparative study we all go through. Through trial and error, we gain the ability to discriminate, judge, control, and guide impulses. Anger's considerable energy can be used to bring the safety and satisfaction it is meant for.

The long journey of human history—as well as your own journey—has been a collection of experiences in the lack of power, poorly used power, and well-used power. All are lessons from which to choose what works best. The learning is more fun in the third form of Anger, Addressed Anger, below, which leads to courage and honor used for the good of all.

Anger: Dammed Up or Flooding?

For some people, their work on Expressed Anger begins a flood of uncomfortable emotions, painful memories, and disturbing thoughts that have been waiting like wounded patients in the emergency room to be treated. It is normal to be concerned, to wonder whether it was wise to invite this Anger, to wonder how it will all turn out. Just know that you are releasing a backlog of well-meaning emotions that are eager to serve you.

For other people, Anger will seem absent, unavailable, or inaccessible. This is a result of well-meaning training to always be nice or to get along, or perhaps it's a result of situations in which Anger was disallowed. In this case, it will take more time to allow this essential power to emerge, but emerge it must for you to be yourself and to claim life fully. Like every emotion, Anger, when properly channeled, is nuanced enough to bring the right amount and type of energy to handle the job needed to protect and increase your well-being.

Relief comes with each release, and even more so when you fully process the emotion by responding to your needs. When you process emotions, however uncomfortable, you are learning to handle their great healing power. Try to reach an increase of peace, which will arise on its own when the emotions achieve some of their purpose. Support your work with any and all of the techniques you know to strengthen yourself, including a nourishing diet, walking in nature, talking with your most understanding friend, or doing yoga, powerful chanting, Navel Center work, vigorous exercise, massage—whatever soothes, strengthens, and nurtures you.

The Third Lesson of Power
Addressed Anger: Human Power

With Addressed Anger, you are a giver, leader, and hero, skillfully using your energies to serve and benefit yourself and others.

Healing Happens Here

When the hostilities and fighting cease, the healing and cleanup begin, which is a better use of energy. After a million mistakes, you are finally starting to get it: power is a medium that can be controlled and used without harm to achieve great things. Can you stop and feel all the personal pain it has taken you to conceive that idea? Even in this stage, you're not done learning this. Feel the suffering happening at this moment in countless homes and hearts—rape in India, genocide in Africa, hunger and poverty in nameless villages, racism and crime in America. All of this is cleaned up one broken heart at a time. The best thing you can do to save the world is to move solidly into this third use of power in your life. Healing the damage done to you and by you is the work. Reading this book is a sure sign that you are ready and have the opportunity to clear up the past and enjoy your power, whether that is, to reclaim it or to temper it.

Well-Used Anger: What It Looks Like

"I can take care of myself and others. It doesn't have to be me *against* them; it can be me *and* them." This realization may come to you while standing broken and alone in the rubble of all your past destruction. It may also be discovered through positive use of your energy in effective action that creates graceful abundance all around. You may have protected and provided for yourself so well that further fulfillment is now found in sharing, giving, and helping others reach the same level. Like learning to crawl, walk, and then run, healthy personal development brings progressive abilities to protect from harm, to get what you need, and then to serve the greater good. Action is effective because accomplishment is made more through win-win situations and less by win-lose competition. Like the master martial artist who defends with subtle elegance long before the harm strikes, who neutralizes the threat early so it never "comes to blows," you no longer need violence. Instead, you can rely on words, reason, and understanding to resolve conflict.

When dealing with an intense and hot person or situation, your internal sensors bring forth the urgency and physical force to match it without causing harm. You can receive the message that harm is near or that harm has been done; you can determine the source and then act to take care of it. Well-channeled Addressed Anger is a steady proactive partner, rather than an enforcer after a crisis. Your skilled use and control of power spreads into your environments; many are protected and provided for by your influence in the home, community, or business. When peace and grace are disrupted, your instincts work to quickly and tirelessly restore order. When anger is allowed to flow, your navel energy handles all the tasks you need to perform in order to get through your day successfully. You are effective, active, responsive, and steadily taking care of things. Boundaries are easily set and maintained. When you are comfortable and safe, you can afford to be kind and are able to be firm.

At this point in the journey of power, you have crossed the desert of struggle, conflict, and separation to reach the oasis of ease, cooperation, enjoyment, laughter, and joy. When confidence is there to handle anything, along with the space to operate with grace, even your enemies are treated well. Diplomacy, negotiation, and compromise replace warfare. Although world events show that we are not operating at this level globally, each of us can reach this refined use of Anger to create Peace in our own world.

Refining Your Power

There are several clear components to training yourself to become more sophisticated in your use of power:

- Learn the first two Lessons of Power (pages 139 and 148): awaken and express that Power.

- Use your energy to clean up past hurts and present sources of harm. Stop the abuse first; then, when you are ready, find the power in forgiveness. Don't give this forgiveness from weakness; be safe first!

- Get your needs met so you don't beg. The chapter on Desire (page 109) takes you through a process to improve that skill.

- Find the power in your choices. Know what is important to you and be willing to make a firm stand for a raise, better treatment, doing what you know to be right.

- Powerful people have strong boundaries; using them well is a refined use of power, enforcing them until they become automatic and effortless. Learn more about boundaries in The Power of Boundaries (page 157).

- Use the power of voice. Learn to communicate effectively to get what you need. I suggest Marshall Rosenberg's *Nonviolent Communication: A Language of Life* (Puddledancer Press, 2003).

- Understand and cultivate the "feminine" forms of power. We can define the yin and yang forms of power in the primal archetypes of masculine and feminine, which equally pervade all people and things. The masculine forms are projective, like going to get things and making something happen. The feminine is receptive: allowing things to happen and embracing what is. The latter is, by nature, quiet and is scarcely recognized as power in our patriarchal culture. However, it is urgently needed to regain balance, both personally and globally.

- Study the virtues of the Spiritual Warrior, such as Courage, Generosity, Nobility, Honor, and Grace. First, what do they mean as ideals, and then, how do they appear in action? Especially in these modern times, if you revive these old-fashioned characteristics by treating yourself and others with these great qualities, you will find the power they convey.

The Power of Boundaries

Strong boundaries are a reflection of personal power. Once established and maintained, they do the work of taking care of you. Strong people have strong boundaries. Can you walk up and slap the president of the United States? No, he has many systems in place that keep him safe so he can focus his attention and energy beyond his well-being in order to serve others. Boundaries are not walls to keep people out. They are like gates that allow beneficial behaviors so you can enjoy and be comfortable with others, but they don't allow harm to come to you, even from those you love the most. They are your way of training others how to treat you. When healthy boundaries are in place, you can relax and be closer to others. Boundaries are simple enough to learn and well worth the effort to establish.

Boundaries range from mild to strong as required to match your need and the sensitivity and willingness of others. When the gentler type is not respected or effective, use the next stronger version until it works.

❶ **Inform.** This first boundary involves sharing your experience, what you see, how you feel, what is bothering you. There is no blame. You own your experience. You take responsibility for what you are experiencing; it is completely valid, but not anyone's fault. The other person is just doing what he or she does. If that hurts you, it is your job to protect yourself. "Do you know that you are speaking loudly?" "It hurts me when you say that." "I never heard back from you." This level works with people who care about you or who are healthy enough to understand and accept the information.

❷ **Request.** The next stronger boundary is used when others don't get it or make a change from the information. Ask them to do or not do something that is affecting you negatively. "Please speak more quietly." "Would you not use the word *stupid* with me?" "Will you return my call, please?"

❸ **Demand.** This is a firmer, more powerful request that can be done gently or loudly—whichever is your own style. You are now telling the other what you require. "Stop shouting right now." "You may not call me stupid." "You must reach me immediately."

④ Warn. Firmly set consequences that you will follow through with. Do not set consequences you are not committed to. Do not back down once those consequences are set, which would train the other that your boundaries are not real or to be respected. "I am not willing to speak with you when you are yelling. If you don't stop now, I'm gone; I can talk again when you are ready to discuss calmly." "I have told you many times not to call me stupid—from now on, whenever you do, I will not see you again until you apologize." "If I do not hear from you by the end of the day, the deal is off."

⑤ Attack. This is the strongest verbal (or physical) effort you can make. "Stop it right now!" "We are through." "You will never work in this town again."

⑥ Leave. This is the last resort if a person will not respect you and your boundaries. You can't control others, but you can control whether you will remain in their presence. Remove yourself temporarily or permanently unless and until your boundaries are respected. "I am moving out for a while until you can learn to communicate." "I am filing for divorce." "I quit." "You are fired." "What you are saying (doing) is unacceptable to me. I am open to working this out with you when you are able to do so reasonably. I am now leaving to protect myself."

This system reduces Fear by creating security. It is graceful way to weed out needy and abusive people who drag you down and to attract support and environments of trust. You can't retrain people instantly, so don't think that communicating a boundary just once will do the job. Help a willing person change his or her habits to suit you. First, get a clear agreement to the new rule or request. Then, the first few times it is broken, remind the other person about the agreement without being upset. Continue to maintain the boundary for a while. It will become obvious whether someone is just in the process of changing habits or is not really committed to respecting your boundary.

Sovereign Self-Command

This powerful practice will coordinate your body, mind, and spirit to find your refined human power. This exercise gives you a controlled situation to handle—the pain in your right arm. The left hand helps you confront the challenge from your nobility, to face it consciously with courage of the heart. It can reset your Fear and Anger to a higher frequency, giving you the control needed to use their strong energies accurately to serve you.

❶ *Begin with Getting Peaceful (page xi). Tune in with the Adi Mantra and continue.*

❷ Grace under Fire.

a.   Extend the index and middle fingers of your right hand, using your thumb to hold down the other fingers. Raise your right arm in front and up to 60 degrees from the horizontal. Keep your elbow straight. Place your left palm comfortably on the center of your chest. Close your eyes.

b.   Make an "O" of your mouth and begin to inhale and exhale powerfully through your mouth with a 2-second inhalation and 2-second exhalation. Breathe strongly and powerfully with emotion. Burn your Inner Anger and get rid of it. Take the help of the breath to get rid of your body's weaknesses and impurities. Continue this breath for 11 minutes.

Access your Anger; the breath and discomfort in the arm will help it come out. Fight and explode inside as much Anger as you need to release. Get mad and see all the ways Anger has done harm when not under your conscious control. When you find enough relief to regain control, rise above it with your consciousness, be the commander of those forces. Work organically and authentically to find your ability to control yourself. Remain clear, calm, even cool within your mind, even while a storm rages in your body. Find within yourself the experience of grace, the feeling of nobility, the meaning of honor. Hold these as your internal posture, and let them carry you through. As you hold strong in this challenge, you will begin to feel exalted. Follow that feeling and increase it. Just as in life, when the pressure creates a demand for more energy to meet the challenge, your nervous system and mind must call for more inner resources. It is more about mind and will than about muscle. Do your best to hold the right arm in position. However, remember that lowering your arm does not mean defeat, unless you let it. Stand firm with yourself and hold your own dignity and honor. Once you find the lift of self-promoting attitude, you have an indefatigable source of empowerment. Call this energy courage and "bookmark it" for easy recall. In time, this feeling can become your new normal.

c.   To finish, inhale deeply. Hold the breath 10 seconds as you stretch both arms up over your head and stretch your spine as much you can. Stretch the discs between your vertebrae. Then exhale strongly, like cannon fire. Repeat this breath sequence two more times. After the meditation, sit and enjoy your Anger in a whole new way. There is no feeling of weakness and no desire to do harm. Power feels pure and wise, able to accomplish anything.

❸ *Follow-Up.* Does this exercise help you feel your power and realize how much you have? You always have it, but can you control it and use it for the good of all? This practice will give you control, which, in turn, will give you confidence to own all your might without abusing it.

Renee Recovers Her Two Forms of Power

Fourteen years ago, my husband and I had happily chosen for him to be the breadwinner, while I set aside my career to raise our two boys. His successful job was highly stressful. Over time, he came to hate it and was no fun to live with; he became a different person. We agreed that he needed to leave his job to relieve the stress and to create more flexibility with freelance work. This solution worked for a while, but when the freelance work began to dry up, he was unmotivated to find new avenues of work. We burned through our savings. With fear creeping in that we would not be able to pay our bills and would be forced to sell our home in an awful market, we became emotionally distant. All I could do was express my resentment and anger; but no amount of bitching got him motivated.

In the middle of all this, I discovered that my husband had created an account on an online dating site. It was beyond shocking and the last straw. I saw only one way out—divorce. Fortunately, working with God, wise friends, a counselor, and Guru Meher helped me see things from a new perspective and understanding. Guru Meher, in particular, shared what I had heard my husband telling me for all of our 20-plus married years—that my husband drew his support, his strength, his everything from me. It was a role I despised and resented. Why should I have to be his support when no one was supporting me? That was my underlying belief. Guru Meher affirmed that men do indeed draw their strength from the women they love, and in turn, they will do anything for those women. I reflected on that thought and recognized that in those times when I did support my husband, he would do anything I needed or wanted. He supported me when I supported him. It was so simple, yet it was as if I were hearing it for the first time. I finally understood what my husband had been telling me all these years. I just needed to hear it from someone else, from another male whose perspective I respected, before I could really get it. It wasn't like the proverbial lightbulb going on; it was like the sun hitting me over the head!

Once I understood that Raymond was hurting, why he felt a need to go outside of our marriage (which he didn't do,) and why he needed support more than my attacks, I realized I had to look at why it made me so angry to be in that position of uplifting him. Why did I feel so much resentment around that? I'm sure that some of it stemmed from what I suspect was sexual abuse as a child. Why on earth would I want to uplift a man when it was a man who had stolen my power? Once I had awareness that this had been going on subconsciously my whole life,

I began working through and beyond it. My only image of female power had been that of "angry woman," but I rejected that role early on. So, without that, what power did I have? As I studied, I began to hear about grace and compassion as forms of feminine power and explored it for myself. I wondered whether I had the power to forgive unjust abuse, to nurture where it wasn't deserved.

It took a lot of yoga and meditation, talking and listening, and releasing through tears to overcome my justified resentments. But now the hard crust over my heart has fallen away. I am revealing a softer, more loving Self that I enjoy. I am learning how to be strong and powerful, but with grace. It's a huge shift for me. I know I am on my way to becoming a different kind of woman, one who has found her power and grace and who can live with them both side by side, comfortably and honorably. Yoga for the third chakra and meditation to expand intuition have also helped me tune into my Soul and allow me to be in a flow.

The results were remarkable. I found that when I supported my husband, he would do anything for me! My soft power of support got more results than the attack-and-withdrawal behaviors and closed heart, which had only contributed to our problems.

Things got better between my husband and me, and we agreed to stay together. But still he could not find work and was lax about trying. I went into sadness and depression that culminated during a vacation in which I retreated and cried rivers late into one night. In the morning, however, I was clear about my other kind of power: I can take care of myself! Rather than waiting for him, I could just handle my fears about money by going back to work. I loved working! My husband had carried us financially for 14 years and got burned out, but I was excited to begin again, especially because our kids were older. I had been working as a teacher part time, but I hadn't seen that as my career. I came home from vacation fired up about work and put together my first résumé in over a decade. I am grateful that my husband was patient and willing to wait for my heart to open to this realization. Almost instantly, he shifted, too. He got excited about starting work he loved and had three interviews in three days—one of which he described as his dream job.

Conclusion? The attitude I bring to a situation does control that situation. I always knew I held great power, but I wouldn't use it if I thought it meant being hurtful. I have found how to express that power with strong words and actions, combined with love, grace, and compassion—all of my powers as a woman. I am at my best when in my positive flow and when I feel my own grace, no matter what the circumstance. A few days after my breakthrough I saw clearly, with a little help from my coach, that with the knowledge and tools I have as an educator and yoga teacher, now is my time to make a difference in the world and to make that difference with love, grace, and compassion. My work is to help women find their power—in mothering, in relationships, and in their lives.

After all you have learned and experienced so far in this chapter, let's take a fresh look at the Purpose of Anger:

The Purpose of Anger is to help you get what you need and protect you from harm by:
Sending a message that you do not like what is happening or has happened
Identifying the harm, its source, and the need it reveals in order to find solutions

Anger has already given you a burst of energy to notice, break through, and clarify the need and the action. It then supplies the passion or physical force needed to stop the harm, take the action, and overcome an internal block, so you can be safe, return to peace, and take care of others.

Once Anger has delivered its message and brought you to a solution to get what you want, it will recede. But healthy Anger is ever alert to the next need or harm. Even in the healthiest loving relationship, Anger is always needed to guard your heart and your honor when there is hurt or lack. When your Anger is channeled in healthy ways, however, it does not push others away, nor does it create distance. Protecting yourself by speaking and taking action to feel safe, honored, and loved creates an environment in which you can open up and be close to others.

Learn to Trust Yourself with Power

In the learning process of our lives, we have all abused and been abused by power. Many good-hearted givers are so committed to *no* misuse of power that they believe they don't have it. Many great leaders and saints remain quiet, invisible, unwilling to do good for fear of doing—or by memory of having done—harm. As you begin to discover your access to power, you may be a reluctant healer or hero, unwilling to accept the responsibility and preferring to remain meek and ineffective, even to the point of continuing to suffer unnecessarily. But trusting yourself to *use your power wisely* is a key step in every journey to the higher stages. Refusal to use your might, even for right, is often mistaken as not having any might. But when the kind and compassionate givers stay out of the game, the world is controlled by insensitivity and force. If you are a reluctant healer, a Spiritual Warrior watching from the shadows with sadness for the conditions out there, then you are needed! You can get in the game if you begin to trust yourself with power, and you can gain this trust though well-channeled Anger. Use it first for self-protection and self-healing, as you experience the good it can do. Then help others from your position of strength. In time, you will gain and use more freely what was always there.

The Fourth Lesson of Power
Finessed Anger: Higher Power

> *Anger is not yours. It is a power channeled through you to break through pain and ignorance and to bring freedom and light to all.*

In the journey of life, it is essential to survival to discover that you do indeed have power. It is also wonderful to discover this! You continue gathering skills, using your power ever more effectively to protect your interests and to get what you want. It feels so good, however, that many a great person-become-egomaniac has become stuck there, creating tragedy. This costly vital lesson occurs when sensitivity is low. If you are unaware of your deeper needs, you become voracious in satisfying yourself with physical rewards, while deeper needs cry out (see Desire on pages 119-126). But when power is used effectively to meet your own inner longings for love and connectedness, that fulfillment becomes a blessing to others. When love and joy truly prevail inside, others feel it too, just by being in your presence. The ability to give, help, and heal is the next stage of empowerment. The scope of interests and activities in this stage naturally shifts from self-serving to serving others, not because "it's the right thing to do," but because it is simply overflowing. Once your own needs are well met, the next need is to uplift others.

When you spend more time in the abundant flow of good things and feelings (even if it takes a lot of work and surrender to get there), your power becomes a pure and benevolent thing: "I can do great things." All that comes to you is received with gratitude and is then shared. As you become the giver and creator of good, you become more God-like, more like the Source of creation that gives all things. You see that all you have and give is simply flowing through you from that Source. Where does all the power beyond you—that which spins the atoms of the stars—

As you become the giver and creator of good, you become more God-like, more like the Source of creation that gives all things. You see that all you have and give is simply flowing through you from that Source.

come from? You didn't create yourself. Your power is not what has kept your heart and lungs working and what has made food available to all creatures constantly. That's a lot of power out there. What if humans could tap into and gain benefits from all that power beyond themselves? We don't have to be religious to define all that power that is above and beyond our own personal strength and will—all that is above our pay scale as Higher Power. Rather, working with it is the final destination in the journey of power.

Your evolution brings a shift in the fundamental operating principles. The ego-based struggle to obtain and retain is over. You enjoy letting things unfold naturally, like sitting and watching a good movie. Your will is used by holding a simple intention of goodwill to all. This is a subtle, almost invisible use of power. But those who have perfected it call it the greatest power. Call it the power of prayer, the power of love, the power of peace. Whatever you call it, it is felt in the presence of great innocence, like a newborn; or of great beauty, like a sunset over mountains; and especially when you go deeply into the depths of the heart, when you feel the Soul. None of this can be conquered and gained by force—the masculine forms of power. Only through the feminine forms of openness, allowing, listening, yielding, and nurturing can you reach it. These feminine powers bring a balance to life by which the Divine qualities of the Soul can shine through a mortal life, unobstructed by ego's cloud of Fear and Force. In human form, that power has a sweet face of Peace, undisturbed in any circumstance, high or low. Sacredness is recognized in all things. Protected by that, nothing can harm; there is nothing to hurt. Individual needs are subsumed; Anger is resolved at its source.

Be Supreme

There are two ways to live. The first way is to exert and assert your strength, fight and win. The second way is to surrender, relax, and allow a higher power to do it for you. This exercise creates a challenge in which you can observe your approach and learn to handle situations using more than just your own force, your higher power. This meditation requires some endurance and practice to perfect it. Your arms will feel comfortable at first, but they often become painful after a period. When that occurs, become very calm and draw your focus onto the breath and the mental mantra. As you focus on allowing some universal force to do it for you, let the images and sensations of your arms fade.

❶ *Begin with Getting Peaceful (page xi). Tune in with the Adi Mantra and continue.*

❷ *Higher Power.*

    a.   Extend your arms in a circular arc so the palms and fingers of each hand face down about 6 or 8 inches over the crown of your head. Separate your hands by about 12 inches. Keep your thumbs separate from your fingers and let them hang loosely. Breathe in a three-part pattern:

        • Inhale in 8 equal strokes.

        • Exhale completely in 8 equal strokes.

        • Suspend the breath out for 16 beats in the same rhythm.

        Mentally repeat the mantra Sa-Ta-Na-Ma 8 times with each full cycle of the breath. Continue with this pattern for 11 minutes. With practice, slowly increase to 31 minutes.

    b.   To end, inhale deeply as you raise your arms high up over your head. Stretch your arms backward and upward. Drop your head back and look up. Stretch with all your strength to extend the lower back and neck. Then exhale and let your arms down. Repeat this final breath 2 more times.

❸ *Be Carried.* Sit very still and imagine you are floating in space, held without effort, sustained by those great Forces that created and sustain your life and that operate the entire Universe. Enjoy doing nothing while everything is being done for you. Do you feel all that power? You don't own or control it, but it is yours. Marvel at all that effortless power: your heart is beating, the world is spinning, your life is unfolding, and you don't have to lift a finger. End with a few deep breaths and some light stretching.

❹ **Capture Your Gains.** This posture releases a powerful stimulant to the pineal and pituitary glands. The result is an increase in intuition, which is a perceptual function of the entire brain and the whole mind. It gives you guidance that seems as if from some great and wise Being—that is your power, your higher power. Did you feel the ease in allowing something greater to take care of you? How could you try and test that in your daily life?

The Gifts of Anger: True Empowerment and Courage

You have needs, and you must gain enough control to take care of yourself. Life has its own built-in urge to sustain itself and an unstoppable cycle of birth and death. There's no fighting it, as some things are beyond our control. There are two sources of self-created suffering. The first is when you don't take control of what can be done. To take this type of control requires your masculine form of power. The second is when you try to control what is not yours to control. Allowing things to be as they must be is your feminine form of power. Learning to use and balance the two forms of power is a sometimes painful, sometimes ecstatic learning process.

In its journey of human consciousness on Earth, the Soul travels from ego to liberation, from isolation to union, from weak frailty through the growing strength of personal will to the full empowerment of Universal Will. We prepare for the greater forms of power, such as Neutrality and Love, by using Anger correctly to create safety and security for ourselves. Then, at the level of Courage, we shift our focus to others by giving, contributing, and living for each other. The shift from Anger to Courage is a lift in consciousness that brings us closer to Truth, Self, and Soul. The ego exaggerates our own importance, while also seeing Self as insignificant. Only a broader perspective—the view from a height beyond Self—allows the insight that leads to true empowerment. The Courage state of consciousness is authentic, not forced. It supplies you with energy to keep going through the unending cycle of loss and gain in order to prevail over temporary circumstances. In that, you become ever more timeless, fearless, deathless.

Self-Study

❶ Use the most relevant concepts and practices you have learned in this chapter in a daily practice. Each exercise in this chapter makes a transformative extended practice. For example, Grace Under Fire (page 159) comes with a specific self-therapy with extensive benefits for venting Inner Anger, as well as for finding and finessing your power. Begin with 40 days of 11 minutes each day. After 40 days of practice with the right hand extended, switch hands and do 40 days with the left arm extended and the right hand on the chest. After 40 days in that position, do another 40 days of both arms extended. This extended practice will do a lot for you in just 11 minutes a day. So don't overdo it.

❷ In conjunction with the exercise, work with thoughts and memories of frustration and anger. The mind brings these to your attention along with emotions in an effort to have those issues resolved. Big issues with an intensity of feeling may ask you to address them first, but you can also start with smaller irritations, which you may find easier to practice. Allow and explore the feelings using the scripted meditation or your own intuitive version of the SOS Method (page 137 or in Resources).

❸ Your meditation is only part of the daily practice. You should also use these 6 weeks to take action. You will hear what needs to be done—you have it written from earlier exercises. Now is the time to act, to take care of the bills and the unfinished projects, to address the unspoken communications. Dip into your well of power daily and use the mental and emotional fortitude to break through fear and resistance. Don't get overwhelmed; you can't do it all at once. Choose one action at a time, and commit to at least one daily. If you resist that, do something else; just move!

Life Projects with Anger and Empowerment

- Your work with Anger will likely include resolving old traumas, which are healed by creating strong protection today. When the psyche feels that what hurt you before cannot likely hurt you now, you are ready to relax and forgive. See Chapter 11 (pages 295–317).

- Anger built up from early wounds and neglect of Anger's clear messages must often be discharged so the present reality can be seen and so appropriate action can be taken to create safety. Holding onto hurts and injustices may *feel* like power, but a far greater power is surrender. The power of surrender may initially feel like weakness, but it makes large amounts of previously wasted energy available that can now be applied to progress.

Ideas to Use

- Recognize Anger as an ally, a bodyguard ready to serve your needs and protect you. Listening to the message beneath your irritations, frustrations, anger, and rage will always reveal a harm that needs safeguarding, an action that needs to be taken to fulfill a need, a boundary that needs to be set.

- Taking full responsibility for all that you experience is an essential lesson in power. It is better to take action to improve a situation, rather than complaining and blaming while continuing to live with it. Shifting from "they did it to me" to "I created this" is a hard pill to swallow, but once accepted, it gives the power to create something better.

- Taking charge of your well-being, rather than expecting and demanding the world to "give me" (as was the case in your infancy), moves you powerfully through Anger. Surrender expectations and entitlement to specific wants. Do the same for approval, agreement, and other behaviors that you often use to try to control others. Focus on control of behavior, body, mind, energy, and spiritual principals. Yoga, for example, is a system that trains all aspects of human self-control.

- Reaching for any higher state will transform Anger. Fear (lack of trust or confidence) underlies Anger. Love dissolves Fear and therefore Anger as well. Antidotes to Anger thus include Love, Compassion, Kindness, Caring, Acceptance, Forgiveness, and Surrender of your "all-important position."

- Find the satisfaction of serving others in order to train your mind to look beyond the self and to discover a broader safety in the happiness of those around you. Higher levels of consciousness see the personal benefit of altruism. You will learn that give and take, peaceful cooperation, and the general welfare of all serve you far better than do individual survival and dominance.

- Become consciously aware of your defensive nature and check it with reality. Even with the help of others, you may not be able to neutralize a particularly challenging situation. (Most friends will always "support" you and will help verify what you already perceive, rather than help you see a new perspective.) You may be able to immediately find allies where you once saw enemies. Self-honesty—that is, the willingness to see yourself clearly, to admit fault, and to make corrective action—is vital to accelerated growth. Self-awareness is the single greatest remedy to all problems. Challenges are part of life, but *problems* are self-created by your perception, which is limited to what is known through the filter of your level of consciousness. Yoga and all practices that increase self-awareness thus result in positive change.

Chapter Seven

Depression
Giver of Rest, Hope, and Help

Depression's strategy is to stop and give up so you can move on and win
Its dead, dark energy forces you to relax, review, and renew until you surrender
to your higher power.

The Purpose of Depression

When you are stuck or frustrated and you can't move forward or accomplish your purpose;
When you don't think you can, don't know how, can't find the power and the way;
When you desperately push harder or feel weak and give up;
When you need to stop everything and reevaluate…
Depression helps you lose interest and give up on what's not working, so you can awaken to new possibilities and approaches.
It breaks you free from attachments that no longer serve you.
Depression forces you to reevaluate your beliefs and approaches by taking away your energy and motivation to continue your old patterns.
Letting go of the old restores your energy and allows you to see life with new clarity.
Depression ultimately connects you to the Source of all power. It teaches you to let go and let the Universe do the work

In these fast and competitive times, there is a constant cultural pressure to go, fight, and win. In this chapter, you will discover and enjoy your built-in faculty to achieve balance and find the way through any block. Please read further to understand the important distinction between Depression and Apathy.

Stop and Listen

"I was really depressed yesterday." I have worked with people and their feelings for decades, but now I hear statements like this much more frequently. The statistics (1 in 10 report depression to a doctor) indicate that there is a lot of it going around. Are you feeling it or seeing more of it around? What is changing? Are we more depressed, or are we just more aware of what was always there? Are we more sensitive, or is it a sign of growing numbness? Is life just getting to be too much to handle, and we're losing hope? Why is this happening now, when access to everything is so abundant? We now know that emotions increase and persist when we aren't listening or responding to their wisdom. So, what is this Sense of the Soul trying to tell us collectively? Since emotions are right even when they are wrong, let's begin to listen more closely.

Depression certainly makes you stop and be still, which is a good condition for listening. Depression directs your attention inward, because you don't care about everything "out there." Depression's energies guide you to your depths so you can listen within for what is wrong, what you need, and what to do. Nanak said, "Deep Listening brings focus easily. Devotion to Self constantly awakens you. Nanak says, Deep Listening resolves pain and errors." Depression can come over you like sleep, yet it serves as a wake-up call. You have been dreaming all along and need to drop something, quit trying, and let new things come to you. Depression will leave once you listen, let old ways die, and resurrect your reality.

Sorting through the Muck

You know the experience of Depression as boredom, laziness, lethargy; the blahs, the blues; a lack of energy, caring, or will; heaviness, sluggishness; feeling helpless and hopeless. It sounds like, "I don't know. I don't care. I can't. What's the use? It will never change. I give up," or just a groan, a weak sigh, and then silence. Let's understand the language of these messages by understanding the actual words we use to describe them.

- When things don't happen the way you want them to or expect them to, you might try harder. If you don't get the result you want, you might feel...

  Discouraged: less motivated, confident, or optimistic

- When all you have tried fails, you may make a big push to attack the problem out of...

  Desperation: a furious but fruitless struggle that may be random, ineffective, and disconnected from the desired results

- When no amount of effort works, you might begin to give up and descend into...

  Despair: a profound feeling of hopelessness in which you no longer try or do anything at all

- Your original need is now more distant, and you have less ability than ever. Your energy drops further as you become...

  Despondent: a state of deep gloom and disheartenment, of hopelessness and lasting passivity; the opposite of respondent; you have no ability to respond to your need

- My dictionary first defines Depression very loosely:

  Depression: a state of unhappiness

  Then clinically:

  Depression: a psychiatric disorder with symptoms such as persistent feelings of hopelessness, dejection, poor concentration, lack of energy, inability to sleep, and sometimes suicidal tendencies

When people tell me they are depressed, I ask them to clarify exactly what they are feeling. They usually find several emotions trying to solve a complex set of unaddressed or unresolved issues. When other emotions have not achieved their purpose after some time, you may go into what we commonly call *depression*. But Depression is not a single emotion; rather, it is a whirlpool of other emotions that have not accomplished their tasks, to which Apathy is ingeniously added in an attempt to help you.

Apathy enters the fray and robs you of energy when you most need it to solve things. Why? Apathy stops your business-as-usual life with a distress signal from the Soul, pointing to serious issues that need immediate attention and action. Each feeling, problem, and solution must be sorted out separately before the natural joy of life will return. You can sort out these problems with the skilled use of any other emotion that has been trying to help you. But if you have entered into Depression, then understanding and working well with your Apathy could be the best place to start. Here's why: We have a tendency to ignore stress, fatigue, and ineffective efforts, pushing ahead harder to solve the issues. But Apathy takes away our energy and drive, forcing us to rest and reevaluate everything. Thus, *apathy* is the word that best describes the

> **Depression is not a single emotion; rather, it is a whirlpool of other emotions that have not accomplished their tasks, to which Apathy is ingeniously added in an attempt to help you.**

actual emotion that gives Depression its distinct character. I will use the terms *Depression* and *Apathy* interchangeably from now on to honor common usage while creating a useful reminder for you to distinguish the primary element of Depression from its many other ingredients.

Apathy

- Lack of energy for or interest in caring about or doing things that once motivated you

- Caused by a state of mind in which circumstances seem too much to cope with

- Absence or suppression of passion, emotion, or excitement; indifference

- Emotional emptiness; inability to feel normal or passionate human feelings or to respond emotionally

---

The meaning of the Greek origin of *apathy* is "insensitivity to suffering, without feeling, without emotion, freedom from suffering." Doesn't that sound like an ingenious solution for our time? Until recent centuries, Apathy was considered a positive quality, an asset. It was seen as giving us the ability to rise above the grip of emotion into reason. The Cynic Movement was a great experiment that tested this approach. The Cynics were onto something that I would call the ability to gain conscious control over emotion. But this movement also failed due to the denial of emotion. In this work we have shown denial of emotion to be injurious and impossible. The Cynic's denial led to unhealthy detachment and a lack of intuitive wisdom that feelings bring; and, a loss of joy. Thus, the Cynics are now remembered whenever we use the word *cynical*. We now know that emotions, as Senses of the Soul, can be used *with* reason—or rather with total sensory awareness—to deal with life head on without being overtaken by them.

How Apathy Happens

There is always a desire beneath Apathy that has been thwarted and unfulfilled. When you don't get what you want, when you want it, exactly how you want it, frustration, mixed with determination, motivates you to keep trying. Desire increases, and you want it even more. Anger and Fear join in the fight with all their energy. You get more attached—you gotta have it. With all that emotion, you lose the rational ability to try another approach, to be patient, or even to decide to do without it.

When your desires outlast your energy and optimism, your efforts are less effective. You see what you want slipping farther away. Then doubt arises about whether you will ever get it at all. Hope diminishes, and with it, the energy to make decisions, requests, or actions—precisely what you need to end all this. These are replaced by more ineffective behaviors, like blaming, complaining, irregular and random efforts, procrastination and avoidance, doubt, confusion, and distractions, all of which give the illusion of progress. Poorer efforts, worse results, and diminishing hope spiral increasingly downward. Apathy is working to help you drop the unproductive pattern, paradoxically by further disabling you to use them. The better you can "listen within" at this time, the more successful your depression will be to truly renew you.

These days, we tend to be overwhelmed with the constant barrage of information and sensations. Changes and choices create increasingly intense and conflicting emotions. We don't seem to be able to move faster or do more to handle it—perhaps it is truly impossible to control it all. With Apathy, our inner wisdom is sending the relief of not feeling, not caring, slowing down. It is sending a message that this is not working, so we need to turn the noise down and slow down so we can sort it out and see what is happening, what is important, and, from there, what to do. In our time in history, sensitivity is increasing, and yet most people don't know what to do with all that sensory information. It makes sense that Depression is increasing, because it initially provides relief, followed by a rejuvenating focus. Paradoxically, this intuitive move to not feel requires that we fully feel—not everything at once, but just this one dark, quiet, inwardly focused emotion that directs us to let go of everything and find our way. As always, the way through emotions is to go through them and allow them to do their work. Whenever our responses to challenges aren't working, Depression helps us drop whatever isn't working so we can pick up something better.

Energy Quality and Relation to Other Emotions

Every emotion has a distinct energy signature and profile that serves its purpose. The intense energies of Fear and Anger are better suited to go get what you want. They clamp down harder onto your goal and won't let go. Desire's burning strength, like a dog on the scent, just won't quit. Grief's softer sadness is designed to loosen your grip, so you can accept reality. But the empty lethargy of Depression can better unclench your fist and jaw. You will fear the loss of control, but that is exactly what you need to give up at this point. You may fear that your mental and physical weakness and the absence of spirit may be impossible to escape, but this won't happen if you gain trust in this natural emotional resource.

As empty as it feels, Apathy is a higher energy state than Shame and Guilt. Compared with their debilitating self-attack and abandonment, Apathy feels relatively neutral. It brings the peaceful relief of nothingness, which can initiate a turnaround toward caring and getting started again.

If Anger has not been able to go, fight, and win the prize;

If Fear has paralyzed your progress;

If Shame has made you feel incapable and helpless; or

If Grief has held you longing for the past rather than engaging the future;

If Desire has you fixed on a mistaken or impossible goal, thus missing true satisfaction…

Then Apathy's quiet surrender is your key to accept what is and to discover what else may be out there in the unknown darkness.

A Safe Experience of Depression

❶ *Begin with Getting Peaceful (page xi).* Become as grounded, clear, and strong as you'd like to be before dipping into this short experience.

a.   Sit calmly, close your eyes, and take several deep breaths. Imagine before you, stretching from far left to far right, the full range of your ability to handle life. Out to your left are memories of feeling small, weak, helpless, and needy. As you move toward the center, you see effort and struggle with frustration, ineffectiveness, and mistakes. As you move to the right of center, there are better results from your efforts, including competence and success. Far to the right are great capability, expertise, empowerment, and ease, which bring freedom and fulfillment.

b.   Can you imagine this full range? Where in this scale do you spend most of your time? Identify your own average level of willingness and optimism, your own sense of what is possible for you to achieve. Mark that spot with a number from 1 on the left (the weaker side) to a 10 on the far right (the empowered side).

c.   Revisit lower states that you have been in or that you have felt in others. Go as far down in energy and despair as you can—feel the heavy, dead feelings. Feel the fear and dread, but don't resist it; let it flow through your body and just observe it all.

d.   Take a deep breath, clear the heavy feelings away, and move as far to the right as you can imagine yourself (or others) in high levels of proficiency and accomplishment. How high can you reach up that scale? Can you allow those sensations, or is it unfamiliar and harder to hold a clear experience?

e.   After exploring as you like, inhale deeply and come back to the here and now.

❷ *Capture Your Gains.* Use your own self-assessed rating first just to know where you stand. Know that there may be somewhere to go, to grow into. Then, as you continue with this chapter and your continued development, revisit this exercise and reevaluate. Mark your number and the date in the margins here and come back in a month and a year for a new "reading" to realize your changes.

The Roots of Apathy Consciousness

As with every emotion, Apathy is a way of seeing the world, and that seeing creates your reality. The pattern may begin in infancy and childhood—perhaps there was scarcity in your environments, maybe you or your needs weren't taken care of, or perhaps your caregivers and role models felt powerless to take care of themselves. When you are small and fragile, there is a very real imbalance of power. When you are abused, you are trapped, with no voice or understanding to handle the situation. You literally only have the experience of powerlessness to cling to. You feel helpless. Even if you weren't abused, if your independence was not encouraged and was supported by a fearful or overprotective parent, you now may be left with the understanding that you are no match for life. When Scarcity Consciousness is in the physical environment, it may feel impossible to prevail against it and find self-power. When this insufficiency moves inside your head, you are imprinted with a lack of belief in your own power, will, and hope. Looking out from yourself, you see a wasteland, a barren world in which there is never enough energy, help, money, time, love, or support.

This early pattern can establish negative beliefs of victimhood and nonexertive behaviors that continue into adulthood. A fully capable adult raised in this way remains unable to get what he needs due to a habitual way of seeing himself. Apathetic patterns can also be initiated in adulthood through trauma or overwhelm. These patterns may be so complete that the possibility of taking care of yourself doesn't even occur to you; instead, you wither away, waiting for "Prince Charming" or "Mommy" to come to the rescue. When you believe that there is no use doing anything, you begin to neglect everything, and life falls apart. In this way, Apathy breeds feelings of low self-esteem and low self-worth. Shame's "I am worthless" and Guilt's "blaming it all on others," as well as pessimism and expectation of failure, blind you, making anything positive invisible to you. When all you can see is black and gray, it is easy to understand how emotions—meant to be a temporary, real-time message—can alter your consciousness when not properly processed. Fortunately, emotions can also be used with awareness to raise your consciousness!

The Apathy Strategy: Stop and Give Up to Move On and Win

When you are stuck and don't know how to move forward to accomplish your purpose, when you don't think you can, don't know how, or can't find the power or the way to move forward, you may instinctively redouble your efforts, forever driving toward a dead end. Apathy is your "Plan B." When you get tired of not getting anywhere but don't see any other approach, intuition takes over to conserve your personal resources with thoughts like, "I don't really need it," "I don't care anyway," "It will never happen, so what's the use of trying?" Your energy shifts to passivity. But there is a genius within Apathy's backdoor approach to accomplishing by way of giving up.

Apathy's stop-everything aspect is designed to take you out of a losing game. Rather than redoubling your efforts when you're down, you withdraw from the goal by not caring. Apathy slowly helps you lose interest and give up on what is not working, so you can restore your resources and awaken to new possibilities and approaches. It breaks you free from attachments that no longer serve you. Apathy forces you to reevaluate your beliefs and approaches by

Apathy slowly helps you lose interest and give up on what is not working, so you can restore your resources and awaken to new possibilities and approaches.

taking away the energy and caring to continue as you were. Apathy puts you in a low state so you can check out, rest, and then check back in to a new, upgraded scenario. When you truly let go of the old, new ways and means that were always there can finally be seen and pursued with restored energy. Apathy ultimately brings realization and connection to the Source of all power. It teaches you to let go, enjoy the flow of life, and let the Universe do the work for you.

In the pursuit of knowledge,
every day something is added.
in the practice of the Tao [the Way],
every day something is dropped.
Less and less do you need to force things,
until finally you arrive at non-action.
When nothing is done,
nothing is left undone.

True mastery can be gained
by letting things go their own way.
It can't be gained by interfering.

➜ Tao Te Ching, 16

Don't Get Stuck Being Stuck

Apathy can't work if you resist it, nor will it be effective if you let it have its way without your awareness. When you don't recognize the purpose of Apathy and don't work with it, you can be stuck forever. Perhaps you've been there before. When you feel it coming on again, it's scary, so you resist it. It feels like it will swallow you, so your instinct is to

When Apathy calls, the more completely and consciously you can give in and give up, the faster your recovery will be.

fight it. So, instead, you hang out in limbo, unable to get out of the pit, but not surrendering completely so Apathy can do its work. It is counterintuitive to give in to that death grip that seems to swallow you forever. However, resistance to Apathy merely delays its ability to help. When Apathy calls, the more completely and consciously you can give in and give up, the faster your recovery will be.

The other misuse of Apathy comes from indulging in it. A client of mine discovered this while sitting with her depression:

> I have felt this way so long, Depression is like an old friend that has been with me through so many hard times. It's like a warm blanket I wrap up in. I can hide under those weirdly safe protective covers. It is my cover-all excuse when I'm scared to try or don't want to deal. It's my getaway escape from every intimidation. I'm not sure what I would do without it.

All of her damage of immobility in her career and relationships became a more comfortable choice, as compared with facing the real issues—no try, no lose. An obvious danger, however, is that the more essential that need is to your survival, the more important it is for it to be dealt with.

Consciously processing Apathy involves neither blocking, resisting, or denying it, nor indulging and wallowing in it; instead, you must welcome, honor, and allow it. Acknowledging Apathy brings a release and a relaxation. As with all lower-energy emotions, there is a fear of being engulfed if you "surrender" to it. But emotion is energy in motion; when it is allowed to flow, it moves things and then moves on in its own time when the adjustment is made.

Consciously processing Apathy involves neither blocking, resisting, or denying it, nor indulging and wallowing in it; instead, you must welcome, honor, and allow it.

As you develop trust in your emotions by seeing the results of being willing to feel bad things, you'll gain confidence to go into that dark valley and work things out. The exercises that follow can help you out of ineffective behavior to get to what your Apathy is really after.

Putting Depression to Work

❶ *Begin with Getting Peaceful (page xi). Tune in with the Adi Mantra and continue.*

❷ *At Wit's End.* Relax your arms down by the side of your body. Bend your elbows and raise your hands up and in until they meet at the level of the chest. With palms facing your chest, extend the fingers of each hand. Cross your hands so one palm rests in the other and the thumbs are crossed. The fingers should point up at a comfortable angle. It does not matter whether your left or right hand is on top. With your eyes closed, focus on the center point just above the eyebrows. Then bring your focus to the tip of your nose. Follow this four-step breathing sequence:

- Inhale through the nose; then exhale through the nose.
- Inhale through the mouth; then exhale through the mouth.
- Inhale through the nose; then exhale through the mouth.
- Inhale through the mouth; then exhale through the nose.

All breaths should be deep, complete, and powerful. When breathing through the mouth, purse the lips almost as if to whistle. Continue this sequence for 11–31 minutes. From this place of stillness, continue into the self-guided visualization.

❸ *The SOS Method for Depression.*

a. ***Stop and Feel.*** Use the following prompts to bring forth memories. Fully allow the feelings and physical sensations to flow through you:

- Poor parental care, abuse, abandonment, poor and harsh conditions, failures

- Dependency, codependency, caretaking, helplessness, victimization

- Laziness, procrastination, avoidance, lethargy, immobility, tiredness

- No one cares about you; you don't care

- Persistent beliefs that life is hopeless and I am helpless

- Helplessness, neediness, blaming, passivity, inertia, inability to handle situations

- Absence or suppression of passion, emotion, or excitement; indifference

Sense the level and kind of energy, your will or lack thereof, or the degree of hope or hopelessness that you feel. Sit with the discomfort until you reach a little stability—a feeling that you can handle—just a slight relief.

b. ***Find the Source.*** Ask your Depression why it is here. What is the source? Can you trace back to something you wanted that didn't happen? What do you want right now? What seems to be in the way—you or something outside?

c. ***Ask for Solutions.*** Ask your feelings, "What do I need to know or do? Is there something I could let go of that would help me feel lighter? Am I now ready to identify a thought, decision, communication, or action to deal with or change something about my circumstances to bring relief?" You don't have to do anything about this; just recognize it. Do you need to just relax and restore? Or is the need to simply shift your focus from past needs to present—bask to the here and now and you. Ask the emotion whether there is another perspective of the need. What is really important? What does your Soul need? Can you feel a sense of control, power, or confidence that everything can, will be, or already is taken care of? All of this takes very little effort. Notice that you can do this work while still in a low-energy state. The energy may even shift or lift with your perspective. A lift that comes from deep within is Spirit. Try accepting, allowing, approving, improving it. Can you feel a shift from just having your needs heard?

d. ***Take Action.*** Act on the wisdom that apathy has brought you.

❹ *Capture Your Gains.* Take notes of any action and attitudes you heard that need to be held and carried through. Follow the voice of this inner wisdom.

Sarah Saves Her Self

I suffered a string of major losses: marriage, house, financial security, and then the new love of my life was gone. I dragged through two months of deep despair and grief; I totally got into it, got lost in it, saw no way out. At some level, I was indulging in the dark stupor of pain like some drug. Maybe I didn't know any way out. It's like I had to wake up and take control instead of leaving my emotions in charge. The switch was to observe rather than to indulge. It took a huge effort to do it differently, but when I finally listened to those feelings, I heard that I just needed to talk to that new love of my life. I obeyed and picked up the phone. Instead of my usual needy pleading or attacking, I simply satisfied the need to talk. It went well. He responded in kind, and I felt better. The turnaround from waiting helplessly, begging, or demanding was to love myself by taking action (and a risk), to get the connection I wanted by giving it.

I was actually in touch with what I wanted, and I was able to act. However, it eventually became clear that my relationship with him was really over. So, there I was again with my familiar friend, Despair, saying, "I don't care." But this time, I came out of it quickly, for the first time ever. What made the difference? The simple ability to sit down and talk to my feelings, to ask what I was feeling. The answer I heard was hard to face: "I am unlovable." That's a sharp pain. But having discovered that I could feel the pain and handle it, I was able to face it. And then, instead of giving up, I asked, "What is the purpose of this feeling, and what is it I need?" The answer came instantly: "Practice giving love to myself." That was a tall order, but once I saw clearly, I could learn to do that.

Going Deeper: Surrender, Rejuvenate, and Resurrect

Like all emotions, Apathy matches diverse situations with specific intensity and results in four time frames: Currently Discouraged, Hopeless History, Bleak Future, and Timeless Patience. Whatever your history and relationship to Apathy, work through the exercises in each section that follows for renewal of hope and strength.

Currently Discouraged: Finding the Resources to Keep Up

Situation: Things don't go exactly how or when you'd like. This situation happens naturally during the course of any day, task, or lifetime. The work with Apathy is to control what you can and accept what you can't control, allowing it all to happen under the joyful fuel of optimism. We learn this lesson slowly by seeing what works and what gets stuck, whether in huge failures or in small frustrations. The little lessons are the least costly, so let's start there with a mild form of Apathy—Discouragement. Think of this as the first virus of Depression; it can be knocked out before it takes over. Discouragement, or a state of less courage, is a partial loss of energy, ambition, and confidence while facing a challenge. Frustration, a mild form of Anger, likely arises first, prompting extra energy to push harder. If you run short on that energy or if it just doesn't do the job, your optimism may drop to Discouragement. You now have less energy and hope, which are the very resources you need to succeed. You hit a wall, get tired, want to give up, or get bored; you are disinterested and don't care. The project stalls. At this point, recovery either can be quick and easy or can lead deeper into Despondency. This is a good time to learn skills that will carry you through life's bigger disappointments.

Our prevailing culture prizes ambitious, aggressive behavior, competitive action, and intense pressure to meet crucial deadlines—*dead* lines! Life seeks balance—a time to laugh, a time to cry; a time to sow, a time to reap. A successful friend of mine was staying at our house a few years ago. She came in from a long day full of exciting meetings and shopping, changed clothes, and had a few minutes before her dinner date picked her up. She flopped down on the couch and asked me, "What can I do for tiredness?" She was hoping for a tip or special herb from my knowledge of nutrition and yoga to keep her going. Instead I said, "Rest!" I suggested that tiredness was her body's way of asking her to relax and replenish her reserves. This thought had never occurred to her. It took a while—after a full collapse later on—for her to learn to balance the spending and replenishing of her resources. Now she enjoys being busy, but she knows when the body or spirit says, "Enough!"

Discouragement's loss of momentum may be resisted, or it may be welcomed as a time to pause, regroup, refresh, and refocus to come out of tunnel vision, avoid burnout, and get back to the enjoyment of your energy in action. Your process to work through Discouragement is the same as it is for Depression, which is much stronger, heavier, and more difficult to handle. So if you practice your skills at this first sign of what can later become Despair and Depression, you may avoid it altogether. (In fact, right now, as I write this, I am feeling stuck and frustrated. I find myself pushing harder to get through it. I have a deadline and need to be finished. I don't like how it's going, and I don't know how to do it. But pushing harder isn't working, and it's sure not any fun. I don't want to stop, I feel the push, but I'd better practice what I teach: Time for a break! Sure enough, I come back from a nice walk and a meal and the ideas are flowing more easily. The work is more enjoyable too. Yes, I practice what I teach.)

Solution: Rest, review, and renew. With practice, you will increase your sensitivity to feel a loss of energy, determination, or hope as it occurs. You can then immediately find out what you need. As experience reassures you that you are more "productive," as well as happier, you will take the time to take care of yourself. When things aren't going your way, it is possible, without ruining your career or upsetting your friends, to back off, lighten up, take a break, and get away from the task. Studies show that the brain works best by alternating use of the left brain's focused analysis with the right brain's unfocused creativity. There are stories of people's intractable struggles with a problem being solved in dreams or idle moments when the mind is at rest. For example, Elias Howe was frustrated for a long time when trying to invent a sewing machine. Then one day he dreamed he was being attacked with spears, which he noticed had holes in the tips, and that clue he got while napping changed the world.

Do you have your own favorite, trusty methods for switching gears from "drive" to "neutral"? A walk, bath, time with nature, meditation, playfulness? The experience that answers can come easily without "trying" presages the highest realizations that you are not the "doer." Even if answers don't come in a bright flash, you can return to the task with refreshed energy and perspective.

Sometimes, however, you need another type of activity, some form of "checking out," to let go, rest, and regroup. Perhaps you need a short break, quick exercise, or a mental health day, vacation, or sabbatical—depending on the size of the change. During that time, you may actually enjoy feeling tired, lazy, and not caring for a while. This leads to a shift into doing by not doing.

Sometimes, what you need might be a shift in attitude: from blaming or complaining about a problem to taking responsibility for making it better; from intimidation and procrastination to believing in yourself; from some concept of how things should be going to allowing for the reality of how it is going. Every emotion begins with a thought. In Apathy, a thought of "impossible," "incapable," or "shouldn't be" starts the sequence. Accepting the situation as a challenge to be overcome, rather than as "something wrong," might be all you need. Or patience and tolerance might be your key. Sometimes you just have to wait for a better day (or year), when the winds of time flow favorably to fill your intentions.

> *Men are born soft and supple;*
> *dead, they are stiff and hard.*
> *Plants are born tender and pliant;*
> *dead, they are brittle and dry.*
> *Thus whoever is stiff and inflexible*
> *is a disciple of death.*
> *Whoever is soft and yielding*
> *is a disciple of life.*
>
> *The hard and stiff will be broken.*
> *The soft and supple will prevail.*

→ **Tao Te Ching, 76, Lao Tsu**

Half-Hour Revival

You can do this simple practice in 30 minutes or less to produce a balance of rest and clear energy that leaves you refreshed and ready. Experience it as a microcosm of the complementary aspects of self-care that you need in order to be at your best. As you go through the different feelings of this experience, notice where your imbalances lie. What do you need more or less of to remain encouraged?

❶ Drink a glass of water. Begin with Getting Peaceful (page xi). Do the At Wit's End breathing exercise (page 181) for 6–11 minutes. Then take a deep relaxation for 11 minutes or more, using Letting Everything Go (Resources, page 334). Wake yourself gently using the suggested wake-up routine.

❷ **Spirit to Move On.** Moses instructed the Jews to do this exercise before long journeys to raise their spirit, correct their slave mentality, and give them the will to fight and not give in.

a. In a standing position, spread your legs as wide apart as possible without losing your balance. Your arms form a 90-degree bend at the elbows, with your forearms more or less parallel to the floor and extending away from the chest in a relaxed position. Rotate your hips parallel to the ground at a moderate pace in as complete and large a circle as possible. The direction can be either to the left or to the right. Continue this movement for at least 6 minutes.

Be completely focused on your body. Feel your feet connected to the floor. Imagine drawing energy up into your body from Mother Earth. Loosen your hips and move in a sensual dance. Be sure to use enough strength that you must remained focus. Feel everything physically moving and allow emotions to flow. Feel earthy, sexy, strong, or whatever gives you pleasure and enjoyment. Lighten up and move; the pace is yours to set.

b. To finish, sit down comfortably to meditate and go through the self-guided inquiry.

❸ *Know How to Go.*

a.   Feel your levels of strength and empowerment. Enjoy that feeling. Without leaving that feeling, look down on now-distant memories of when you did not feel this way. Recall your fits of Depression. Your energy level may dip as you recall that familiar state. Feel the difference but don't go all the way there this time. Hold on to your current reality.

b.   Explore the source. See clearly whatever it was that was being hampered, obstructed, or thwarted. Recognize the concept that you now have of what you want and what ought to be happening. See the whole history of your efforts and what it has come to now.

c.   Come to a full stop. Declare everything on hold for now and let it all go, just for a short time. Do you feel any resistance or any insistence that you must make it happen in a certain way and when you thought? Even racecars take pit stops; this is a very calm one for you.

d.   To the extent that you can, let go, rest, and relax. Enjoy temporarily losing focus as you let everything go soft. Everything's fine. You haven't a care. You don't care if you dare. Detach further. Let all your fixed concepts drift. Maybe there is something else out there. What if some new and better idea is out there that works so much better for you? Actively and creatively choose to know nothing. Can you feel safe in the unknown zone for a few minutes? Let not knowing be okay—even relaxing and fun.

e.   See the whole play of life on Earth. You have never had to carry all this life. Let gravity work to hold Earth together while you enjoy it. Know that there is an answer out there somewhere. Call on the vast darkness to work things out. Send out your intention for things to flow in harmony, but leave the details unformed. Your order is in, that's all you need to do now. So relax and feel that all is well, it has been all along, and it always will be. Can you truly feel that?

f.   Don't go after a new plan. Instead, try a something different—let it come when it is ripe and ready. If patience is difficult, agree on the most time that you are willing to give for it to happen, and then commit to being open and relaxed at least until then.

❹ *Capture Your Gains.* Be sure to create this kind of inner environment at least daily. If, from your unattached attention, you feel, hear, or see something at any time during this practice, receive it gratefully. Plan to go about your business, participating in life in the most enjoyable way you find. Develop your trust in this process. Write what you learned, commit to an experimental new approach, just for a while, and track your results. Wait for some time before you evaluate the usefulness of the approach, and then measure not just your "results" out there but also your quality of life, enjoyment, and emotional well-being.

Jan's Rejuvenation

Jan is a political activist who has worked hard to promote important global issues. When I met her, she had already been angry at the "opposition" for years and frustrated that all the injustice and ignorance still hadn't changed. She no longer saw any hope and was in a slow process of giving up. "Why should I care anymore?" she asked. Jan looked pretty lifeless, with an undercoating of remaining Anger that flew out occasionally. After just a little conscious work with her Apathy, she brought on some accelerated "giving up." First she gave up the idea that the world should be—and soon would be—without struggle, that people would ever all agree on something. Her inner vision showed her that differences were all part of the creative Universe, that nature loved to keep things interesting by mixing us all together to work things out. Life is just as it is meant to be; all Jan had to do was play her role and be on her side of issues, while also seeing the importance of diversity. This has helped her enjoy the dance of opposition. As her energy and enthusiasm returned, she also let go of the view that there had not been any progress. Issues she had fought for 30 years ago were done and won. She has now raised her standards to fight for further change.

Depression is a way your Soul gets you to wake up and listen. It pulls you out of the game and sits you down to make you look deep inside for what matters most, what you need to get rid of, how best to move forward, and finally the nature of power itself. Your energy, spirit, and enthusiasm will return on their own when there is balance within and without. You might be charging down the wrong road. But if you work with your Depression, the right way can open up to you without so much effort on your part. This is very different from all the motivational "just do it" approaches that ask you to assume someone else's level of energy, ambition, and source of satisfaction. Only your heart can reveal what is right for you at any time, what motivates you, what you care about, and how much you want it. When you are tuned in and ready for it, your Soul always has up-to-date best practices and information available for you.

Hopeless History: Memories and the Patterns They Create

Situation: Early training and old memories cause you to feel weak or to try too hard. Your psyche can take over once Apathy's inertia moves into it. Your thoughts and feelings of Despair may have been learned at an early age from your parents, other role models, and environments. Or you may have discovered them yourself in reaction to outside influences, such as insensitivity to your needs, aggression, perfectionism, shoddy environments, and abandonment. You react to all this by adopting a clever way of coping with the situation, using the resources you believe to be available. Here are a few common coping patterns, all of which carry a belief that you are incapable of having things the way you want them to be.

>   **Nonexertive strategies:** "I can't do it. Help me. Poor me." You suffer to get sympathy. You suffer personal neglect. You are wasting away or living in substandard living conditions.

>   **Exertive strategies:** Martyrdom; extreme sacrifice and suffering; excessive caretaking of others; resentment; blaming and complaining; intense, ineffective, and misdirected efforts with no productive outcome; energy spent to destroy yourself or to sabotage the success of others; hoarding and other addictions.

These coping strategies can be mixed most creatively. Once the energetic signature is a well-worn path in your experience, it can be a very difficult ditch to climb out of. But Despair will tell you how, once you are listening.

Solution. The first step is to cut your ties to the beliefs, their patterns, and the energy signatures that make them so familiar and even comfortable. Releasing the deep fatigue from years of neglect can open room for deep rest and fresh energy. Only when renewed possibility wells up will the psyche release its dependence on the poor strategies that had served as lifeboats in more desperate times. Rejuvenation requires physical recovery, as well as reorientation, deep inside yourself. A fresh, up-to-date, and thus more accurate appraisal of your resources and capabilities gives new definition of what is possible. That is the beauty, and the point, of Despair—it works at the foundation of your beliefs, your being, and your spirit. Working with the slow, low energy without resisting, fighting, or thinking something is wrong is part of the package. That surrender can be so beautiful for you and may not even be accessible to all those happy, busy people you have envied.

You may be very reluctant to trust that dark, fearsome state of no energy. You may wonder whether if you surrender to "no energy" whether energy will ever return. But remember that this is also how the body heals from illness. When you are ailing, energy seems to be gone, so you must rest in bed. But the energy isn't really gone; it is just being used for change and healing. In this section, we're talking about consciously participating with the Depression process, rather than languishing in Despair with no awareness. You may know from experience that it is particularly tough to see others in that languishing state. If you have tried to help, you know when they are not ready. The best advice in this situation is for you to be willing to help others while allowing them their own process, without guilt and without taking responsibility for them. The same is true for helping yourself in this same state.

Rest and Rejuvenate

❶ *Begin with Getting Peaceful (page xi). Tune in with the Adi Mantra and continue.*

❷ *Emotional Fatigue Buster.*

a.   Raise your right hand up by the shoulder, palm facing forward as if to make a pledge, with the fingers straight up and the elbow relaxed and hanging down. Bring your index and middle fingers together and your ring and little fingers together, with a "V" shape between them, like a "Vulcan" greeting. The thumb points toward your shoulder. With your left elbow relaxed by the side, bring the left forearm parallel to the ground across the front of your body. With the left hand facing palm down, spread your fingers wide. Pivoting from the elbow, move your left hand back and forth, parallel to the ground, like a pendulum. Move steadily with one complete stroke— left and right—per second. Breathe through an "O"-shaped mouth, keeping pace with the movement of your left hand. Continue for no longer than 11 minutes. To end, inhale deeply as you interlace the fingers of both hands and stretch them above your head. Stretch. Exhale. Repeat 2 more times and relax. This step will take away your internal fatigue forever. The fatigue that your body cannot remove, that makes you old, that makes you weak, will disappear in the first 7 minutes. Yawning is natural and normal. Let it come.

b.   Move your arms vigorously. Let your entire torso go wild! (Do not play any music; you don't want to become systematic or rhythmic.) Go wild for 3 minutes!

c.   Bring the tips of the thumb, index, and middle fingers of each hand together. Lift and swing the arms alternately back over the head like a backstroke. Move quickly for 1 minute.

d.   Release the fingers and sit straight. Whistle loudly for 4 minutes. Then begin singing for 1½ minutes. Whisper for 1 minute. Whistle for another 30 seconds.

e.   To end, inhale deeply. Concentrate at your Navel Point as you hold your breath. Pull your navel in strongly toward the spine. Exhale. Repeat two more times. Then relax.

❸ *New Review.* Sit still. Be in total awareness of how you felt in each part of the exercise. You know how your energy has flowed in your life; you know the feeling of your highs and lows. Just take in the panorama of your life's enthusiasm-and-despair profile. Instantly understand how you have squandered wasted energy. See clearly what has drained your lifeblood the most. How are you currently out of balance or unsustainable? Your body will tell you that you need rest, or that you need more stimulation, or what you need to work better, to feel just right. Don't think. Just let your body and feelings tell you exactly what you need to do in life to rejuvenate yourself physically.

❹ *Capture Your Gains.* Take notes on what you learned. You may need several years to release old fatigue and recover your health, optimism, and willingness. Be sensitive to what your system is asking for; be kind and caring in response to those needs. Whatever effects those damaging beliefs and habits have caused, healing is always available. It is important to actively let go, which you may not be able to do as a leap of faith. Your subconscious will cling to old sources of safety. What will be your new sources of security, modes of operation, basis of trust? Honestly find them with new eyes within and around you. Opening to the future can be very difficult when all your energy is gone. Allow time to heal, knowing you will move on with greater joy and success when the extra weight you've been dragging around has been dropped and new resources take over. Don't push. You may have to wait for a slight break in the clouds of Depression to make use of bits of motivation as they come. Listening to all the underlying emotions and clearing up their intended tasks will take time. But careful attention to the layers of emotion and their distinct processes will release Depression in its own time and rhythm.

Awakened to Her Apathy

In the past, I would get stuck in shame for so long without relief that I would get depressed. After years of this, any time I felt bad or when someone was "mean" or displeased with me, I'd go straight into Depression.

I had experiences this weekend that would normally have sent me into Despair. But this time I was watching. When I didn't go to Despair, I was amazed that I became happy. Going into Despair has been such a habit; it required a lot of focus and effort to go a different way. I asked myself, "How will it serve me if I fall into Depression right now?" I saw that the old benefit was that someone would have pity on me and help me, even though that never really worked.

Just this new approach to Apathy made the difference. To know that Apathy possibly has a function and benefit made sense and changed everything. I love the analogy that Depression takes you out of the game with a purpose. Something's got to change, so step back and take a different look at it. I now know I can get back in when I'm rested and ready.

When I "stayed awake" in that feeling, I could just stop and let go of something that was obviously not going to work out. It gave me more kindness to myself to know that nothing is wrong with me when I feel this. Asking, "What is a new way to approach this?" became a source of energy.

→ *SM*

Bleak Future: Finding the Resources to Move On

When your needs remain frustrated and you just don't know what to do, you begin to believe "it" is big, and you are small. Once "Impossible" and "I can't" enter the mind, you begin to go progressively weaker. Depression creates a reverse momentum of spirit, energy, and effort that spirals downward and collapses into itself like a black hole that pulls in all surrounding light. Without emotional training to know what is happening, you can be held down by Depression for a very long time. You may need to go all the way to the bottom before you can climb back out; that may be what it takes for you to completely give up before abandoning your defective programing and patterns of helplessness.

Moving on requires the release and rejuvenation described in the Hopeless History section. Here we will work on improving the resource management that is required to sustain yourself. You have an amazing supply of energy, ideas, and enthusiasm available. Don't take my word for it; you won't believe it until you feel it. But when this supply is recognized and utilized, life is fun, and happiness flows. Knowing what you have to work with and having the confidence to use it wisely bring trust in yourself to let go of old ways and move forward.

When time and advantages are mismanaged, you can come to believe that things just don't work out for you and never will. But it may just be simple logistics. Experts and coaches are available who can teach and train you to be effective. Here are a few practical areas to consider. Do an honest self-assessment of each of the following:

Daily use of time and energy: Of everything you do, ask, "Is it time effective? Is it money effective? Is it impact effective?" Review and, if need be, revoke commitments. If they are not serving you, there is likely someone else who can serve them better.

Safety of relationships you are investing in: Are you looking for love in the wrong places?

Projects and situations: Deal with whatever you haven't handled. Complete or cut your losses on unfinished business. Don't leave things hanging and weighing over you.

Health and energy: Heal imbalances of the body, mind, and spirit. Get help if you don't know what to do or won't do it.

Acceptance rather than resistance: See where you are wasting energy. Change what you can control, accept what you can't, and learn to know the difference. Allow what is to be so.

Let go: Let go of concepts or behaviors that don't serve you. If you are depressed, that is what is being asked of you.

Situation: Stuck and feeling helpless or hopeless. One warm afternoon, my son and I were taking a walk on a country road when he was 4 or 5 years old. On our way back to Grandma's house, he said he was just too tired to go one more step and miserably plopped down. It was hot, and I did not want to carry him home, so I said, "I'll teach you that your attitude and spirit control your energy more than your body does. I'll race you home, and if you win, I'll give you (whatever it was I knew would excite him at the time). Go!" He jumped up and ran full speed all the way to the house.

While physical depletion is a real cause and effect of depression, it will always have a mental, emotional, or spiritual basis. Willingness comes when purpose is being pursued. Hearing from your heart and soul are the only ways to know what will bring fulfillment. I hope you have experienced by now how well emotions can help your inner wisdom.

Solution: Better allocation of subtle energy. Breath is your most vital physical resource, but it is subtle enough to help you work with your nonphysical assets. Your breath is a key to the invisible inner world, where all your undying hopes and dreams come from. Your subconscious mind is closely attentive to your breathing, even when you are not. When the constant, effortless rhythm of inhale and exhale are interrupted, all your survival fears and instincts are on full alert to protect you. The following practice uses the conscious mind, where willingness and optimism are directed, to intentionally take charge and manage the breath in a way that increases both calm and active energies in a balanced way. The use of breath in this exercise represents your ability to recognize, access, and utilize all your resources, such as health, time, money, friends, challenges, opportunities, luck, fate, and destiny. Moreover, it teaches, practices, and enhances your ability to draw on your infinite energy, called the Source, Soul, or God.

Energy Sustainability

You live and spend energy. What inner and outer resources have returned to you from that investment? Do you use that capital well? Does all that energy exchange serve you and your purpose? Are you able to handle the demands of your life and reach your destination? Do you know your own definition of *success* and how to fulfill it?

❶ *Begin with Getting Peaceful (page xi).*

❷ *Managing Your Resources.*

a. With your elbows relaxed by your sides, bring your hands to the heart level, separated the width of your chest. Hold your palms facing up, as if to catch water. Your eyes are one-tenth open. Regulate the breath:

- Inhale slowly for 20 seconds until you reach full lung capacity.

- Hold your breath for 20 seconds; be relaxed and steady.

- Exhale slowly, taking 20 seconds to fully empty the lungs.

Repeat the parts of this breath for 11–31 minutes. It takes time for most people to develop this capacity and control. You may need to start with 10 seconds each segment and slowly lengthen the time with practice. Whatever you do, just keep the three parts of the breath of equal time.

b. While maintaining the same position, immediately begin to chant "**Har**" at a steady pace on each exhale. With each "**Har**," pull in the navel strongly and pull the fingers into the palm, like calling someone toward you. Continue for 3 minutes. Then inhale deeply as you make tight fists. Exhale and relax.

❸ *Self-Assessment.* During or after the exercise, sense the following: What is the source of your energy? How is the supply of your energy? Where do you get your sense of purpose and enthusiasm, your deep-down motivation? Where do you want to invest your time and that energy while here on Earth? If you often feel empty and meaningless, feel it now and let it reveal what is missing. What would make your heart leap? What would get you out of bed willingly? Attitude and spirit are the source of energy; they are the switch that turns it on. Ask your spirit what would totally resurrect your attitude and spirit within you? Take note of every insight. These are your Soul's marching orders. These orders will guide you to manage your gift of life to reach your destiny.

❹ *Capture Your Gains.* Write about your experience. Use honest reflection and deep introspection to understand how you can better align your personal energy and environmental resources with your purpose.

Timeless Patience: Will and Willingness

Fear, Desire, and Anger teach about getting what you need and want. They motivate and help you develop strength of Will to reach a goal. They are like your car's accelerator. If a car is going in the wrong direction or is headed into a wall without brakes, it will either run out of gas far from the destination or crash and never make it. Depression is your braking system; it seeks to enhance your "drive" with maneuverability so you can get where you are going. Once you get good at pushing, you need to balance that with patience, because not all things can be won by force. Love is a good example: You can't make someone love you. You can act favorably, but Love happens on its own clock.

> **Once you get good at pushing, you need to balance that with patience, because not all things can be won by force. Love is a good example: You can't make someone love you.**

Imagine for a moment that the Universe actually operated such that everything you wanted could totally be yours. However, being the Universe, it would actually know better than you the best time and form in which to bring your wishes to you. But by then, you would have become disappointed and moved on to some other Desire. You would miss recognizing it altogether. So, you would constantly think the Universe did not care very well for you, while it would wonder why you keep refusing the gifts. The difference in receiving all or nothing depends on what is called Surrender. This is not "giving up" but "giving in"; it is allowing *what is* to be what it is, and to let what you know to be augmented by what you don't know, to have what you intend be enhanced by how things actually go.

Depression is a sign that your balance of Will and willingness is off; Depression forces you into submission. When ambition is high but vision is missing, Apathy helps you stop and see what is really happening beyond your limited scope and concept. Sooner or later you discover that it works better to use your Will to make something happen and to blend it with willingness to let that something take its own course. When you reach the dead end of your own power, you realize you need some higher octave of power outside your best limits. We very practically call that a "higher power." Surrendering to Higher Power (capitalized to show respect for its awesomeness) or accepting Divine Will is a concept and a practice that helps us learn this more refined way of operating here on Earth. Doing so requires skills very different from "willpower," like the subtle and archetypically "feminine" forms of power— sensitivity, humility, and patience. These powers are neither in vogue nor in the spotlight of world power at this time, but your heart may be achingly calling for their soothing benefits.

The timeless lesson of Apathy is to transcend limitations of body, mind and time in order to be helped by that Source of all things.

Going Into that Dark Night: Sacred but Scary

Before you learn by experience to trust your emotions, it may seem dangerous and ill advised to let them have their way with you. None is more frightening than Apathy, which sucks you down into a seemingly inescapable tar pit with no energy to fight it. To completely surrender is what you are being called to do, but to give in and give up feels like certain death. Those of us who have been there know that fighting with ever-diminishing resources is truly hopeless—as they say, "Resistance is futile." To really truly give up, to embrace the relief of not caring, to really let go, and then possibly risk letting things take care of you? That is a scary but exciting possibility.

The following exercise requires both effort and surrender. It allows you to examine how you use these two complimentary forms of power to find your best blend. Although it takes strength to maintain, try to relax and let energy come from beyond yourself to carry you through effortlessly and joyfully. This might not happen right away, but all skills require practice. Once you understand how well it works to "let go and let God" in a practical way, you can use it throughout your life.

Rise and Renew

This exercise will challenge you. To pull it off is an exercise in will and willingness.

❶ Begin with Getting Peaceful (page xi). Tune in with the Adi Mantra and continue.

❷ Resurrection. Read the following passage and replay the words in your mind while you do the exercise. (Ideally, play the recorded version as you practice.) Use the words to learn to give up your own effort and to succeed using a power greater than your own. When it gets hard and you don't think you'll get through it, remember that it is your nonphysical resources, like Hope and Determination, that control the body to keep up and keep going to the end. This will train your Will to win whenever you need it.

> Patience pays.
>
> Wait. Let the hand of God work for you.
> One who has created you, let Him create
> all the environments, circumstances,
> facilities, and faculties.
>
> "Oh individual, why are you in a very
> doubtful state? One who has made you
> will take care of you."
> One who has created this Universe,
> all the planets, planetary faculties, and
> facilities in us,
> He is the one who has created you. Wait.
> Have Patience. Lean on him.
> Then all best things will come to you.
>
> Dwell in God. Dwell in God. Dwell in
> God.
> Befriend your Soul.
> Dwell in God and befriend your Soul.
> Dwell in God and befriend your Soul.

*All the faculties and facilities of the
Creation that are in your best interest
shall be at your feet.*

*You need a million things. A million
things will reach you if you are stable,
established, firm, patient.*
*Remember: Creator watches over you,
and Creation is ready to serve you if you
just be you.*
*So please, take away the ghost of your
life and stop chasing around.*
Consolidate. Concentrate. Be you.

*And may all the peace and peaceful
environments, prosperity approach you,
forever.*

Sat Nam.

→ Yogi Bhajan, "Patience Pays"

a.   Extend both arms straight forward, parallel to the ground. Curl the fingers of your right hand into a fist. Extend the right thumb straight up. Keep the right elbow straight as you move your fist to the center of your body. Wrap the fingers of your left hand around the outside of your right fist. Extend the left thumb straight up. Adjust the grip of your hands so that the thumbs can touch along their sides as they point up. The tips of the thumbs will form a little "V" like a gun sight. Focus your eyes on the thumbnails and look through the "gun sight," seeing both far away and the "V" at the same time. Follow this breath:

- Inhale deeply as you fill the lungs for 5 seconds.

- Exhale completely as you empty the lungs for 5 seconds.

- Suspend the breath out as you stay still for 15 seconds.

b. Continue this breath cycle for 3–5 minutes, slowly building up to 11 minutes over time. Do not exceed 11 minutes.

❸ *Use Your Senses.* During the exercise, when the pressure is on, work with this self-guided meditation:

Imagine you are working with two sources of energy, one internal and one outside yourself. Feel your own effort, as well as something else beyond you, doing the work. Try less and yet continue more easily. Look for a new experience about who is in control and where your power comes from. Can you feel a deeper confidence, maybe a sense of trust that everything can, will be, or already is taken care of? You may have the experience that you are complete at every moment; that all is taken care of for you. In that reality, stress vanishes. When you feel you have no energy of your own, you can call on that other type to take over completely until you are back on your feet. Once you know the power is out there, you can tap into it at any time. Your soft energy can help you accept and allow it. Rejuvenate to resurrect. When you feel Willingness and Optimism, that light keeps you going through any darkness.

When you are finished, relax and rest.

❹ *Capture Your Gains.* This meditation is known to conquer normal depression and discouragement. It builds tremendous strength in the nervous system. This meditation must be cultivated and built up gradually. That is why you start with 3–5 minutes. Be sure that you can do the meditation perfectly for the entire length of time you choose to practice. If not, lessen the time and build up. As you master the practice, you can increase the time that you hold the breath out from 15 seconds up to 60 seconds; pick a time that is realistic for you. Then build the practice time up to 11 minutes, but do not go any longer. Remember to keep your elbows straight during the entire meditation. If you feel dizzy or disoriented in this practice, be sure you are doing the suspension of the breath properly and that you are holding the neck straight by pulling the chin back just slightly. You may want to have a partner supervise your practice by timing it, having a glass of water handy, and giving you a massage at the end. Build your nervous system's strength with this exercise; you will feel a new stability and trust in yourself.

The Gifts of Depression and Apathy:
Willingness and Optimism, Hope and Divine Help

Energy will ebb and flow; success will come and go. You have the sense to know what to do when both are low.

The timeless lesson of Apathy is to transcend limitations of body, mind and time in order to be helped by that Source of all things.

When feeling hopeless, you feel small and incapable. At that moment, you don't feel connected to anything greater; it's just your Self against the world. There is no help out there. "In low spirits" means you are not feeling Spirit. Spirit is, by definition, invisible, vast, not completely knowable. Any amount of connection to that Spirit is both the purpose and the solution to Depression. Soul has access to all power, it is always in control, and it never gives up. The ultimate lesson of Apathy is to confront the limits of Ego and Personal Will to see that you are not the doer at all. Your birth, your breath, every good break—all of that is power you enjoy but don't possess. The timeless lesson of Apathy is to transcend limitations of body, mind, and time in order to be helped by that Source of all things.

When you can't see the beauty, the opportunity, the love, the God all around you, staring into the dark nothingness for a long while forces a change in perspective. A glimmer of light somewhere may be undeniable, like staring at the sky until you see the first lone star appear. When that happens, Hope may return—if you can find what previously seemed impossible, anything else could also be possible. So maybe there is Hope, or there is a way, or there is a God. You didn't make the star appear; it happened. You don't make your heartbeat; it beats for you. Can you appreciate its beating, the gift of it, and accept that now as well as when it stops? Accepting things as they are, trusting what is and will be, allowing for the entire universe to take care of you and everything—these are the elevated truths of the Soul. We are born with needs and the ability to meet them in a Universe that is fully able to take care of us.

If you want to become whole,
let yourself be partial.
If you want to become straight,
let yourself be crooked.
If you want to become full,
let yourself be empty.
If you want to be reborn,
let yourself die.
If you want to be given everything,

give everything up.
When the ancient Masters said,
If you want to be given everything,
give everything up.

→ **from Tao Te Ching, 22, Lao Tsu**

Self-Study

Choose from among the exercises in this chapter to create a regular practice that will give you the changes in perspective and energy you need.

Projects for Growth

Make an assessment of your relationship to Depression and its purpose in your life. What has fallen, and what will it take to resurrect it? How is your balance of personal willpower and your patience to let things take their course? Write what you now know about your own Apathy. How has it manifested in your life? What does it require of you now? Is there more work for you to do here to clean up unprocessed issues from the past? Do you feel equipped to work with these as needed when they come up in the future?

Chapter Eight

Grief
Sadness Helps You Heal

Grief nurtures you to awaken and heal your heart.
Its bittersweet longing dives deep within to find wholeness after any loss or change.

The Purpose of Grief

When things change;

When something is lost or dies;

When you are heartbroken, sad, and lonely, pining for the past, longing for what you miss;

When the hopes and dreams you have set your heart on look like they won't happen;

Or when you need to get cozy and quiet to get in touch with your heart, to mend your wounds and care for yourself . . .

Grief and Sadness slow you down and bring a soft energy that allows you to look deep inside and feel what is most important; to know what you need to be complete and full; to move forward to getting it; to be able to adapt, change, and flow; to constantly renew and grow.

Grief ultimately opens your consciousness to love and reverence for all things that come and go.

You are invited to safely explore your depths, awaken your heart, and return from that inner journey ready to live fully.

Greet Your Grief

According to the dictionary, *grief* is "suffering over loss; remembering with sorrow; mourning; feeling anguish, heartache, woe, sadness, melancholy, moroseness." From mild temporary regret to prevailing bitter anguish, Grief feels like dropping into darkness and emptiness. You deflate; you want to cry and wail, rail against the unfairness, or collapse like a child lost and alone. This low-energy state feels heavy of body, heart, and spirit; thoughts are dark and cloudy; the pain can be intense and visceral. The blues, mournful country songs, and ancient ballads of lost love; collapsed chests and heads hung low; deep sighs uninterested in the next breath—all express some of the flavors of Grief.

Thoughts dwell on the lost one, with past joys biting deeper with each memory and cycling endlessly to recapture and hold on to what was. You want to get back to a time, a place, an experience that you miss. It feels like part of you is lost, and the only way to be whole again is to go back—back to when you were happy, to remember and re-experience it again. In remembering, you may feel connected to the desired experience, but this route is full of pain.

When something has opened your heart, expanded your horizons, and filled you up, you feel on top of the world, like Leonardo DiCaprio's character on the bow of the *Titanic*. However, when things change, when that moment is gone or that person leaves, your bubble bursts; you feel deflated and brought down. The greater the joy associated with that moment, the deeper the fall and the more painful the landing. At the moment of loss, the mind brings only positive memories back. Life suddenly seems empty or even impossible. If you ever for a moment didn't appreciate it, its importance is clear to you now; life is empty without it.

Gain and Loss at Work

Here's how the dominoes fall: You need something, you desire it; that need motivates action, and you work until you get it. The effect is positive—you feel good and want more of that same feeling, naturally. In this fashion, you begin to connect your well-being to the object. Happiness becomes attached to and dependent on maintaining things as they are. You want to do what you can to maintain the status quo. The positive outcomes of this dynamic are self-care and responsibility; the negatives are attachment and resistance to change.

But as we know, the only thing in life that doesn't change is change itself. Every source of pleasure diminishes with time. Every treasure becomes boring, loses its shine, changes or departs altogether. When that happens, you are no worse off than you were before, except that you have now become accustomed to the benefits, and your baseline of happiness has shifted. Suddenly, you feel the loss, and it's unacceptable.

Initially you try to protect your happiness and maintain the status quo by holding on to the past or by resisting, or even fighting, the change. It feels unfair that life gave you something but then took it away. You may blame God, the world, or yourself and your bad luck. When the fighting doesn't work, you become Despondent. The Latin origins of *despondent* imply a broken pledge or promise. Life interrupted the flow of love that it had been sending; it took away something important and broke the joy that was yours. The assumed deal was broken. When you become Despondent—the opposite of respondent—you enter a state of deep gloom and sadness.

Impermanence: *Change Is the Only Constant*

In the time it takes you to read this sentence, about 5,000,000 cells throughout your body will die and new ones are being born. It is a constant process that continues until your body dies. After you die, other bodies will come and go. The nature of this universe is that it is continually being created and destroyed. Yet the urge of any individual life is to be permanent and survive. We seek safety and stability in the known, in the unchanging. That is why we invented God and hold on to Him so dearly. We reach for the unchanging, and it can be found—just not in material form and function.

Think of all the things that change: the seasons change, youth grows old, good times end, memories fade, friends move on, pets and loved ones die. A babbling infant grows into a marathon runner; your thoughts change from bad to good to bad again; hopes are realized or lost; opportunities are taken and missed. Would you have it any other way? You don't want to get old and wrinkled, but how else will you experience everything you're supposed to experience or learn what you need to learn? Movies and myths have long told of the hell created when every day is the same, when we never grow old—the curse of living forever. No change means no learning, no improvement. Change is how we learn: Growth is a drive within each cell. Change is the essence of life, and life is unrelenting.

Adjusting to Change and Gaining from Loss

Your ability to let go of what was, adapt to change, and move forward is cultivated through your experience of Sadness and Grief. If every loss left us weak and alone, our species would never have survived. But it only *feels* like we can't go on. "It is better to have loved and lost than never to have loved at all" is true; if it weren't, you wouldn't have known what love is. Usually you are not even aware of the lesson until Grief delivers its truth.

Your ability to let go of what was, adapt to change, and move forward is cultivated through your experience of Sadness and Grief.

The process starts with an attention-getting pain that focuses you on what was lost; this brings a humbling appreciation for whatever was lost. In this way, Sadness reveals what is important to you. Every single thing comes and goes, but knowing what you gained and appreciating its presence and its passing allow you to enjoy that gift. The things that change us stay with us forever. You can't keep people and things, but you can live with the permanent imprints they leave on your heart. And that may be enough: to have had the best love of your life, to have enjoyed a fantastic career, to have had an exciting youth.

It can't go on forever, and yet we act as if it should. Even the most delicious meal only tastes good when we're hungry. Once we're full, we push back from the table—nothing can tempt us when we've had enough. So how do we get to enough?

When you identify and relate to the underlying qualities of an object—its inner essence—that essence is abundantly available within many other things. A flower has beauty, fragility, freshness, to name a few of its qualities; it might even convey Hope or Love. These qualities are not just held in that one flower, but in all flowers, and all living things, even stars, depending on the beholder. And the qualities of an object remain with you; their effect on you leaves a lasting impression. You can enjoy the sustenance, flavor, comfort, and good company long after a particular evening is over or after a particular meal has passed. The essence of pleasure is available from countless other sources as well. Loss can lead you to feel unsatisfied and insatiable, but when handled with awareness, it can bring you into a deep state of healing, wherein love and reverence for all things flow. These are the gifts of Grief.

With the loss of a close loved one, you may think that all love and joy are gone with them. It's true that you'll never have those exact experiences again, but "good" grieving can leave you grateful for and enriched by the person. You will be able to enjoy the same level of happiness that the person helped you rise to, while going on to find new and different—and possibly even better—ways to experience joy.

The Right Tool for the Job

I was helping Alexandra through a recent breakup with a boyfriend. "He treated me so much better than any man I have ever been with, the way I had always dreamed of feeling with a partner: safe and respected. I have been really depressed since it ended." I asked her to check with herself more closely: Was she feeling Apathy? Was she powerless and unable to do anything about this? Or was it Sadness in dealing with the loss of a wonderful relationship? She shared that she had ended it, because after his initial show of kindness, there had been some betrayals on his part. She had made a powerful and courageous decision to end it despite how well it had started. So it was Grief that she was feeling. This feeling was needed so she could adjust to the change. But she also had to acknowledge that it had been her choice—she had chosen to end it; she had regained her power. Recognizing this difference allowed her to work more accurately with her emotions. She was able to heal by trusting her decision to let go and, thereby, experience her own power.

Depression usually includes a host of emotions, including Grief and Apathy, both of which have similar energies—low, dark, slow. These energies take you deep inside to get intimate with yourself—cozy up, lick your wounds, let go, review, and regroup. Grief cares. If you try to avoid the pain in Grief and become numb, its process is blocked. You remain stuck in the past, unable to move on and enjoy anything but the memory of that which is gone. When you feel that there is nothing worth living for, that all is hopeless, you are in Apathy's realm. In Grief, you can get stuck in regret, recurring memories, and comparisons of your current darkness with the bright past. In Apathy, you despair that there's nothing to be done. Both Apathy and Grief work by making you stop business as usual to look beneath the surface.

A Conscious Encounter with Grief

❶ *Begin with Getting Peaceful (page xi).* From this place of stillness, continue with the guided visualization.

Go deeply inside yourself. Imagine and feel your chest as a huge, dark space that is cold and empty. Let your body be soft and listless. Think of something that you had and lost or that you wanted and didn't get. Let any and all previous losses you can recall come back into your mind now. Keep breathing deeply and slowly as you observe with great interest the sensations in your body and the subtler emotional feelings. Be curious to experience them fully, as if you were deeply engaged in a movie. Stay with the feelings until you are not afraid or until you wish to end them; the more you can relax and surrender into the feelings, the sooner they will subside. But ending them is not the point; rather, the point is to realize that it is okay to feel it all. Once you have a little equilibrium, can you proactively pursue the empty feeling as you would enjoy a warm, dark room when you want to sleep—as something restful, peaceful? Imagine floating in warm water or deep space or whatever image works for you to feel you can completely let go and let the world take care of itself without you. Let everything be taken care of for you. Let go and let things flow as they will. Notice equally any unwillingness to go soft. What are you holding on to? Speak kindly to yourself, as a mother would soothe a child scared of the dark in his own bedroom. Can you encourage yourself this way to move into feelings of safety, coziness, and love? Enjoy as much of that as you can for as long as you like. Then breathe deeply, stretch, and return to activity.

❷ *Capture Your Gains.* Compare that last state to the memories of the loss(es) that you first recalled at the start of the exercise. What do you make of these two very different experiences? How are they related? Did you recognize the physiological signs of Grief? Take note of your breathing patterns, your posture, your energy level. Make notes of what all of this reveals to you about Grief and Sadness.

Grief Consciousness

When loss happens early in life or repeatedly or with dire consequences, it may create Grief Consciousness, a lasting belief that all of life is sad and lonely. Mourning and bereavement come to dominate your worldview: "I am always left alone in the end, so why bother to love or enjoy anything?" Blaming yourself is common, too. "It is lost" becomes, "I lost it," and concludes, "I am a loser."

When we feel that we are small and our perspective is limited, when we focus only on the finite, when we fear for survival and cling to the known, then change is dangerous. Grief Consciousness believes "I am incomplete, alone, and can't make it on my own without _____." Only what we've known, the way things were, is safe. Through this filtered view of reality, the unknown future is ripe with fear and anxiety. We become resistant to change and fight to prevent loss. We refuse to accept what is. Our Soul wants to expand that view of life. This battle between impermanence and our resistance to it is played out in every grieving heart and is observed in the widely accepted list of stages that people generally go through in the grieving process. There are several versions of the Seven Stages of Grief, and they all help to understand this intense experience. Any and all emotions may be involved, and it is a process as varied as humans are. Remember, don't let anyone—including me— tell you how to feel when you are grieving!

The Senses of the Soul offer a valuable contribution to our ability to recover from loss and change. I will be provocative to make the point: Although the Seven Stages of Grief are helpful and widely experienced as a progression of emotions and behaviors associated with loss, *not one of the Seven Stages is the actual process of Grief*. Again, one should expect to go through these stages and much more, but in this book, we are engaged in an advanced understanding and direct personal training in the skillful use of emotions. So let's distinguish the role of each stage in the traditional list. Then we'll learn the essential and indispensable role of Grief itself.

> **Although the Seven Stages of Grief are helpful and widely experienced as a progression of emotions and behaviors associated with loss, not one of the Seven Stages is the actual process of Grief.**

The Traditional Seven Stages of Grief

❶ **Shock or Disbelief.** Physical and emotional disorientation is a protection from the massive assault of major loss. Energies are intense and mixed; though you feel a lot, it is a form of numbness. This stage prevents overwhelm and buys you some time, since it will take time to accept and adapt to the loss. This is a natural defense as you prepare to grieve.

❷ **Denial.** This is a form of resistance or an effort to maintain things as they were. You are not yet ready to grieve.

❸ **Anger.** After being knocked over by the loss, your energy returns, and you get back up to fight the assault on your world. You'll complain, rant, and rail; you will feel the injustice and will attempt to protect yourself from harm. You are fighting to avoid the change that has already happened. Although it is important to feel that you have some power, this form of power doesn't change anything.

❹ Bargaining. This is another form of resistance that is softer, reflecting the beginning of acceptance of the inevitable, and yet your hope to undo the change remains.

❺ Guilt. In this stage, acceptance of the loss has settled in. There is an urge to explain it or to blame something. The last bit of resistance is melting. The energy is lower, and your attention is focusing inward and toward responsibility to deal with this unwanted reality.

❻ Depression. This is a swirl of many unaddressed emotions stepping up to help. Apathy as a major component shows that resistance is gone, replaced by powerlessness, or the realization that there is nothing you can do about it. See the chapter on Depression (page 171) to understand that it can help you realize what can be done. Grief will reveal what that thing is.

❼ Acceptance and Hope. These are two outcomes of successful grieving. However, before you can experience grieving, you must first go through resistance, blame, and giving up. Through pain, fatigue, and defeat, you are pummeled into accepting the loss. Finally, after your wounds heal with time, you come to Hope.

All of these stages are certainly natural reactions to loss that lead to resolution in their own time. The supporting roles of other emotions are helpful, but they are not able to do the essential work that is required and for which Grief is uniquely equipped. Grieving is painful and messy. All of us must do it in our own time and in our own way. With the understanding and cooperation of our sensory system, there will be a return to strength and joy as soon as possible.

The Modified SOS Method for Grief

While you may need any of the first six stages of the traditional stages of grief, the modified SOS Method for Grief goes through the actual work of Grief. When you go through this process—and it will likely take time and many repetitions that bring a little more healing each time—you will come to enjoy the seventh traditional stage of grief. Read through these four steps to first understand the process intellectually, as this may trigger feelings. Then go back through the steps in a meditative process to let your Senses of the Soul do what they know best.

❶ Stop and Listen: Feel the Pain. Because the pain is great, your initial reaction is to run from it. You feel that you aren't ready and can't handle it. True self-recovery doesn't begin until you listen and feel your pain. Thus, the first focus is on yourself: You are the one who must be taken care of. You need to feel and process the pain in order to get back to balance. You will experience protective mechanisms and resistance of all kinds. And you need to support yourself physically for this challenge. It can be all too easy to neglect your health.

❷ Identify the Loss. In this stage, you clearly name what was valuable. What exactly has been lost or changed? An obvious but essential step is to shift the focus outward to name exactly who or what was lost. However, this step is not so obvious when the change is slow, as with aging, or when loss is accumulated over time, such as the regrets of wasted opportunities or lost time. The recognition of two distinct parts—what you lost and how it affects you—is crucial to not lose yourself in the process. The harsh glare of loss is always a wakeup call to your complacency. It's not wrong to be happy and to get accustomed to having things as you want them, but any expectation, entitlement, ingratitude, boredom, or numbness to joy and appreciation will be shaken by loss. This is a humbling experience, where nothing is taken for granted. "You don't know what you've got until it's gone" is a sentiment that will not likely be felt as Appreciation or Gratitude at this point, but only as Pain and Suffering.

Recognize its importance to you. It may sound harsh, but the truth is, you care for something not for its own sake but for the experience it gives you. Yes, you are self-centered; it's your job alone to sustain and fulfill the life you've been given. So, you do your best to surround yourself in relation to people, things, and activities that you enjoy. You love others because of how you feel with them in your life. You give and serve and sacrifice because those things fill your Spirit. To heal the hole that opens up with loss, to feed that gnawing hunger, you need to know what your heart wants. You need to be clear about what you gained from the relationship. Was it security, safety, belonging, love, respect, honor, a purpose? If you didn't value those qualities or if you didn't need those experiences, then you wouldn't be grieving. You are only sad because you've lost that which brought you those particular qualities or feelings. Grief's relentless search for connection—primarily through memories—is the craving to feel more of that good stuff. In this way, Grief can be used to discover what matters most to you. Grief is the gasping for air of the drowning man. Grief identifies the "air" in your life—you have always needed it; loss just helps you see it more clearly.

❸ Getting to Solutions and Resolution. In this stage, you shift focus from what was lost in form to what you found through it. Perfect lovers may be in short supply, prized possessions may be one of a kind, and successes may be fleeting, but the qualities they carry and the experiences and feelings they bring are not. No one person delivers or takes away all the love available to you. You tend to regret most the loss of those rare "peak experiences." Those once-in-a-lifetime experiences may have changed your life, but they also leave you with the impression that it was that person or those circumstances that were the key to your happiness. But really it's your own capacity to create that happiness within yourself.

If you change our perspective just slightly, you can use these peak experiences to know and touch the possible. You can then go in search of it again or, better yet, within. The unchanging permanence you seek is impossible within one form; but if you release your attachment, you will find that it's available in limitless supply within the entire realm of reality. The love you want is there for the taking; or you can suffer while holding out for your one-and-only and ignoring the other seven billion possibilities. Memories can also bring that love, as can sun and trees, as can the breath you just took. Take another deep breath and feel the love. In meditation, you can enjoy that infinite ready supply, any time.

Impermanence includes loss and gain. There is always something created in the ruins of what was destroyed. Particular joys may fade, but Joy will always be. You will die, but life will continue. Grief helps you look beyond the illusions of this temporal world to the undying and regenerating nature of things.

Before you go out to get more of what you lost—like another pet, job, or lover—you must complete the current transaction. You must complete the Grief before you can truly be available to anything new. Now that you have identified the essence, you can shift your focus from what was lost in Form to what was gained in Essence. The pain in grieving comes from the loss of pleasure, but pleasure is always within you and is not lost. That pleasure has survived; the joy is still there in memory and can be felt any time now that you have known it. You can leave behind, reluctantly at first, your requirement for that particular experience and instead embrace the equally satisfying ability to experience it again, now. That wonderful person, place, or thing left you with a permanent gift that lives within you. You begin to enjoy the memories, to feel gratitude rather than sorrow, knowing you can fill yourself to satisfaction any time. The power to fulfill yourself is not out there but within you. In fulfilling yourself, you steer yourself from only experiencing pain to spending more time feeling full, contented, and whole again—like nothing is missing, because it isn't!

❹ **The Action Is to Let Go and Move On.** Don't imagine this is a big one-time move; it happens thousands of times. These times add up, little by little. When you try to "get over it" and "move on" from loss with the idea that you now have to do without, you will have an instinctual, survival-based resistance to this net loss. But once you learn how to receive, in some form or another, what you got from your lost love, it will be like realizing there's no need to starve because one restaurant closed; there are countless ways to feed yourself, and you do. One day at a time, you make the choice to live again.

In those moments when you are filled rather than empty, when you are strong, resilient, and happy, not weak, needy, or clinging—in those moments of strength, you no longer feel dependent on any single temporary source of happiness. You can release attachment to the object and enjoy what it brought you. You let go without struggle. It's easy to accept an exchange: "I lost that, but I got this." "She is gone, but she left me with this joy." You aren't desperate; there is no urgency to go out and get another one. But you are ready.

Your next lover doesn't want to fill the hole left by another, nor does he want to be with someone who feels incomplete. When you are healed, you are whole, and that makes for a good life and satisfying relationships. When your memories are able to bring you strength and joy, you are healed, whole, and ready to move on to wherever you'd like to go or wherever life may take you.

These steps can be followed straight through, but know that grieving has its own rhythm. Clarity, answers, and relief will come, by degrees and in due time, as you repeat the process. When the intensity of your feelings shifts into love and gratitude, that is the sign that healing is happening.

Get to the Heart of Grief

This exercise relieves the stress of attachment and loss, especially in matters of the heart.

❶ *Begin with Getting Peaceful (page xi). Tune in with the Adi Mantra and continue.*

❷ *Relief from Emotions and the Past.* Put your hands at the center of your chest, with the tips of your thumbs touching each other and each of the fingers touching the corresponding fingers on the opposite hand. Keep space between the palms and point your fingertips upward. Look at the tip of your nose and breathe 4 times per minute: Inhale 5 seconds, hold 5 seconds, exhale 5 seconds. Continue for 11 minutes or until you feel relief.

❸ *Heart of the Matter.* During or after the exercise, follow this guided visualization:

a. Recall memories of loss of any kind: objects, relationships, any contest or goal, opportunity, love, respect, health, youth. Focus intently on the loss and the pain. Allow the discomfort to be felt freely throughout your body. Notice where you feel it and exactly how it feels. Breathe deeply and stay present with these feelings until you gain a little equilibrium, knowing that you can handle the feelings.

b. Continue to see images of the person, thing, or event. Shift your focus from that to yourself, to your heart, to the feelings of exactly what you long for. What is it about the object of your grief that's so important to you? You can recall how you felt because of that person or thing. So shift your attention from the object to the experience it brought you. Do you see that what you miss is that feeling? Follow that feeling and find out what is so vitally important to you about that experience. As you leave the physical messenger of that experience and go into its effect on you, you'll come to the core of the loss. Now is the time to fully grieve. Let yourself be as sad as you must be, in light of how very important it is to live qualities, values, and feelings that your heart and soul long for. It may take time and will require great openhearted honesty to see the essence of your loss. And it will certainly take courage to face it.

c.　This heart of the matter that you have found is a quality that is not in limited supply. Your heart wants more of this, and your mind even demands the source you just lost—with good reason. This was likely the best source of love (or whatever it was) that you had ever found. Are you willing to accept that this wonderful messenger brought you an understanding that this level of experience is possible? It opened your heart to handle more. You need courage to let your heart lead you to new sources of this same experience. So now, without any thought, let your heart direct you to those new and diverse sources. The mind will object that only the one now gone will satisfy. Yes, you must adjust to what may currently be a far-distant second best; but in time, you can become as full or fuller than you ever were before.

d.　Once you accept the "substitution" and allow your heart to be full from a variety of new sources, the pain in your heart will begin to dissipate, like a hungry belly after a meal. And just like with food, you must actively go search out these new sources. It was easy when you lived with the previous source, but now you must do more work to fill that void. You begin to see that you can fill your heart and that no one person or thing can prevent that. From this place, the memory of your lost loved one shifts from a painful experience to one of great joy. If that person, event, or object brought you an ample supply of what your heart needs, recalling it becomes one of your best sources for that experience. The messenger has departed, but the message remains with you. You may also find a bonus in all this, and that is deep love and a reverence for all things. Part of your pain comes from a limited view that only certain things are special or yours. When you see them as part of a Universal pool, however, in which there's a constant flow and exchange, you never need be sad and lonely again.

❹ *Capture Your Gains.* When you feel complete, take a few deep breaths, stretch, and return to activity. Make some notes for yourself: What stands out most from this experience? List the object(s) of your Desire, the essence(s) therein that you long for, and a list of other sources or other ways to get more of that good feeling and experience. Continue to add to this list as you discover wonderful new ways to fill your heart. Make it a priority to pursue and allow these varied sources to enrich you.

Paola's Sadness Turns Sweet

When my mom was in the hospice, I had a moment with her when I hugged her as if she were my baby and I were the parent. She just said, "I am so tired." I have this memory of love that I cannot describe with words, but the feeling is there, the memory is with me, very real. In the past, I did not want to bring this memory up, because it made me sad since she passed away. But now I can see how that powerful feeling is so precious to me; it is cuddling me even if she is not there anymore physically to hug. I can feel the sweetness of the moment without interpreting it as being sad. I guess I can just bring back the experience I am longing for. The connection is strong—very strong and real—any time I remember to bring it up again and be hugged by it.

Self-Complete, Self-Contained

Grief grabs on to what felt good, what made life better. It tries to hold on, because without it, life can feel frantic and fruitless. You miss the messenger, but it is the message that's really important to you. Her smile brought you Joy; his strong voice brought you Security; your dog's loyalty and companionship brought you Contentment. Those subtle essences of Joy, Security, and Contentment feed and sustain you. Although you attach to the smile or the voice or the dog, the inner experience is the real endgame.

Sources of love come and go, but each reveals that more love is always available, everywhere and within you. Fear of the impermanence of form yields to trust in the stability of essence.

Through this process, you have discovered that you never really have to give up anything that deeply matters. Experiences change, but you remain and are enhanced by each experience. Lives are created and destroyed, but life is ongoing. Sources of love come and go, but each reveals that more love is always available, everywhere and within you. Fear of the impermanence of form yields to trust in the stability of essence, which pervades through time and space and your being. Everything that is out there is in here, too. You are self-fulfilling, self-contained, and content. Life never breaks its support, but you have to stay connected to Source to receive that support.

Going Deeper

Let's look at Grief's roles in the present, future, past, and timeless time frames.

Immediate Impact

We create security through the stability of routine, familiar environments, and friendly faces. Our brain is wired to maintain these as a map of our place in the world. Sudden loss threatens all of this. When a big piece of the map falls away, we are truly disoriented, unsure of who and where we are. Hence, you have the universal experience of shock and disbelief as your mind and heart are forced to reorient so you can find yourself in relation to this changed world. The tendency is to be absorbed and distracted from self-care just when you most need strength. Yet there is much you can do for yourself in this early impact zone. In times of peace, you can actually prepare yourself to handle disasters by building resilience and your ability to adapt. The Brace for Impact practice will help you both before and after your world gets shaken.

Brace for Impact

This meditation will help you be more intuitive and sensitive to prepare for changes or personal and natural disasters. This exercise "feeds" the brain, eliminates fatigue, and gives a constant flow of energy so you won't sink into depression.

❶ *Begin with Getting Peaceful (page xi). Tune in with the Adi Mantra and continue.*

❷ *Shock: Prepare and Repair.* Hold your hands at the solar plexus level in fists with your index fingers pointing straight and the forearms parallel to the ground and held slightly away from the body. Hold the right hand palm down and the left hand palm up. Put your right index finger on the top of your left index finger, with fingers crossing exactly in the middle of the second segment so that a special meridian contact takes place. Inhale deeply and very slowly (15 seconds) through the nose. Exhale through the puckered mouth (not whistling) forcefully and completely, directing the breath at the tips of the index fingers. (Never do this with a quick breath.) Feel the fingertips getting cold or vibrating. You may yawn or stretch, but keep breathing. Meditate on the life that is carried by your breath. Continue for a maximum of 11 minutes. When you finish meditating, lock the fingers and stretch.

❸ *The SOS Method.* During or after this practice, work with the Modified SOS Method for Grief (page 212) to talk with yourself and find what you need. Know that you can handle all change and thrive.

Avoid Adversity by Accepting Little Losses

Situation: You can't let go of what is taking you down. Let's turn to a practical application so you can get more comfortable with Sadness and put it to use in your daily affairs. You can use Sadness to let go of something bothersome that you get stuck on. Let's say you are on a first date, and it is going well. A topic comes up that brings you to a difference of opinion. You feel strongly about your position and can't believe anyone could feel differently. From that difference, a distance is created; your buttons have been pushed, and you can't let it go. Feelings get hurt on both sides; there is no kiss goodnight and no second date. In longer-term relationships, if it happens often enough or over big issues, the fun, partnership, future plans, or even the marriage may be over. Such is the story every day. You may have won the fight, gotten your way, proved you were right at the cost of the greater good or the long-term benefits, but you will probably suffer later. As it's often been said, "You can either be right or be happy."

Solution: Give a little to get a lot. You may need to step back and get some perspective to somehow shift to the bigger picture. Come to terms with what is most important to you: Is it being right and standing by your principles, or are you just being self-righteous? Is it really no big deal compared to the bigger picture? This type of review will clarify when to hold and when to fold. If you already know your true values, these decisions become easier and easier. You may feel some sadness as you willingly give up something that you thought was important: perhaps she doesn't think like you or share all your values, but she likely shares other values with you. It may hurt that you aren't always right; you might feel disrespected or overlooked. It can actually feel like vomiting as you release something deep in your belly that feels like your life depends on it. Or you may feel a little weepy. But remember that this thing is likely just an opinion, a source of pride, a belief, a need to be right, a search for power or revenge. It may even be an old wound from a loss you haven't dealt with yet. If you are honest, you will rebound and return to intimacy and relationship with a full heart.

Sweet Surrender

Recall a past standoff or conflict, a win-lose situation that you lost. Perhaps you won the immediate fight but lost out later because of it. Once you identify the memory or situation, rewind to the part of the story where you couldn't let it go. Think about how you were dug in to your position like a dog on a bone. Pause and step back. Reflect on what is most important to you in the long run. Is it this issue or this partnership? Once you see it, are you are fighting for it? Can you see the smaller turf you were trying to claim? What was the cost of winning that turf? Feel and review it all. If you are off, you could lose the battle but win the war. Choose instead to focus on the shared goals and common ground. Use enduring values as your motive to work out or drop differences. See the happy outcome as being worth taking the higher ground.

Follow-Up. Experiment with generously giving up some things you find this way. Not with a sense of defeat, but with generosity, largess, and a view of what really matters. I think you will enjoy the results.

If you were just willing to be a little sadder, you'd actually be a lot happier! Sadness helps you review a situation and feel what is really important to you. It helps you let go of things that don't matter or that must be relinquished due to circumstances, while holding on to what is most valuable. When that process is fluid and flexible, you can be consistently present and empowered, come what may. You can use your sensitivity to those twinges of regret—for a missed deadline, being late for a meeting, forgetting Mom's birthday, gaining weight or losing health, making a poor choice, overcommitting—to remind you of what's really important to you. If it's not really a big deal, you can drop the guilt. Or if it's more important, you can be more careful to take care of it. When you live your life knowing what it's all for and acting in support of that, you will die with no regrets. Losses, even the little ones, serve to connect you more deeply to life through your heart.

Lori's Longing

It's interesting—exploring my emotions, rather than suppressing them, made me realize how sad I am. I've allowed myself to feel the sadness that I can usually mask and hide. Through feeling, I have discovered the desire to find a partner and of wanting children. My response has been self-care, like eating better, nurturing myself, exercising, being in nature, and loving myself. Now I'm less despondent and just more cautious and conscious.

Clearing the Past

Emotions are a portal to the past. Anytime you feel an emotion, a door to the past opens up, and you have an opportunity to heal past events that created similar emotions. Emotions reoccur until all previous injuries are healed and you are better equipped to handle them in the future.

If you feel weak or incomplete due to a loss in the past, any current loss, even a minor one, can feel like a life-and-death issue. It is important to be able to differentiate current losses from older ones so you can address them appropriately. If you are sad about losing your job but the death of your father has never been resolved, or if you lament your children growing up and leaving home when your own loss of youth needs to be addressed, you will remain stuck on both issues. Without some movement and relief from sustained Sadness and Grief, you will eventually drop into Apathy.

Death Revives the Living

I've been depressed ever since my divorce. When I finally sat and went into it, out of nowhere came sadness I felt about my twin sister. All these years, I have never really felt the "loss" of her. I kind of acted like we have never been apart. Going deeper, I discovered feelings of guilt and shame that I had lived and she hadn't. I also felt sadness for all the life experiences she wanted and couldn't have. I let myself finally feel all of that and let some of it go. In the early hours of the next morning, I dreamed that I was with my sister. She was laughing so hard and joking with me; at one point, she showed me her body as if it were ready to be buried. Standing next to me, she looked at me and said, "I'm not really dead." I woke not long after this. I felt very light and was happy for the reminder.

Mahan

The power of the mind to transcend time and space, to live with the past even in the present, has a benefit: You can complete things previously left unresolved. You can speak to loved ones long gone. You can make peace with those unwilling or unsafe for you to be with. You have the power to heal and make peace with the Universe and, finally, to feel complete—all within yourself.

Clear the Way to Happiness

This set of exercises will help clear historical loss and standing patterns of grief in your consciousness, while bringing the life-affirming energy needed to move forward. Freely work with your emotions in the safe space this practice creates.

❶ *Begin with Getting Peaceful (page xi). Tune in with the Adi Mantra and continue.*

❷ *Absorb the Blow and Let It Go.*

a.   Keep your eyes wide open. Rest the back of your hands on your knees, with your elbows relaxed by your sides. In a single motion, raise your hands in an arc so the fingers and/or palms bounce off the tops of your shoulders as you exhale and stick your tongue out and down as far as you can. Inhale powerfully as you return to the original position and pull your tongue in. Alternate between these positions with a strong rapid breath for 6–11 minutes. At the end, inhale deeply and hold your breath as you press your tongue to the roof of your mouth. Hold your breath for 20–30 seconds. Repeat this breath suspension a total of 3 times.

b.   Extend both arms over your head with your elbows straight, palms forward, and thumbs extended stiffly toward each other. Press your eyes upward. Begin to rotate both arms from the shoulder and armpit areas. Move the left arm in a clockwise (if you are looking up) direction and the right arm

in a counterclockwise direction. The movements of the two arms are not necessarily synchronized, but they do move continuously. Breathe as needed! Continue for 11 minutes. Inhale at the end as you stretch the spine and arms up.

c. Inhale fully through the left nostril as you block the right nostril with the thumb of your right hand; your other fingers are pointed straight up. Exhale through the right nostril by blocking the left nostril with your right index finger curled across. Continue for 3–11 minutes.

d. Rest your palms face down on your knees. Grasp the knees firmly. Keep your spine straight as you sway forward and then backward in a steady, powerful rhythm. Inhale back and exhale forward. Continue for 3–11 minutes. To

end, inhale; hold your breath as you tighten the body and shake for 15–30 seconds. Then exhale. Repeat the breath suspension and shake a total of 5 times.

❸ **Follow-Up.** Memories of past mistakes and traumas can make you insecure, unwilling to risk, and slow to change. You close your heart to pain and joy alike. Instead, be present. The gift of your temporary body is that it never dwells in the past or future. That's why focusing on breath and sensations, as well as doing yoga, is so calming. Happiness too is sourced only in the now. A memory can trigger happiness, which itself is occurring *in the present*. So focus on what is here and now to bring Joy. The present is always fine when the mind is clear of past pain and future fear. (See the Self-Study section at the end of this chapter for additional notes on making a regular practice of this exercise.)

The Soul's Lesson in Loss

Only from a larger view—the Soul's perspective—can we trust the process and know that we will always have what we need, that things are replaceable, and that love is everywhere.

Moving on from Grief requires letting go and accepting that change is a part of life. In spiritual terms, the lesson is to surrender to what we often call the "Will of God." Only from a larger view—that is, the Soul's perspective—can we trust the process and know that we will always have what we need, that things are replaceable, and that love is everywhere, not just in the one person we loved or who loved us. This insight shifts our empowerment from outside us (helpless victim of irreplaceable loss) to within (responsible for and accessible to infinite gifts). We go from being dependent on fleeting things "out there" to having control of and constant access to our source of well-being, independent of material objects. At the highest level of this realization, we become the master of our own well-being. Even loss of our own life is no longer a threat. We accept not only change but also the very flow of the Universe as it is.

The highest power comes from understanding that everything comes and goes by "God's Will." In this way, we accept and even enjoy both pleasure and pain. At this level of consciousness, there is no loss and gain; the only pain of separation is in relationship to the Soul, the Source itself. The final stage of human awareness is the recognition that no separation exists, even for a moment.

Conscious connection to our own essence is the only protection for the heart, which embraces all loss and gain, stability and change. With that Spirit as a constant companion, we learn quickly from the past, we rapidly come up with new ways to move ahead, and we find joy anywhere that we find ourselves.

The effects of the Safeguard Your Heart meditation in the Love the Everlasting exercise have been well researched and touted in recent medical journals to help in many ways—most specifically, for help in cognitive function, such as mood, memory, feelings of peace, well-being, focus, and attentiveness. Researchers at both UCLA and the University of Pennsylvania found that practicing just 12 minutes of this meditation a day can create beneficial effects that could not be duplicated even within groups that were listening to classical music or doing a relaxation exercise. The results were astounding. (See Resources for further information on these findings.)

Love the Everlasting

In this exercise, the brain hemispheres will balance; the past will be processed and dumped; and insecurity will vaporize. You can learn and benefit from the past without getting caught and then move ahead.

❶ *Begin with Getting Peaceful (page xi). Tune in with the Adi Mantra and continue.*

❷ *Safeguard Your Heart.* Cross your forearms below the wrists and hold them in front of your chest. Hold the arms out slightly, with palms up and facing toward the chest. Look down the tip of your nose. Begin to chant "Sa-Ta-Na-Ma", one cycle per inhale and one per exhale. With with each syllable, touch the thumb tip to the fingertip of the index finger with "Sa," then thumb to middle finger with "Ta," thumb to ring finger with "Na," and thumb to little finger on "Ma." Continue for 11–31 minutes. To finish, inhale; hold your breath and roll your the eyes up; become completely still. Exhale and relax. From this place of stillness, continue into the guided visualization.

3. Impermanence and Reverence.

a. Go to thoughts of death—your worst fears from memories and movies. Imagine your own death. Go through Fear into Sadness for the future loss of your own dear life. Sit, breathe, and fully feel; allow it to flow. Accept the fact that the hour will come for you to go. Imagine it. Let go of your body and feel that ultimate loss. See your resistance but stand your ground to face it.

b. Look back at your whole life, including this day, this moment. You have it now and then it will be gone. Can you feel the preciousness of each moment and appreciate its fleeting nature? Your today will pass but another will come. Everything you see and hold dear will change and move on. Your body will go, and other bodies will replace you. This love will fade, but Love will always be. Your spirit will change forms, while Spirit is everlasting.

c. Do you feel that delicate line between resistance and acceptance, between holding on and letting go? This is just practice, so practice a surrender to this reality. As you give up Fear and make the transition, watch for Awe to arise—sense a deep appreciation for the power and beauty in both life and death. Feel the reverence. Great love may swell up. It may be bitter and sweet all mixed together. When you know death, there is no taking life for granted.

d. When you are complete, take a few deep breaths and return to activity. In what way can this experience change things in your daily life? In your attitudes, bring appreciation for the preciousness of all things into your day. In your actions, maintain close regular contact with what you feel most reverence for. Have relationships with people and possessions reflect their importance to you; treat things as sacred to you.

Love and Reverence: The Gifts of Grief

Many books are full of stories of near-death experiences. Whether the approach is medical, mystical, or deep survival in disaster, there is commonly a profound impact. Lives are transformed; people say, "The little things no longer bother me. I feel peaceful all the time now. I see love everywhere. I am in awe of all things." In the spiritual literature, countless saints and sages share the same experiences, gained through a variety of approaches, from asceticism to devotion. These experiences differ from those in the first group in that the sages and saints set out on an inner journey in pursuit of those experiences. Those in the first group had no such intention; instead, they had this consciousness thrust upon them. Both are dearly grateful. How will this realization come to you? You know that loss and change will visit you. How you receive it makes all the difference. Your Soul has a set of Senses—your emotions—that can bring you either closer to or farther from your Self. Some simple intention on your part to consciously follow the lead of your emotions will bring you through every loss into Love and Reverence for all things past or present, and to enjoy them all as eternal.

Self-Study

Continue to practice Absorb the Blow and Let It Go (page 224). There are shorter times listed for a 31-minute version, but I recommend doing the full 44 minutes at least once. Continue this practice daily for 40 days for a full self-therapy to release centuries of grief. During or after the exercise, sit with, observe, and work with your feelings. Use the meditation to give you the energy to handle and process Grief safely. Explore, let go, heal, and elevate yourself. Then journal your experiences.

Absorb the Blow and Let It Go is an ancient practice that will help heal the body and rid the mind of old emotional blockages. The best results occur when the diet is light, preferably with many melons eaten during the day. Practice this only at night. The first step opens the lungs and releases centuries of old grief and mourning. There are many things that pass on but which you long for. The loss that is unresolved, unexpressed, or painful can hold you back from a full commitment to the present. It's as if you honor the past by denying the present and betraying the future. Thus, this first step centers you into the present with a vision toward the future as the old patterns are changed. The second step creates emotions with lightness; it adjusts your ability to welcome positive experiences. The third step creates deep calmness and focus. The fourth step activates the body's healing resources; it soothes and is self-calming.

Life Projects

There are as many ways to work with Loss and Grief as there are individuals and events. Your Soul, speaking through your emotions, will always give you the best solution. Here are some approaches to use:

- Work with Death in order to accept transience and change. Come to enjoy that all things come and go. A medical death sentence often brings people to fully live more so than all the pleasure money can buy. *A Year to Live: How to Live This Life as If It Were Your Last* by Stephen Levine (Bell Tower, 1998) will take you through an experiment in dying. He created the practice while working with terminal patients, realizing how wonderful it would be to live with their clarity and appreciation for life, even when you still have many years to enjoy that life. Another book on the subject is Rinpoche's *The Tibetan Book of Living and Dying* (HarperSanFrancisco, 1994). Learning about conscious dying will help you find safety and sacredness in dealing with death and will give you more reverence for life. Likewise, hospice volunteer work gives you direct experience. We're all going to die, and as with any big trip, it's better to be prepared. If you can deal with the mother of all fears, then you can handle anything

- Examine the concept of ownership and specialness. Everything you touch, including your body, is a gift on loan. You come naked and leave with nothing. Be grateful and generous. See how free you can be to enjoy life when you feel that none of it is yours to keep.

- Actively transfer your sources of security, love, and happiness from temporary things to subtle and universal qualities, from object to essence. You may lose your health, youth, or beauty, but you can always enjoy youth, newness, and rejuvenation in other ways or in others. Move from one lost love to all love everywhere. Train yourself to find sources of joy that become ever subtler, less temporary, and more sublime. Be flexible and creative in your demands. All of these qualities are plentiful and can be found everywhere and within. They are universal and undying; therefore, their supply will never dry up. Replace Grief with the pleasant pain of longing for only Spirit. Unbroken union with Spirit is our final human desire.

Chapter Nine

Guilt
Your Guide to Truth

Guilt is an internal compass that uses mistakes to teach responsibility and integrity. This strict internal judge guides you to be true to your Self.

The Purpose of Guilt

When you are unclear about your actions, ethics, and sense of Good and Evil;

Or when you want to learn about consequences, responsibility, and intended or unintended results…

Guilt helps you realize and rise to your highest caliber and conduct.

When you have violated a set of values or code of conduct, a painful pang of Guilt tries to stop you.

It asks you to check yourself—to reflect on the facts, recognize your truth, and correct with integrity.

Guilt returns your power to respond in your best interest. It sharpens your ability to sense the consequences of your actions, avoid mistakes and harm, or learn from them quickly.

Guilt ultimately guides you to trust Truth—and that will set you free.

You need never go wandering in doubt or wondering what is right. Go beyond the polarity of right and wrong and get to neutrality. The battle is over when you learn to Trust.

Get to Know Guilt

Guilt is self-guiding; it shows you your values and helps heal your behavior. You know it by a tense, sick, or dropping feeling in the belly, as if the ground has fallen away from under you. Or it may be a fluttering in the heart and a caved-in feeling in the chest. You may feel a sense of danger, sudden exposure, and vulnerability. You may be disoriented and confused, trying to piece together what happened, followed by an urge to conceal, cover up, and scramble for an excuse. You may feel like there's an alien living inside you. You may wonder about yourself, "Who is this person?" You may feel alone or distant from yourself, the situation, and others. Sadness and Regret might join with Guilt to urge you back to before this happened, to start over again. Anger may join in to attack you, your bad luck, or whoever "outed" you.

Together, Shame and Guilt serve to discover your values and live to your standards so you are happy being you.

Shame is most likely to accompany Guilt; they work together so closely that they can be hard to distinguish. Whereas Shame teaches acceptance so you can be you, Guilt teaches responsibility—that is, how to do what's right for you. Shame is about image; Guilt is about action. Both deal in duality—comparison and judgment, estrangement or separation. In that pain of separation from Self, there's a strong motivation to find a way back to unity, to being included. Together, Shame and Guilt serve to discover your values and live to your standards so you are happy being you.

Guilt: Your True Compass

The dictionary describes *guilt* as though it were a fact: you are guilty when acting outside the current law or some established standards. As an emotion, Guilt certainly lets you know when you break with what is expected of you in society. However, Guilt's deeper purpose is to warn you when you are off track with your own values and with Universal Truth. When Guilt strikes, you may need time to get clear about the right thing to do before responding. It may warn you in time to stop what you're about to do, or it might show you that apology and amends (a mending process) are needed after the fact. Recognition and corrective change are all part of Guilt's essential process of locating your truest self and aligning with it.

You are known by your actions. Your behavior is your projection. Actions arise from character, and character is molded through action. Both character and action drive you either closer to or farther from feeling true to yourself, to being strong and comfortable in your own skin. By constant trial and error, you test this mixture of inner values and outer actions to slowly find and live your truth, to fully be who you were meant to be. Alignment between your deeds and your values is called *integrity*. When both are aligned with self-realized universal values, it's called *enlightenment*.

From Jesus on the cross to abolitionists on the Underground Railroad, from rebels before despots to those defying laws outlawing who one can love or marry, history has been changed by those found guilty of standing against prevailing norms because their hearts told them they must. When a person acts on his own higher values, he challenges everyone to rise to that standard. Living your Universal Truth, at all costs, brings a deep soul satisfaction that makes bearing persecution a joy. It seems that individually and collectively, we sometimes find our best truth by obeying the rules but also by breaking them. Life is a comparative study—we sift through the results of our actions and learn what works best. But how do you decide what is good, better, best? The mind has many conflicting choices, but your heart and Soul always know. Guilt asks you to listen.

An Experience of Guilt

Sit still and breathe deeply to become calm. Use Getting Peaceful (page xi) to become focused and clear. With your eyes closed, recall a time when you felt really badly after doing something you felt was wrong or when you were caught and told you were bad. It may be something you are currently doing that you hope won't be found out. Did you cheat, lie, steal, betray, let down, disappoint, double-cross? Was it you against the world, or did you have supporters on your side? Was the urge to save your skin, to save face, or to save your soul? Were two or more conflicting motivations and truths vying for the right to justify it, competing to tell you what to do next? Get familiar with the feelings and know that their purpose is to preserve something and clarify your Truth so you can be safe and certain within yourself and society. Observe the different levels of Truth operating and begin to understand these valuable messages from your Soul.

Guilt Consciousness

When you look at life through the filter of Guilt, you see a world colored in only black and white, polarized into good and evil, right and wrong. In that duality, you endlessly bounce back and forth, exhausted by the impossible task of holding back evil in an effort to create a haven of only good. Winning this battle is not about admitting that both sides exist; instead, through judgment and punishment, you seek to make the bad into good, to make things "even." Guilt Consciousness believes that everyone, including God, is doing things *to you* from meanness and on purpose; things don't just happen. You compare everything—categorizing and ranking people's goodness and worth according to your "right(eous)" measurements. You assign guilt based on your values, your truths. Groups and entire systems form and take self-validating sides of right and wrong. The judged are forced to accept the opinion of the prevailing side. Guilt Consciousness thus contributes to the colonized mind, and you begin to take on the ideas and attitudes of the powerful. Everyone operates under the currently popular viewpoint, forced to lose their inner moral bearings. Direct access to integrity and truth are lost, with no lasting agreement or collective compass. Here's how Guilt has been misused for the past few thousand years:

Guilt Consciousness: An Old Paradigm

1. The world is either good or evil.
2. Bad people commit sins.
3. Sin causes suffering. All suffering is due to sin.
4. Good people judge, accuse, blame, deplore, or condemn the wrong.
5. There is a price to pay to make it right; the sinner must suffer equally.
6. Punishment or suffering will make things equal or right again.
7. A good person imposes suffering to make things right.
8. Suffering is the price that then earns redemption.
9. Forgiveness is granted.
10. There is renewal and rebirth.

Which of these beliefs have you observed within yourself? I imagine most of us have plenty of experience with this consciousness in ourselves and in others. Many a person who grew up Catholic has told me, "Jews invented Guilt, and Catholics perfected it." The church did discover a clever way to control an entire population without an army. It simply used a set of beliefs—that we are all born in sin—guaranteed to indict and condemn every being. If your innate, natural, and unavoidable sexuality is decreed evil, then your very existence must be a constant apology. The idea of a price for purity has led to an entire marketplace with specific costs associated with various sins. There are social and legal systems, self-punishments, or surrogates, from animal sacrifice to the whipping boy to Christ himself on the cross. These all serve to appease the angry judges; as long as someone suffers, justice is done. Regular payments are required, but relief is always temporary. This is certainly not the consciousness of Christ, and yet it has been carried forward in His name, and we are all its inheritors.

When Guilt has you feeling bad, it is an opportunity for honest review, self-purification, and personal resurrection. When that invitation from your Soul is ignored, however, the emotional message still remains. Like the reminder light on your phone, your Soul keeps flashing those feelings. This constant emotional message leaves you vulnerable, because your head's not "in the game." You are easier to control. Conquerors have always used this feeling to dominate a population; men use countless ways to blame their misbehavior on women; one race convinces another it is inferior; the enemy is always demonized. In the absence of the internal guidance of well-functioning Guilt, these messages are not used to check and correct. You believe yourself damned; so you fall from your own Grace. But this fall can only happen with your cooperation. Has the voice of a parent, an institution, or a localized opinion moved inside your head? Is Guilt weakening what you know to be true so that you can be controlled? When you internalize Guilt, you become your own critic, judge, jury, and punisher. You ignore all the signals that guide you to recognize what's right for you and align with it; as such, your suffering continues.

> **When Guilt has you feeling bad, it is an opportunity for honest review, self-purification, and personal resurrection.**

Here's an illustration: The damage of Hurricane Katrina was seen by some as the vengeance of an Angry God punishing the "guilty." Others saw it as an unfortunate event for which we should take responsibility by addressing our role in climate change. The first view is shaped by something people were told to believe; the second, by an interest in observable connections between cause and effect.

Consciousness, or the window you see through, determines your ability to perceive the difference between an attack, or intentional harm; an accident, or an unintended sequence of events that could be avoided; and a coincidence, or something that just happened at a time and place that affected you. You respond according to your perception. Do you protect and defend, plan and prepare, or accept and move on? Guilt Consciousness sees everything as an attack and either reacts defensively or turns righteously offensive.

Anywhere you find Guilt, you will find a painful polarity—a division between God and sinner, the wrongdoer and the injured party, your guilty conscience and your inner peace. The cycle of Guilt Consciousness is unending, because polarities cannot be solved; they never go away. If you see only the bad in a person, punishing that person will never "make" her be good, because it won't change your assumptions, which is that she is bad; that's your truth. But getting even doesn't work; as Gandhi said, "An eye for an eye makes the whole world blind."

It is possible to see the good that is also there in the guilt, to accept that the sinners (who are just like you) also have good in them. When you embrace the reality that the priest and the hero both have their dark sides, just as sinners have their virtues, you will find it impossible to judge and label. We all contain everything. Only when both sides are embraced is there freedom to be a whole person and to choose whichever brings the best results. This is the very definition of *union*: the freedom to live with the opposites in balance, without being limited by either but empowered by both.

What Is Your Consciousness Up To?

Why do we suffer? Our consciousness explores the darkness until it finds more light. If the universe is one cohesive whole, what is that light in the case of Guilt Consciousness? What is the darkness? The universe manifests in the form of pairs of opposites. Night distinguishes day, "you" helps define "me," pain helps identify pleasure. But these opposites attract like the poles of a magnet. The separate parts long to join and be one again. Thus, consciousness goes deep into the pain of opposition to motivate the urge to merge and find peace and wholeness.

Check out both sides of a polarity—being righteous versus condemning and punishing evil. Try playing the role of the bad one, fighting the law, and expressing your dark side. When consciousness expands, it becomes possible to see opposites as more than "opposition;" rather, they are mutually fulfilling parts of a whole. That merger of opposites brings peace; the blending of differences defines harmony. These opposites seek each other out in a dance, through play.

The Shift: Taking Responsibility

We were trained to believe that others know best. Since ancient times, people have been told what to think and believe, how to behave, what is right. Children have been told this by fathers; subjects, by kings; and followers, by priests. We are trained to trust and obey those in power, to comply with their wishes, and to conform to their consciousness. We forget how to listen to ourselves and lose trust in ourselves. We become dependent. We go searching for help, strength, and truth outside of ourselves. We want someone to tell us right from wrong; we want someone to take care of us. However, without self-reliance, there is no self-esteem. Easily shamed and feeling guilty, we give up control and are exploited. We are indebted to any good that comes to us, and we likewise blame anything outside us for our misfortune. In doing so, we lose our capacity to respond; we lose the intuition to know our own needs. We don't know what feels right or what went wrong, what we need, and how to make things right in light of the highest truth. Guilt is a sure sign that you are in this consciousness. It is also a sign that your soul wants to return to your ability to respond in your best interest. This is responsibility.

Guilt helps you feel when you have caused pain. It informs you to make a correction yourself without being told to do so by an outside judge. In the process, you sharpen your intuition, your ability to foresee the outcome of your actions. But it would be better to call it "fore-feel"—that is, to know how you would feel if you did a thing—and thus avoid any mistake before it happens. Your intuition—that infallible internal GPS—is in vital need of restoration in these Aquarian times so it can work faster and fall less often. Guilt is your ability to sense the consequences of an action and to adjust your response to the desired result ahead of time. No one else can tell you what you need to do; no one else can do it for you. Your truth is only in you. Listen to your feelings, heart, conscience, self, soul, and consciousness. Talk with yourself openly and honestly. Face yourself; face the truth. The teacher's job (Guilt's job) is to teach you to do this, to sense your own of truth, to help you find your power, to train you in self-correction and self-healing, and to teach you how to use your inner wisdom for guidance.

The Universe teaches us through cause and effect. We are causing every effect we experience. If you don't like the effect you caused, try doing something different until you get the desired result. This is as automatic and unbiased as gravity. But we load this process with judgment and self-sabotage, instead of using it to learn and grow. We often resist the consequences that we cause, deny the learning opportunity to change, or blame some outside force for our fate. Responsibility represents the shift from being controlled by forces outside ourselves to owning the power within to correctly discriminate and guide our own lives, our own destinies.

The New Paradigm: The Power of Responsibility

❶ The world works by cause and effect—consequences follow actions.

❷ I take action, unaware of the consequences.

❸ When my action causes suffering, this is an error or mistake.

❹ Suffering is caused by my ignorance.

❺ No one wants to suffer. Thus, even intentional wrong is evidence that I don't yet know how to prevent it.

❻ A teacher, nature, or time and pain eventually helps me see the connection of action to result so I can make a better choice. I recognize the relationship between the cause and the effect.

❻.❺. (Meanwhile I have the right to protect myself from someone else's trial-and-error process.)

❼ Awareness is the price I pay to avoid more suffering.

❽ Until I learn the lesson and make the correction, more suffering will occur to help me learn.

❾ This process is a law of nature; I can resist or accept, but I cannot avoid this education.

❿ I accept responsibility and deal with the consequences.

⓫ Responsibility, or the ability to respond in a way that creates a better outcome, is found.

⓬ I make corrections or amends for past or future actions.

⓭ I have found a preferred new outcome.

⓮ Learning has occurred. I have discovered a better way. There is rebirth.

⓯ I redeem myself by asking for forgiveness, by forgiving, and by making amends.

⓰ I am a new person. I am not as ignorant as the one who unknowingly did that before.

Lessons Learned

This exercise is a form of ancient self-therapy. When inner conflict blocks your ability to think and act clearly, you often end up confused and held in deadlock. This meditation resolves many inner conflicts so you can be clear and responsive and learn quickly from accidents or mistakes.

❶ *Begin with Getting Peaceful (page xi).*

❷ ***Convicted and Conflicted No More.*** Close your eyes nine-tenths of the way. Place your hands over your chest, with your palms on your torso at the level of your breasts. Point your fingers toward each other across the chest. The key to this meditation is attention to the breath. Inhale deeply and completely for 5 seconds. Exhale completely for 5 seconds. Hold the breath out for 15 seconds by suspending the chest motion as you pull in the Navel Point and abdomen. Continue this breathing for 11 minutes, slowly building up to 31 or 62 minutes. To end, inhale deeply as you stretch the arms up overhead. Relax the breath and shake the arms and hands for 15–30 seconds. Relax. From this place of stillness during or after the exercise, continue into the self-guided visualization.

❸ ***The SOS Method: Using Guilt for Guidance.***

    a.   ***Stop and Listen.*** Recall memories of blunders, mistakes, accidents, or screw-ups that you caused or that happened to you. See the images from throughout your life that stand out and let yourself feel those uncomfortable feelings.

- See the judgments on stern faces, the tone in voices, words of good/bad or right/wrong.

- See reactions of scolding, blaming, yelling. What does it feel like to be you now? How is your self-esteem?

- See all the punishments—hitting; distancing; silence; the removal of love, freedoms, and privileges.

- Are there other emotions? How much fear and anger are present? Grief and despair?

- Allow all thoughts and feelings: Blame, Guilt, Remorse, Self-Hatred, Vindictiveness, Unforgiveness, Undeserving, Wrong.

Continue breathing deeply and remain aware that you are also present and safe here and now.

b. **Find the Source.** When you feel stabilized, ask these questions directly to your wise feelings:

- What harm was done? What was the real harm to objects, to others, to myself? If the message is from another, assess the actual damage to that other. Then assess the damage to you, your body, and your reputation, relationship, career, heart, integrity, self-esteem, future.

- What was off? Your attitude or behavior, or theirs, or some of both?

c. **Ask for Solutions.** What needs to happen to make it right for the other? For you? What behaviors will serve the greatest good for you and for others? Imagine saying and doing whatever you see that will make you feel right again. Keep going as you observe your own inner response, doing what it takes to feel increasingly bright and strong, clear and pure about yourself. Enjoy the happy reunion of love with self and others.

d. **Take Action.** Sit and enjoy this relief and peace. Then gently return to activity. Follow the voice of your Guilt, the voice of your Soul, by taking any actions or making any amends you were given.

❹ Using the Messages from Guilt. Write some notes of your experience and anything you learned. Solutions may include repairs, amends, or boundaries set for yourself and others, as well as higher standards to be met. When you hear the voice of your Soul through these feelings, obey it! This is the true voice of authority. When you obey your Self, a new and better way will be found; a newer, truer you will be reborn! As you develop a skillful relationship with Guilt, you will begin to quickly resolve anything that disturbs the peace with yourself.

> When the healing influences of free-flowing guilt and shame flow gracefully through your psyche, you won't be painfully shame-ridden or guilt-laden; instead you'll have a compassionate sense of ethics, the courage to judge and supervise your own conduct, and the strength to amend your behaviors without inflating or deflating your ego unnecessarily. When you successfully navigate through your honest guilt and shame, you'll feel proud of yourself, and you'll move naturally into happiness and contentment.
>
> → **Karla McLaren, The Language of Emotions**

Going Deeper with Guilt

Guilt will guide you in any of the four time frames: present, future, past, and timeless. We'll see how each situation helps guide you to Truth, but first we must understand Truth itself.

"Truthiness": A Sliding Scale

Guilt's job is to help you find the truth—but which truth? Have you ever noticed that there are many truths to choose from? In fact, there are as many conflicting opinions and rules as there are people, and even people change their minds over time. What was once evil becomes legal, and crusaders change camps. So, when you want Truth, who are you going to ask—a politician, a judge, your mother, a religion? Even God's truth seems to vary depending on who you ask.

I have found that there are three types of Truth. Understanding them will help Guilt sort it all out so you can act clearly and confidently amid all the noisy voices clamoring for their version of Truth.

- **Personal Truth:** Add the word *truth* to anything and it sounds noble—even "truth in advertising"! But Personal Truth comes from your animal nature; it justifies your individual instinct to take what you want, in the moment, with little concern for your effect on others or your own future. It self-validates your actions so you feel good about yourself, whether or not anyone else agrees. Technically, it is the source and expression of all your neuroses, though it is more "polite" to say that a neurosis is the most extreme adherence to a Personal Truth that distorts reality. Irrational, fact-defying, self-contradicting, fanatical rants are the high art of Personal Truth. Its moderate expressions are those things we tell ourselves to rationalize, and thereby excuse, all the bad behaviors we don't want to change. We each have our own versions of truth that fit neatly with what we are doing. Can you identify some of your truths without judging them?

- **Circumstantial Truth:** Originating in your human nature, Circumstantial Truth thrives in the fertile realm of ideas and ideals. It lives in groups that share the same background, needs, or current interests and common understanding. Circumstantial Truth is truth by consensus. Interest groups, religious organizations, political parties, and nationalists engage in passionate logic, reason, and arguments with their ideological rivals to constantly reinforce and support their own beliefs. This type of truth enjoys broad validation from others who see things your way; however, it is still limited to local circumstances and contemporary (and temporary) times. Whether referring to fashion, food, or religious fads, *popular* means that the population likes it. Slogans are used to push circumstantial truth, tenets are recited to confirm membership, and beliefs are promoted to further the cause, whatever it takes. In balance, this form of truth gives you confidence and allows you to check your reality and its temporary individual need to sustainable group interests.

- **Universal Truth:** From the Divine in all of us, the deepest wisdom of the heart and the highest aspirations of the mind make up Universal Truth. This truth deals with the invisible qualities and transcendent desires of every soul. It uplifts and awakens your most noble qualities and inspires behavior that serves the best interests of all. Words of Universal Truth live forever and are unchanging, even in changing times; their impact penetrates across time and space. Not everyone will be receptive to this truth at every moment, but when Universal Truth penetrates the heart, all heads bow. Every religion is based on it, and every faith experiences a decline as Circumstantial and Personal Truths take over. Throughout time, great souls have accessed and conveyed the highest levels of Universal Truth and have infused us with its healing sustenance. These great souls are called masters, saints, and even gods, and yet we all have access to that same source. This truth transforms a simple life into an extraordinary experience. When you transcend the limits of ego, you live in freedom, your reality expands; there is no smallness that can harm you. This is how spiritual heroes are able to go through all kinds of torture in peace.

There is a time and place for each truth. In Personal Truth, you will act to save your skin. In Circumstantial Truth, you will act to save face, to save your place in public standing, along with that of your clan. In Universal Truth, you will act to save your soul; you will act for peace, grace, and love for all. You can trust your Senses of the Soul to take care of you at the level needed, while they steadily guide you to realize your highest reality. As you climb a mountain, your view widens; as you look through a telescope, you can see worlds beyond your own. Just so, the more you see and the broader your scope, the greater your options, choices, and freedom. Guilt's gift is to get you to Universal Truth. In that big picture, you can see consequences, and you are free to choose the outcome you desire. Here's the first proving ground.

Present Guilt: Caught in the Act

You are certainly familiar with the dreaded sensation: "Gotcha!" The horrified reaction of others clearly shows when you are out of bounds; then that cold flash runs through your body. Or you might realize on your own that what you're doing just doesn't feel right; you get that sinking feeling that you can't seem to shake. Then comes the famous "moment of truth." Do you conceal or reveal, cover your ass (tracks) or come clean? The Truth or The Lie is your choice, and each has its own consequences, in the short and long term. These choices affect your consciousness as well. This is not a question of morals; the results are for you to receive and learn from.

When you feel Guilt and act anyway, what are you up to? Awareness of consequences is working, but you are not yet clear and committed to your values or the results you prefer. Are you wishfully hoping for an easy way out, or are you simply testing for more proof before you surrender to that? Sometimes you watch yourself make the same mistake repeatedly until you are ready to courageously step into new behaviors.

Back to the Future: When You See the Mistake Coming

When you get that heavy heart and sinking feeling in your gut in anticipation of your actions, congratulations! Guilt is working. You now have enough awareness to pre-correct, avoid the mistake, and save yourself the trouble it will bring. In other words, you have choices: When your motive overrides or hijacks caution, you can continue. Or you can check in with the highest truth accessible at the time to make a more conscious choice. Will you serve your immediate need, the socially acceptable choice, or the voice of Soul? Which truth you check in with is key! Is it the right truth? Can you trust it? If so, are you willing to take the consequences and obey them? There are two steps to acting consistently in your best interest. The first is to know the truth you are acting under. The second is to live it.

First Choice: Which Truth?

When you ask, "What should I do now?" the answer will depend on whom you ask. Every opinion you gather—from a mother, priest, friend, or expert—will reflect that person's training, experiences, and motives. You have been trained to listen to all of these other voices but not your own. Yet you are the only one who must bear the consequences of your choices, and you are the only one in a position to know what is best for you. That truth—the one that best serves you—can only be known to you. But it may not be available when you need it. We were taught to obey the truths of others and not to listen within—that is the source of human suffering. We all lie about and betray our feelings. It takes practice to hear and obey the truth that beats in your own heart. Yet that truth will never fail to save and exalt you. Guilt serves to find and live that truth.

Once you know to ask yourself for the truth, the confusion isn't over yet. If you listen to your Personal Truth, you will react and protect. It will have you preserve the moment, save your skin above all others, and fight back with tooth and nail. If you rely only on your Circumstantial Truth, you will be clever and calculating according to your priorities:

money, family, reputation, position, mission, and popular cause. These priorities may serve you well, but they can also lead to rationalization and justification. You want to hear from the highest authority. When you check with your Universal Truth, your timeless values, you stand down a tank in Tiananmen Square or chain yourself to a tree to save it. You stand tall, even if alone, and fight for freedom for all. Actions derived from this highest truth are long remembered and inspire others into the future. Universal Truth calls on your own highest consciousness to emerge and prevail within you.

There is no resolution to Guilt without the Neutral Mind. The highest truth is accessed in neutrality through the Neutral Mind. The physical universe is based in polarity, or the contrast of opposites. When the mind tries to navigate the pros and cons in order to decide what is best, your thoughts become like Ping-Pong balls batted back and forth. There is no resolving right and wrong through the polarity of good and bad, because they are relative to each other. It is done only through the Neutral Mind—the calm, clear judge that sees all at once. This neutrality takes you beyond the pressure of personal needs and temporary truth, giving you access to the whole truth. Mindfulness and meditation are well-proven methods for achieving the Neutral Mind. Coming into this state of neutrality through yoga, breathing, and centering exercises is an important practice before sitting with your emotions and doing this level of work on yourself.

Neutrality takes you beyond the pressure of personal needs and temporary truth, giving you access to the whole truth.

> There's no good or bad. There's no right and wrong. There's no high or low. A Yogi is a person whom the opposite polarities do not affect. He recognizes there are polarities.
>
> ↠ **Yogi Bhajan, July 29, 1996**

Second Choice: Live Truth or Lie

Once you have your clearest truth-as-basis-for-action, you must still act from that, rather than try to escape it. Escaping it is called a lie. A lie is anything other than Universal Truth coming through you in word or action. Living truth is a tall order that few of us yet match. But remember your choice isn't good or bad; it simply has consequences that you will take to learn from. The consequences of a lie are that it diminishes you. It weakens your confidence, weakens your will, drains your energy, cheapens your own self-image. You lie only when you feel unable to handle the consequences of truth. You may be so accustomed to lying that you don't notice the contraction of aura and consciousness. But when standing for Truth, you can always feel that power return.

You lie only when you feel unable to handle the consequences of truth.

The opportunity to practice truth and enjoy its benefits is not limited to major life events. There are countless choices you make every day to either present your brightest and best qualities or be ordinary as you go along with personal and popular pressures. When you stand down rather than speak up, manipulate rather than be up front, you betray the noble soul. That guilt may be so subtle and habitual that it is unnoticed, but it is there, always encouraging you to stand tall as a fearless spiritual being. Train yourself to hear truth and live as if there were no guilt, only greatness. Integrity is the integration of your highest truth made real in word and action.

Guilt from Past Events: **IT Happened

When you feel bad about something that happened, whether 5 minutes or 15 years ago, Guilt persists; it insists that you learn a truth you didn't know at the time. You may remain stuck in the past until you realize how to act in such a way that the mistake and its repercussions don't happen again. Your lesson may be small, requiring just a twinge of Guilt, or it may be so life threatening that Guilt is all consuming. The issue may not even be yours; rather, it may be something you are blamed for, and you take on Guilt from others. In every case, cloudy vision caused the problem. It will only be cleared up when greater truth is found and followed. Here is a true story of a perfect storm of Guilt.

Jamie's Story: When Everything You Do Is Wrong

When I was little, I didn't know what was wrong. I just thought I was a bad person because my mother was always punishing me. I couldn't figure what I was I was doing wrong; I just thought I must be a bad person. She'd take me into a corner and say, "Shame on you, you are my daughter, and I do everything for you, and this is how you thank me?" She wouldn't say why . . . or at least I couldn't understand why. "I worked and slaved for you, and this is the way you treat me; this is how you pay me back." I tried hard to please her, but there was always something wrong. I felt shame and guilt, but there was never any way out; I was just defective.

It was an impossible situation. But I was born with a stubborn perseverance that meant I couldn't give up; so I kept trying to please her. I would jump to do anything she asked. In this way, she controlled me totally. I tried so hard to be good. As I grew older, I never got into drugs and sex like others my age, and yet she always accused me of the worst. I couldn't do anything right; I was stupid and bad. And if I tried to explain or stand up to her, there was worse hell to pay for that. If anything at all bad happened to anyone, it was somehow always my fault.

"It's your fault, you didn't listen to me, you didn't do it right." When I brought my first boyfriend home, she laid into me; I was even bad for being loved. Every message was that I was ugly, inadequate, and undeserving of love.

At school, the nuns [Yes, Catholic school! I told you it was a perfect storm.] were equally as hard and relentless in their attacks on me. I now believe that my mother was jealous of me for being attractive and for going places, and she tried to keep me unhappy along with her. It was the same with the nuns. Although they told me I was stupid and wrong, I discovered I was good in math. It was great, because at least there I could be right. Mom liked that I was smart; she used it to feel superior to her sister.

Even though I had no power to be right at home, somehow I was allowed to be tough outside the house. Mom encouraged me to fight back. I discovered she thought it funny when I beat up the mean neighborhood boys. So men + love = I'm bad, but men + fighting = okay. That fit in with her as role model: love = abuse.

I went on to put up with a lot of abuse from two husbands. I could never defend myself, because I was trained and shamed by Mom anytime I protested and stood up. She supported those loveless relationships and blamed me for any trouble in them.

When I left home and the trap Mom was making for me, I made a life for myself with the only two things she allowed me: to be smart and aggressive outside of my relationship with her. I became a corporate lawyer, one of the first women to do so. I was wildly successful. But in that cutthroat world, I was attacked by the male partners; so I worked harder than anyone to prove myself. I never got away from feeling stupid, but I believed my hard work and perseverance would win out.

My mom died when I was 25, but her voice lived on in my head. I have two grown daughters and constantly feel I am to blame for every bad thing that happens to them. They somehow have replaced my mother. Although I was a great career role model, they grew up seeing me as abused. They blamed me for not being feminine enough, for being selfish, when all I did was work and give everything to them and my freeloading husband. It was always my job to take care of everyone; I never thought of myself. Yet all of their misfortune is always my fault, again.

> My mother hijacked my life—my purpose was to serve her. If she weren't happy, I wouldn't be either. My daughter and husbands continued that after her. I would like to feel that it's okay do what I want to do and not be punished for it; that I deserve love and can receive it in a healthy, loving way, without feeling bad about shining my own light.

This is an extreme story in which Guilt and Shame were used to debilitate and control. The Guilt was not Jamie's; but once internalized, it colored everything she did. There could be no escape until she learned to hear a higher truth from within. As a child, she couldn't self-recognize her beauty and innocence without help, but Guilt has stuck and prodded painfully until she could find that truth. Her healing has begun with just being able to recognize all of this as abuse. Working with her emotions to get to compassion, she began to feel worthy of taking care of herself, to think more highly of herself, and to not believe her mother's early abuses. Her mother's neurotic Personal Truth had been imposed on her and colored Jamie's relationship with her daughters, gathering a consensus that then gained strength and became her Circumstantial Truth. Although she did no wrong, the rules she depended on to know what was right were flawed, to say the least. Even so, Guilt pointed to an inner wisdom that she could tap to heal this tragic imprint by bringing her to a truth she could not have known at the time. This was a case of Guilt gone wild. For most of us, however, it is more common for Guilt to go idle.

Where Is Guilt When We Need It?

The more prevalent misuse of guilt is that it is ignored and overridden by Personal Truth. In the age of information, we see pedophile priests who prey on parishioners, violating their vows while the highest church elders hide them from law. We see banks steal from their customers on a global scale, while no one goes to jail. Laws are changed, or those who commit these crimes feel they are above the law—too big to prosecute. Governments act against the people they are meant to serve and send death and destruction to innocents. How do all these people sleep at night? Individual truth—that is, "What I want now"—is their validation. It is codified by consensual truth—"Everyone else is doing it!" Healthy, course-correcting Guilt has been lost on this larger, systemic, cultural scale. Rudeness is in fashion, and crime is glamorized, even institutionalized. Corporations have the "divine right of kings," without the statesmanship required.

Whether you have too much, too little, or just the right amount, Guilt gives you direct access to the truth that brings you into balance. To act clearly, you must see clearly and be present. Guilt, regrets, and memories of misdeeds that remain without resolution mean you are literally living in the past, operating on old information. Learn to let go so you can live as your most excellent and up-to-date self. The following is an adaptation of the SOS Method that helped Jamie. It can work with any of these three time frames of Guilt, bringing you to the Timeless. Test for yourself how acting on higher truth can resolve any issue.

Self-Renewal: Washing Away Patterns of Guilt and Shame

If there is some past wrong done to or by you and it still bugs you, wash away the act and the cloudy judgment, get clear, and start over all the wiser for it. This practice will help you get to Neutral Mind, so you can hear Universal Truth, obey it, and act on it. For this practice, be ready to draw upon any memories of guilt, blame, and punishment.

❶ *Begin with Getting Peaceful (page xi). Tune in with the Adi Mantra and continue.*

❷ **Pittra Kriya.**

a.   Rest your left hand on your Heart Center and cup your right hand in front of you with your elbow relaxed by your side. Focus your eyes are on the tip of the nose. Lift your right hand up so it passes the ear, as if you were splashing water over your shoulder. You will feel the wind pass your ear as the hand moves toward the shoulder. Your wrist must cross your earlobe. Continue this for 11 minutes. As Yogi Bhajan says, "Get rid of this inner mental and physical tension."

As you move, dig up and recall your entire inventory of memories involving Guilt, Blame, Remorse, Self-Hatred, Revenge, Being Unforgiven, Being Wrong. Recall any blunders, mistakes, accidents, screw-ups that you caused or that happened to you. Think on judgments, scoldings, punishments. With each stroke of your hand by your ear, dump those memories and feelings behind you. Put that earlier, less-conscious version of yourself in the past where it lives. None of it is real now; realize they are all back there, behind you. You are not that person now. Purge, cleanse, and wash away with each stroke; then go back in for more. Keep digging, remembering, and feeling every incident that comes to you; then release each one. The eyes help you hold steady in the here and now. Regain the control you didn't have back then. With love and determination, swim toward strength, responsibility, and your higher consciousness. Get free.

To end, inhale and suspend the breath for 15 seconds as you stretch your right hand back as far as you can. Exhale. Repeat twice more. Sit calmly for a few minutes with close self-awareness. Enjoy the clear and clean space—or whatever you feel now.

b.   Place your elbows on the second rib below the base of your breast in line with the nipple, by pressing the upper arm against the front of your torso. Hands are slightly wider than the elbows, and the palms are facing up, with the thumb on top of the nail of the middle finger. Focus your eyes at the tip of the nose. With each exhale, chant the sound "Hud" as you flick the middle finger out and away from under your thumb. *You have to touch the tongue firmly to the meridian points in the upper palate that relate to the hypothalamus in order to regulate the pituitary to bring you energy.* Continue this for 11 minutes.

The sound "Hud" has three very specific sounds: an aspirated "h," expelling breath with enough force to feel a strong pull backward at the navel; a deep guttural "uh," coming from the belly and felt in the chest; and a precise "d" or "duh," where the tip of the tongue quickly flicks the upper palate behind the front teeth. The mouth remains slightly open as you generate this strong sound (it is very important to maintain this position). With the power of the navel, feel your power.

You lightened the load of Guilt in the first step. The balance of power has shifted in your favor, and you are on top now—stronger and in control. Flick away lies like so many flies. This makes small the annoying opinions and judgments against you. With that same finger, you defiantly tell the world to get out of your face; you proclaim there is no power over you, nothing you are in doubt about. You are open to learn who you are and live free to be that.

Continue to release and repel any belief in your weakness and badness. It is all part of you as a whole being, but you are choosing your strength.

To end, inhale deeply. Continue moving the fingers as you suspend the breath for 15 seconds and let it open your ribcage. This will balance you. Then exhale powerfully through the open mouth. Repeat this 3 times more.

c. Bring your arms out in front of you in a "V," about 15 degrees above shoulder height. Your hands are flat and facing down. This is the Superman Pose. At the rate of one repetition per second, repeat "Hud" as in the second step, but this time, alternately cross your hands in front of you and keep your arms straight; do not bend your elbows. Focus your eyes at the tip of the nose. Continue for 11 minutes.

This step will challenge your arms. You must find the strength within yourself to maintain the movement. Feel free to get mad, determined, and defiant to stand your ground. As you call up that energy, use it to confront and prevail over every past and future challenge to your self-esteem; every insult, failure, attack, weakness, fear, lack of faith in yourself. There is no hiding or blaming. Just channel the energy straight into your courage and excellence. This is the real you. Don't stop; find your hidden strength. Even if your body crumbles, you do not. Salute, praise, and honor yourself. Feel the power.

To end, keep moving the arms as you inhale; hold the breath for 10 seconds and exhale explosively out. Repeat 3 more times, moving your hands as fast as possible during the last repetition.

(**Note:** These three steps must be done together for 11 minutes each—no more, no less. Together, they will eliminate Guilt and Stress and relax you. Do this practice daily for 40 days to be done with guilt. Then do it after that as needed.)

❸ *Envision Your Higher Truth.*

a. Sit and enjoy the mental clarity and stillness you have created. Guilt brought you to this review, but there is no need for that guilt now; you are elevated and aware. Feel your power to face and handle anything. Sit as a wise seer holding court. Recall the problem incident or issue, the source of any feelings of wrong; bring it before you. Stay neutral and see it all without being caught up in it. See the action, the motives, and perhaps the underlying pattern and flawed belief. Don't take any of it personally; just watch.

b. See and accept the animal in you—the need to grab that made it seem right at the time. Feel justified in that impulsive urge.

c. Be in your clever, calculating, and careful Personal Truth. What rules directed your decisions? Whose rules were they? Did conflicting voices pull inside and outside of you? Was there resistance? Uncertainty? Did you sense that you couldn't handle it straight, so instead you looked for more convenient rules that gave what you needed?

d. Leave that feeling and rise again to neutrality. Go deep into the heart and ask it to speak to you. What truth do you hear? What does Soul want in all this? Sit with whatever it is.

e. See all three levels of truth and how they are related. See that you acted in agreement with something in each case. Can you see how the agreement made sense from each point of view? Could you forgive a decision made from limited scope and consciousness either from you or from the other party?

f. You can now rewrite any agreements you may have been unknowingly acting upon. Consciously declare an end to any outdated understandings, pacts, or promises. Behold the higher truth you wish to live by. Can you agree to this? Seal that covenant in a sacred way within yourself.

g. Imagine yourself obeying that truth. How will you live this promise to yourself? How will it decide your course for you? Is there any unfinished business in your life, any letter to right, conversation to have, fence to repair that will better align you to this vision? Can you see how, even if difficult, these actions will strengthen you? It might be relaxing to just follow one truth with no doubt.

❹ *Capture Your Gains.* Come back with eyes open and make some notes. What did you rid yourself of forever? What did you gain? What did you learn about yourself? What do you need to remember to live in that clarity? What do you need to do? Is it a one-time action or a new way from now on? Write down your new truths, agreements, and actions, and then live them!

> *Such is the identification with Truth; it makes you pure. When you agree to agree, your mind becomes sure.*
>
> → **Guru Nanak, Jap Ji Sahib**

Skilled Guilt

Clearing up the past is the most commonly needed use of guilt. Guilt only persists until it is able to get you back on track with your deepest commitments. This Sense of the Soul insists that you come clean: identify the error, set new and improved boundaries, make behavioral changes and social repairs, and forgive yourself for the error that made all that happen. Mistakes are made, and things are broken. Destruction is part of the cycle of life; it allows new and better things to arise. Enjoy the flow of your trial-and-error learning process. Take the blowback as a blessing, the price of lessons learned. Improvement through learning, rather than revenge and punishment, is the intended purpose of Guilt. It's an evolutionary training process of positive and negative feedback that guides you to your best behavior. Guilt is a comparative study using cause and effect: "I didn't like the effect of what I did. I feel guilty. I don't like that feeling. But when I do this other thing, I feel good about myself, so I'll do it that way now."

Acceptance and Forgiveness

Forgiveness is when you understand what this mistake was *given for*. You forgive in exchange for grace and the embrace of greater goodness. In this way, you learn to trust yourself, act confidently, and avoid mistakes—or at least learn quickly from them. You let go of the past and the person you were when you made that mistake, even if it was just moments ago! Your sensory system will give you immediate positive feedback. You feel good about yourself again and move forward with restored strength, self-respect, and integrity. Taking full responsibility for your actions, their results, and your total life circumstances, while allowing others to learn in their own time, is the fastest way to reach no guilt, no blame, and ultimately peace.

Your consciousness is continually expanding, as is the Universe. Because learning is continuous, you can expect to be greater than you were yesterday and less than you will be tomorrow. Action/reaction is a physical law; we learn by making mistakes. It's not personal. Claiming goodness and blaming evil is false ownership of the whole process. Guilt is a reminder that you are in the ego-based belief that "I did it." Instead, simply play your role in life observantly, allowing lessons and growth to occur without resistance. When Yogi Bhajan made mistakes and was scolded by his teacher, rather than get down on himself, he would say, "What a day this is!" and then learn from it. This guilt-free acceptance of the effects you have caused is stress free.

The Power to Bless

We each have the power either to curse ourselves and others or to bless. As you have seen, deciding which one is deserved and "true" may be a matter of opinion and circumstance. Right or wrong, we can bless the person and the situation and then move on. A blessing is a projection of love and good wishes, of good will and positive intention. A blessing is unconditional. You can bless your enemies even as you protect yourself from them. Forgiveness is a form of blessing, as is a smile, a hug, a helping hand, a dollar in the hungry hand. When you feel blessed, it flows through you to others. Your very existence can be a blessing to others, even though they may not like you or even know you. If you can't bless yourself, if you can't receive your own blessing, no one can bless you. You may be facing death and feel blessed, or you may have all the riches and feel cursed. The power is yours. How do you use it? Practice!

Bless Yourself

This meditation is a noble act that brings you into a deeply personal experience of Blessing and being Blessed. You may not understand what Blessing can do. It's no secret: If you Bless, God immediately, spontaneously blesses you. A person who blesses will not go empty.

⟶ **Yogi Bhajan, December 4, 1993**

❶ *Begin with Getting Peaceful (page xi). Tune in with the Adi Mantra and continue.*

❷ *Being Blessed.* Extend your right arm out in front of you, sloping up slightly at about a 45-degree angle. Your right palm is flat and facing the ground. Your arm should be relaxed; the elbow doesn't necessarily have to be kept straight. Place your left hand flat against the Heart Center. Close your eyes . Look toward and focus intently on the navel. Imagine that you are very angelic. Begin to bless the Universe, Earth, and even your enemies— all of humanity, good and bad. Feel very caring and kind. To bless is a noble act. And don't forget to bless yourself! Use the word *bless* constantly and consistently in your mind. Open and deepen your heart. Do this for 11 minutes, spending the final 2 minutes just blessing yourself. To end, inhale deeply. Hold the breath as long as you can as you feel the blessings circulating throughout your body. Exhale. Repeat 3 times total. Relax.

Guilt Leads to Timeless Truth

No one wants to be wrong—not the child in time-out or the criminal at his execution. Every trespass begs a look in the mirror, a closer scrutiny, a search for understanding or clarity. When we resist that inquiry and harden in our views, the pain persists. But when we are willing to see what comes to light, when we yield to the lessons gained and face the consequences, we become lighter and stronger. In the meditations in this chapter, you may have realized something you didn't know before. When through the Neutral Mind your heart speaks Universal Truth, you have found the gift of Guilt. You have entered the Timeless realm that is Soul's steady destination through every experience and emotion. Living in and acting from that Truth is the highest human experience. Even so, the transition from living in your lesser truth and lies can be daunting. Having leaned on your cleverness for so long, how do you learn to trust this quiet voice that commands so simply and yet feels so foreign?

Have you ever been in an earthquake? When the one solid thing you assume you can rely on to support you—that is, the earth you stand on—is unstable, it rattles you to the core. Uncertainty is stressful. We've all spent lifetimes wondering what's wrong, who's right, how do we act, what do we do. In contrast, when you know where you stand—on the solid ground of self-reliance based on the fact that inner guidance is reliably available—you are relaxed and carefree, even through shaky times. This is the state of Trust.

Bless and Trust

Building trust is usually approached by working toward a preconceived idea that fits our needs: that a mate will never leave or hurt us, that people will never cheat us, that God won't make bad things happen. We bargain with whatever we think will win those outcomes: gifts, prayers, best behavior, or forced compliance, if necessary. But because we can never bend the world to our personal will—how could the world bend to the constantly changing wishes of seven billion people—this trust is never achieved. What we seek is the security of knowing what will happen. All we want is something steady to go by. We all have that within ourselves. This practice will bring it out.

❶ Begin with Getting Peaceful (page xi). Tune in with the Adi Mantra and continue.

❷ Spiritual Stamina.

a. Fix the eyes one-tenth open. Extend your arms up in a circular arc, so the palms and fingers of each hand face down about 6 or 8 inches over the crown of the head. Keep the hands separated by about 12 inches. The thumbs should be separate from the fingers and should hang loosely. Breathe in a three-part pattern:

- Inhale in 8 equal strokes.

- Exhale completely in 8 equal strokes.

- Suspend the breath out for 16 beats in the same rhythm.

As you breathe, mentally repeat the mantra "Sa-Ta-Na-Ma" with each part of the breath. Continue in this pattern for 11 minutes, slowly increasing to 22 and then to 31 minutes over time.

b. To end, inhale deeply as you raise your arms high up overhead. Stretch your arms up and back. Drop your head back and look up. Stretch with all your strength to extend the lower back and the neck. Then exhale and drop your arms. Repeat this final breath 2 more times. Relax.

❸ Comments. This exercise requires some endurance and practice. The arms will seem comfortable at first, but they often become painful after a while. When that occurs, become very calm and draw your focus onto the breath and the mantra. Let the images and sensations of the arms fade. This releases a powerful stimulant to the pineal and pituitary glands, which results in an increase in intuition. Intuition is a perceptual function of the entire brain and whole mind. This meditation gives you the blessing to be still and to discriminate the real from the unreal, truth from illusion, fantasy from imagination. It gives you guidance and relentless dedication to your vision.

True Trust

Through the clear and quiet Neutral Mind, things can be seen as they are, free of your projected will—or what you think they should be. When you get to know a person, you can predict her human weakness. When you learn how life flows, you can expect the entire variety of ups and downs. You can trust with certainty that life will flow as it always does, predictably unpredictable. You begin to trust in yourself to handle what comes. You trust in God to surprise you, so that you are never surprised, disappointed, or betrayed. This is true Trust, and it is an extremely powerful state that paradoxically comes through acceptance and surrender, rather than through projection and control. Like any good relationship, Trust in your Self and in Truth is built over time with familiarity and regular interaction. Through the proven method of daily practice, through quality time focused on the vast invisible world within your heart and mind, you become timeless; you become Universal; you become Truth. Your innate innocence is felt and preserved though time. Your honor is protected in advance. You act with an intention to serve Truth and let the Universe handle the outcome. When nothing is personal, there is no personal consequence. When you flow within the rules of dharma, there is no karma. The very purpose of Guilt has been achieved and is resolved at its core. If you do get off track and need a new course correction, Soul will be sure to let you know.

Self-Study

Check in with Universal Truth daily through a regular practice.

❶ Practice Pittra Kriya (page 250) for 33 or more minutes daily to solve incomplete lessons of Guilt once and for all. Early morning before sunrise is best, as this is the time when the subconscious can open up and release while the conscious mind is clear and alert. Evening is second best, because it clears your day to relax. Of course, any time you can is also fine. It is also best to start with some yoga or exercise and deep breathing to clear the mind and increase your energy before you meditate.

❷ Use the exercises and your stillness afterward to reach Neutral Mind, where you have few thoughts and can see clearly. This is the time to ask questions and allow your highest truth to guide your decisions and solve your dilemmas. You'll know if you need to change your ways, forgive yourself or others, or take action to makes amend.

❸ Finish with Bless Yourself (page 256). You can ask for blessings, forgiveness, and love. But don't wait for God to grant it. Giving yourself what you want to get is always the best. Ask for forgiveness of your Higher Self. This way, you control the response, and it is instantaneous.

Chapter Ten

Shame
The Teacher of Self-Esteem

Shame drives you to accept yourself.
You will hate or hide until you come to love all as perfect in its imperfection.

The Purpose of Shame:

When you feel embarrassed, disgusted, ugly, or bad about some part of yourself;

When you are told or believe that you are different, defective, unwanted;

When you want to hide or die;

When you are abandoned, rejected, alone, and lost, even to yourself;

When you've had enough and you want to rise, stand strong, and believe in yourself...

Shame shines a light on the shadows, those places where you don't live to your own standards and values.

It drives you to accept your worst, accept yourself as perfectly imperfect, and rise to your best.

When you live within your integrity, you feel comfortable in your own skin.

Your identity is your Divinity. The ultimate lesson of Shame is unshakeable self-love.

Shame teaches you to take control of your self-esteem. This chapter will let you safely go to your darkest places to compassionately embrace every ugliness and beauty. You can then enjoy that clean, newborn feeling that is the reality of your Soul.

Do You Match Up to What Is Expected?

Every day of your life, you deal with your own many needs, while being confronted with the demands of others. You cannot live without the social network of support, yet you are also competing—as are we all—for your own happiness. You are constantly negotiating this blend of personal needs and group expectations. To balance what it means to be you with what it takes to get along with others is an essential challenge. To do it successfully, you need to use three faculties. First is your capacity to listen to yourself—to have an awareness of your unique qualities, capabilities, and values and to know what is important to you. By listening to yourself, your goals and the personal resources you have available will be revealed to you. Second, this listening ability must be tempered by sensitivity to the world around you, so you know what is expected and required by others. Too much of the first, and your own uniqueness will be disharmonious, undervalued, or even distorted without feedback. Too much of the second, and you will be a chameleon, selling out to fit in and losing touch with the only real thing you have—you.

Awareness of self and others must be moderated by a neutral party, which is the third faculty—the ability to see it all at once, even beyond all those short-term circumstances. We call this the *voice of Soul*. I hope by now you know how to hear from it, for it is the arbiter of all disputes between pleasing self, pleasing others, and fulfilling the Divine Order of All Things! You have your own special sensor to detect and sort out internal information about your Self, external demands, and how well you are balancing both of those with your essential purpose. This sensor is called Shame. I know, you don't like to say its name much less feel it, but it is your own EGS—Emotional Guidance System. It guides you by providing the only thing that will allow fulfillment: Being You.

Like a car's gas gauge, which lets you know if you have what it takes to reach your destination, you have a measure for how well these three awarenesses are working together—your self-esteem. Shame reveals the condition of your self-worth at any moment and serves to raise it. Whenever it feels bad to be you, Shame detects and reflects that you have forgotten who you really are. It transforms those debilitating feelings of being "worthless" into the experience of being "priceless."

Shame reveals the condition of your self-worth at any moment and serves to raise it.

Self-esteem is your picture of yourself. It is a subjective and sometimes arbitrary estimate of how you think you compare to others. How you compare is how you will fare out there. Your value—what you think you are worth—defines what you deserve. What you deserve is what you can expect to receive. Results always match self-image. You may not have natural physical ability or you may even have compromised health, but if you somehow believe your body is strong and resilient, you may enjoy sports, taking risks, running fast, and going on playful adventures. However, if you believe yourself, for whatever reason, to be fragile and easily hurt, you won't take risks or play hard; instead, you'll move slowly and not extend yourself. Therefore, self-esteem is everything; it is a self-fulfilling prophecy.

What Do You Have to Work With? And Does It Work for Them?

When you are born, you try to figure out how it works "out here." Who gives you what you need, and how can you influence that in your favor? What is it about you that motivates their desire to care for you? Is it smiling or crying? As you grow older, you try to figure out how to get the teacher to give good grades, the popular kids to pick you as a friend, the boys to notice you. You respond to the feedback and adopt that as your Self. This external validation is how you first come to define yourself. Your environments, which may support or reject you, form your initial self-concept. If the random needs and moods of others are your only source of self-esteem, then you will forever be a beggar, asking, "Do you like me?" The only way you can answer the questions "Who am I?" and "What is my proper place here?" is to mold and conform yourself. This is exhausting, because you can never please everyone, and you never get to enjoy being your Self.

Shame, from *skem*, means "to cover," which implies a way to hide whatever is unacceptable to others. "To survive, I have to behave!" How did Shame start for you? If you are "different," like the runt of a litter of kittens, you are pushed aside at feeding time. A school of fish finds safety in being nearly identical and moving in perfect synchrony; those on the fringe are preyed upon first. A black sheep stands out and may be left out on the fringe of the herd where the wolf strikes. When we lived in primate groups and later as cave-dwelling people, both appearance and behavior had to be in line with the clan for survival, and the consequences of rejection were great. If you were an outcast from the shelter of home and tribe, you didn't survive. As I wrote this, the poor and elderly were the last to get food and power after Hurricane Sandy. You don't get or keep your job unless the company has the feeling that you fit in. You learn by reward and punishment, obedience, conformity, fidelity, loyalty. Social animals perish without group support, so you have a primal instinct for the "right" behavior, as well as a fear of strangers, both of which can result in the extremes of sectarian warfare, ethnic cleansing, racial prejudice, or gender bias.

In which group of people are you most "at home"? Where do you feel that you fit in and belong, are accepted and welcomed, even honored? Is it with your family, a friend, your 12-step meeting, or your yoga studio? What do you have in common with those you most often commune with and call your community, where everybody knows your name? It may be a bar or the NRA, your neighborhood or your country. Do you feel as comfortable with all of humanity? Whom do you consider the weirdos, the fringe, dismissible, wrong, bad, crazy, and unimportant? When you focus on the differences, it can be lonely, even with seven billion others. There is a deep, even primordial, history of the dangers of being different.

The Fall from Heaven

Imagine being born with everything perfectly taken care of. Parents who protect and nurture you; the feeling of being safe and loved. Being you seems to be a good thing, and you are free to explore the world. Everything you discover about it and yourself is full of wonder. There is no self-consciousness of the body and its functions; it's all natural, all you. Then you had the first of many moments, a sharp stinging sensation, when someone suddenly did not approve of you. You could see in the mirror of their face or the tenor of their voice that they were now looking at something horrible, something they didn't like. In that moment, it all changed—you could no longer just be you; you had to watch yourself; you became self-conscious and had to quickly figure out how to get them relaxed and smiling again. It may have happened to you very early. You might not even remember the event, when everything changed about how you felt—from happy and normal to miserable, humiliated, unsafe, unclean, unworthy, unloved, unlovable, unwanted.

Shame Makers

Here are some situations involving and creating Shame, all from true stories. As you read, note which are familiar to you. Write down any memories that are triggered as you read this so you can work with them in the exercises that follow.

- Baby Ellen poops and pees anywhere. It's natural, but she still remembers the day when her mom told her it was disgusting. She still feels that way about her body.

- Ray is just 10 months old and loves to crawl and to explore everything with all of his senses. One day, his mom's friends are over laughing and enjoying his cuteness, even when he pulls off his diaper. But when he plays with his penis, an uncomfortable silence stops everything. Mom slaps him hard and says, "Dirty." That cold feeling still comes over him when he tries to ask his friend for a date.

- Sweet 6-year-old Beth crawls up on kind Grandpa's lap, like a hundred times before. Today he is sexually frustrated with his wife, mad, and drunk. When she kisses him, he slaps her so hard she slams against the wall across the room. She doesn't know what is so horrible about herself to make him mad, so she hides her affection from him and all men for the rest of her life.

- A 12-year-old Maria has always been praised for her beauty. She dresses up carefully for the big dance, and that cute boy really notices and asks her to dance. Later, alone, he violates her. Being attractive is never again safe.

- On Shari's first day at her new school, she wanted to make friends, so she wore the special dress her mom had bought for her in Mexico. All the popular girls pointed and laughed. Ever since then, she thinks of herself as an oddball, and she blames her mother.

- Scott knows all the answers in class and loves to learn. The big guys call him a nerd and beat him up; his grades go down.

- Carla's mom and dad used to get disappointed and mad when she as not the best in gymnastics class. She won every competition but always felt that she was not that good. Now she always feels fat, and she is careful never to eat more than a few bites. Her mom worries about how bony Carla is, but Carla keeps her not eating as a secret.

- Jim would really like to talk to girls and go on a date, but he just feels awkward and stupid. He doesn't know what to say. It's easier to just be lonely.

- Senator Russell grew up being told men loving men is sinful, but he just can't help checking it out. His gay affair is found out. His career and marriage are over.

- Ricky blew that last point, the team lost, and no one will speak to him now.

- Gerry took some money from her dad's wallet and now can't look him in the eyes.

- Daddy's little girl is caught making out in the car on her first date. Dad hits her and calls her a slut.

- Jenny talks mean to her friends so the popular kids will think she's cool. They never speak again, and Jenny feels bad every time she sees her old friends.

Your Own Experience of Shame

As dark and uncomfortable as feelings of Shame are, you need to know what you are feeling; that's how emotions speak to you. The physical sensations help get your attention and demand that you listen. What is called a loss of innocence is the loss of your "inner-sense," the loving connection to essence that gives you the freedom to be you.

❶ *Begin with Getting Peaceful (page xi).* From this place of stillness, continue with the guided vidualization.

This meditation is about your personal story of The Fall, when you left your own Garden of Eden. Be aware of all your sensations. Invite these darker memories. Continue to breathe deeply and be present as you discover that you can handle the feelings that arise. When was your innocence lost? Do you have memories of being abused, laughed at, ridiculed, ostracized, despised, left out, picked last, unwanted, neglected, abandoned, rejected, attacked personally, embarrassed? You may have had strong feelings of humiliation or being unclean, unworthy, unwanted, miserable, unlovable. You or your environments and caregivers may have been shabby, unkempt, uncaring, neglectful, or embarrassing to you. You may have felt great urgency to be liked and included, of trying to please, of trying to fit in by being smart, cute, funny, tough, hardworking, serious, sexy. Or perhaps you felt like you were not enough, didn't belong, or were undeserving, wanting to disappear or not be seen or known. Perhaps you felt self-loathing, inner anger that manifested as self-destructive thoughts and behaviors, or a desire to harm and self-annihilate.

What was that Shame for? Was it something you did, how you looked, your family or home? Who did it come from—was it public and blatant or behind your back, subtle, implied? What were the consequences of not fitting in? In each case, you were just being yourself, but that was suddenly a problem. Some characteristic, idea, or action of yours was seen as bad. But it was not seen as a separate quality; instead, it marked you as inherently and entirely flawed. You didn't change, but your feelings about yourself changed in response to the feelings of others. You were no more or less pure, beautiful, and innocent, but somehow you lost that awareness.

When you are vulnerable, when you need the food, care, acceptance, approval, love, and any other need from those other people, you just go along with what they think and feel about you. They are big and powerful; you are dependent on them. So you stand with them—and against yourself—to survive the moment. You trade "it feels good to be me" for their approval and what it brings you. In a deal with the devil, you look back at yourself from their viewpoint with their disgust. You see yourself as ugly, no good, defective, gross, worthless, less than. You become embarrassed, even disgusted, with your own precious self. Then you blush, feel hot, and want to hide. You feel apologetic for who you are. You may think you are alone, lost, and vulnerable. You might even feel nauseated or sick.

Shame can be so painful that it will even hide from you! When it does that, it goes underground to affect you subconsciously, without your ever having a memory of the incident. However, it is there, waiting to heal you from whatever happened, to restore your innocence once again. But first you have to restore your inner-sense, which is the only way to return unwholesomeness to wholeness.

❶ Capture Your Gains. Take a moment to write down any memories that have come up so far.

Surviving the Challenges with Your Dignity Intact

"Am I enough? Good enough, beautiful enough, smart enough? Will I be loved? Am I worthy? Do I fit in, measure up? Do I honor myself, feel my inborn purity and grace, and have an inner sense of my innocence?" When you feel bad about yourself, all of these questions arise and challenge you to work with them to find the answer to the question that is You! Doubts from within and attacks from outside constantly challenge you to connect to and strengthen the trust in yourself. You are more than adequate to be here and to handle your life. These attacks—and they are lifelong—will take you closer to or farther from the strength and joy of being uniquely you. It all depends on how you respond. The choice is either to save yourself in the short term by selling out and fitting in or to stand your ground. When you modify yourself, create the camouflage needed to fit in, at the cost of your own self-approval, you create an inner conflict.

> **Doubts from within and attacks from outside constantly challenge you to connect to and strengthen the trust in yourself. You are more than adequate to be here and to handle your life.**

The only possible, sustainable comfort comes from that one person you live with 24/7—that would be you! But when you lose your bearings, begin to feel lost, and start wandering outside, you leave home in search of shelter. And yet, what you have to work with, the life you were given, the mixture of defects and excellences that are uniquely yours are *always* sufficient to live your life. But when insecurity sends you scrambling after the likes and lives of others, it's like walking away from your own survival kit in search of supplies. Choosing to work with what you have is the early beginning of self-love. Your fundamental doubt is, "If I am just purely and authentically me, will I be okay? Will that work? Is it safe to come out now, to show myself, to be myself?" Life is a proving ground to discover who you are and how well it works to be so. Shame lets you know how it's going, what you need to work on, and what you need to improve. It gives you all the information you need, right when you need to address it.

The Journey from Zero to Hero

How much you enjoy being yourself and how much fulfillment you realize for yourself are both entwined with beliefs about your worth and your place in the world. Those beliefs, which are revealed in your thoughts, fall somewhere between complete self-loathing with no right to exist, a "zero" at the low end of the spectrum, to a complete loving merger of the micro self with the macro Self, a "hero" at the peak of human experience. When a belief of unworthiness dominates your view of your place in the world, it's called Shame Consciousness. You may compensate with perfectionism to earn your keep, or you may project this inner war of aggression on others, becoming disapproving and intolerant, unaccepting of defects in others that you fear in yourself. When you attack the only thing you have—yourself—or when you attack others whom you need, you create your own obstacles. This makes Shame the most debilitating of all emotions, because, in this way, it is devoid of the self-love it so desperately calls for. Apathy seems neutral and peaceful when compared with Self-Hatred, though the two often work together. Every one of us is somewhere on this road from the pain of aloneness to the bliss of oneness, always moving toward that union that is the goal of all yoga and spirituality. As you read through this chapter, feel for any resonance with beliefs you have had, note what each one feels like, and see how each step is stronger than the last. Use the following spectrum to determine where your consciousness currently resides.

I am All.

I am love.

I love myself.

I accept all that I am and am not.

I can receive love.

I have some value.

I can earn your love.

I want to hide.

No one cares.

I'm unlovable.

I loathe myself.

I don't exist.

Do you recognize some of these in yourself and others? Where do you spend most of your time now? You likely have a familiar range, with occasional visits to states above and below your norm. Mark your current predominant self-concept with today's date. Do the same at monthly intervals while working with your emotions. Mark in the scale your perception of several other important people in your life. Include famous people who you think are extremely high or low. Can you imagine being at the next level for yourself? How might you get there?

Each step forward is an incremental healing of your relationship to yourself. Self-loathing worthlessness is a living hell. Every time Shame speaks, that awful emptiness motivates you toward more self- acceptance, so you can

Shame leads back home to the unequalled, excellent experience of Self.

embrace your perfect imperfection and love who you are. This, in turn, leads back home to the unequalled, excellent experience of Self. Now use your Senses of the Soul to help you along this road.

Finding Your Worth

❶ Begin with Getting Peaceful (page xi).

❷ Modified SOS Method for Shame.

a. **Sit and Feel.** Cross your arms left over right, holding opposite shoulders. Relax and let the shoulders carry the weight. Breathe very fully, deeply, slowly and evenly for a few minutes while feeling held, safe, and cared for. Bring forth any memory that this chapter has stirred up or any that comes now—a time when you were embarrassed, when you wanted to run and hide or "just die." Go through the memory clearly, including what you saw and heard. What were the physical swwensations? You will likely feel them again now. Let the thoughts and feelings flow as you continue to breathe slowly and deeply. Just watch it all with great interest, long enough to get accustomed to the feelings without resistance. As uncomfortable as it may be, slow down and feel, rather than avoid; face the feelings, rather than hide.

b. **Ask and Listen.** Once you settle down within the feelings, you can communicate and get their wise messages about who you really are. Stay present to the feelings and let them answer in the same feeling language. Notice that you are viewing yourself, and you are having opinions and feelings about yourself. Are you comparing yourself? If so, with whom or what?

- Where did the attack or the message that you are defective, bad, or wrong come from? Was it words from others, their attitude or silence, something you saw, something "everyone" thinks? If it's coming from you, when did you first think it? Where did the thought come from?

- What exactly is the judgment? Is it about people like you, about you overall, or about a very specific part of you?

- Can you see the desire to be accepted, the pain of rejection, a wish to change and make it stop?

- Did you question, disagree, defend verbally or mentally? Or did you believe what they said about you? Is there a voice from within your own heart telling you that there is a problem with you?

- Do you feel doubly alone when others don't approve? When you don't approve of yourself?

c. **Seek Solutions**. Take charge. Do you see that you could have stood your ground or loved yourself no matter what others say, even if what they say is true? Follow your heart and your own internal, compassionate voice. What does it value? Do you see something not aligned with who you know yourself to be? Be very specific about the source of any bad feelings about yourself; name the badness, wrongness, or defectiveness that is at the heart of it. Can you honestly admit whatever your heart tells you is not who you really are? Can you still see your other good qualities and hold a balanced perspective? Whatever your own heart wants to improve, see the image, qualities, or behavior it is leading you toward. There was some rejection and disapproval by others and yourself that initiated your feeling bad about yourself. It has all helped you see yourself more clearly. Either it was never true and you have reaffirmed who you are, or it poined out an opportunity to better align yourself with your vales and course-correct your behavior. Do you have any remaining conditions to give yourself the love and approval you wanted from yourself or others? Which quality did you want to see in yourself then? Was that quality it always in you? Can you bring it out right now?

d. **Resolutions and Corrections.** Is there a correct action (a correction) that feels better just to imagine? Imagine yourself doing that correct action, being that person that it feels right to be, living true to that image of yourself. Can you give that love and approval to yourself now?

❸ **Self-Care.** Use the following breath practice to complete your experience. It will raise your energy level, which is needed to counter Shame's debilitating force. This practice brings strength and cleansing.

a. Open your mouth and form a circle that is tight and precise. Place your hands crossed over the Heart Center, right hand over left. Close your eyes and sense the area under your palms. Breathe a steady, powerful breath where the exhale is like the burst of a cannon, flowed by an equally strong inhale through the mouth. Let your mind focus on the tight ring of the lips that shapes the breath. Continue for 5 minutes.

b. Inhale. Relax the mouth while holding the breath as you mentally repeat: "I am beautiful. I am innocent. I am innocent. I am beautiful." Exhale through your nose. Repeat a total of 5 times. Then relax.

c. Slowly return to your everyday awareness. Use Self-Care breath any time you need to get right with yourself.

❹ *What Is Shame's Purpose for You?* Do you feel better after this exercise? Relief is your reward for listening. Immediately make some notes about all that you experienced and learned in the guided meditation, even if you don't fully understand it. What were Shame's most important messages? They may be for you to accept yourself, stand up for yourself, or make some correction, or for you to behave differently next time in order to align with your best self and highest values. Know that you can cooperate with others without compromising yourself.

Now is the time to let the mind help by implementing the heart's wishes. These amazingly accurate answers come from a place of knowing that has much more clarity than the mind's thinking. The mind's proper use is to handle the details and to execute the instructions that come from your Soul. In this way, you will always feel better; life will be enhanced when you follow the advice that comes through you. You can be sure that your patient Soul will continue with the feelings and situations you have been reviewing until you advance and live with the consciousness gained from the lessons of Shame.

Remember and record these insights and answers. Will you commit yourself to them now? It may help to go to someone who supports you for encouragement. Tell that person who you are and ask for support in your excellence.

Free to Be

I grew up with the belief that shame was experienced if I did someone wrong. By this I mean, not doing exactly what others wanted me to do in their way. I saw guilt in much the same, only I thought it was used to manipulate me into doing what they others. I didn't believe I had either of these feelings. But I did. I just didn't recognize them because I thought it was just normal to feel wrong, small, and like a failure. Now I see that I did feel guilty for a marriage that didn't work out. I did feel guilty because my life had been successful, happy, and free, while my twin sister's life had been cut short. I didn't realize how any good thing that happened made me feel bad!

I have discovered that I often do what others want of me, regardless of what I want. Watching myself do this is now frustrating; I see it as being very self-destructive. By letting all of this come to the surface, I have found myself in a very unfamiliar place. I've felt a very deep sadness; I feel that this is my spirit longing to just be me, to lead my life from within, without being pushed aside and neglected. To use my emotions as guides from Soul is very powerful and essential. It is great to be free, to make my choice, and that makes me happy.

→ *Mahan*

Going Deeper: The Four Sources of Self-Esteem

Once you cultivate them, self-acceptance and self-love can feel so good; you will naturally gravitate toward what feels better. It's simply a change in the habit of how you see yourself. Upgrading to a more satisfying self-image will be easier once you understand the four sources of self-esteem. I introduce them here and then offer tools for you to take conscious control of and to benefit from each one.

- **External Validation:** Messages from others and the environment about who you are
- **Historical Validation:** Memories that become the false internal basis of your self-image
- **Internal Validation:** You take control by acting on the qualities you choose
- **Universal Validation:** You relate to Infinity within and act from your timeless virtues

Each source of your self-image presents a challenge and an opportunity. Whatever your current sources of self-esteem may be, you can use them all to serve you. Use the following practical information and exercises to help you recognize each source and to benefit from it. Take time in daily practice to work through each exercise so you can get the full experience; you want to become familiar with every influence upon and aspect of your self-image. As you progress from the illusion that you are lost, defective, alone, or unlovable to the enjoyment of your excellent self, you will experience an increase in self-awareness, self-control, and self-love. Shame is only here to help.

The First Source of Self-Esteem
External Validation: Filtering Public Opinion

In the first stage of life, you absorb self-concept from external sources. The purity and sacredness of every newborn life is clear to all. But then the work of living sets in, and the baby loses touch with that essence. Not yet having the security and self-awareness to establish yourself, you take your first clues about who you are from your caregivers and environments. Your sense of Self is built on external messages that will support or attack you. The earliest, strongest, and most frequent cues establish the picture firmly, and they largely determine the landscape in which you will live. We all depend on external validation as our first foundation, but if we remain dependent on that alone, we become beggars, always blown by the winds of public opinion.

Situation: Judgment day. A judgment, disapproval, or rejection from others triggers your instincts as a social animal to quickly conform or hide. The reaction is to either reject the person and his opinions or accept him and conform to the pressure, thereby rejecting yourself. With no internal guidance to check the message for accuracy, you are forever dependent on others' inconsistent moods and needs. From this perspective, every event contributes to how you see yourself. If left unchallenged by your own will, a false negative impression will be built about you, your worth, and your place in the world. Either the other person's view wins, or you stand up to it, evaluate the information, and adjust yourself on your own terms.

Solution: Let the heart decide. When you get hit, you feel the dip of energy and esteem. But don't let that energy-sucking alien thought stay in you. Here is a quick practice to use when you have taken a blow to your sense of self. It clears away the fog of confused behavior and thoughts, gives the clarity to see yourself (and messages about you) neutrally, provides the strength of will to make adjustments when you are off, and builds the energy to act from your own truth.

Keep Clear

❶ *Begin with Getting Peaceful (page xi). Tune in with the Adi Mantra and continue.*

❷ *Self-Care.* Use Self-Care breath (page 271) right away. As you breathe, listen to your emotional message. You can use this variation of the SOS Method to help.

a. ***First, Feel.*** The mind can spin and run through the story, rationalize, and defend. There are always two—or a thousand—sides to a story. The issue cannot be resolved this way. Instead, accept the full impact of the message and the feelings it brings to hit you. Appreciate that it is an attack, a blow to your sense of self. It's appropriate to feel hurt. Although it's instinctive to run and hide from the message and these feelings, or to attack the messenger and defend yourself, or perhaps even to attack yourself, don't react! Don't think right now, as that will just lead to confusion. Be fully aware as you feel everything and resist nothing.

b. ***Listen Consciously.*** Ask the feelings and feel the answers directly, before thought enters in. Was the message you received about yourself real? Did it happen, or did something trigger a memory and then the message was imagined and projected from your past? Is the message from someone else, or is it truly from your own conscience?

c. ***Find the Solution.*** If your consciousness can now see that there was no basis, you are free to move on, more clear about who you are and more able to stand up to scrutiny. If your consciousness sees some possible improvement, be grateful for the opportunity and proceed to do that work.

d. ***Act on the Information.*** If any part of the message seems to fit, feels right to you, it's not personal. The Universe is just showing you how to be yourself. In your clarity, ask and discover the correction that is needed within you or out there in the world.

At the end of 5 minutes, inhale; as you hold your breath, ask your heart: "What am I?" Just listen. Repeat whatever you feel or hear with each of your following held breaths for a total of 5 breaths. Then sit quietly and let all other true statements about yourself effortlessly come forth from your heart and soul.

❸ *Capture Your Gains.* Your Soul used the event as a self-esteem training exercise. To complete that training, you want to rise even higher. Be sure to finish your process with authentic recognition and acknowledgment for your virtues, both inherent and earned. Write them down! So be it. Be it so. Live it so.

The Lesson

Shame means "to cover up," so *a-shamed* would mean to "un-cover." If you are willing to consciously and compassionately feel ashamed of yourself when your Soul calls for it, you will uncover any neglect or injury to the infinity within. Judgments from outside yourself increase the feeling of separation and emptiness; when you don't know yourself, you believe whatever others say, and you feel an even greater internal divide. Judgments also present an opportunity to strengthen your connection when you find the strength to stand tall and back yourself up; in this way, you can consciously and impartially review your actions and make compassionate corrections. Shame shows you the gap between your highest self and your current beliefs about yourself; it helps you recognize and live to your highest values and standards, even as it shows you the path to acceptance, self-actualization, and fulfillment of your potential and ultimately your destiny.

The Second Source of Self-Esteem
Historical Validation: Releasing False Impressions from the Past

The second source of your self-image is the accumulation of past impressions from outside yourself that are stored in your subconscious. The random experiences you encounter are internalized and crystalized as reality, so that you perpetuate a false, incomplete self-image. You have become the preserver of that external source; you inherited it, and now you own it. As you grow, learn, and advance, your body and mind become stronger, and your abilities improve. In every moment, you are the best, wisest, and most capable you have ever been. However, you carry the memory of every previous, younger, weaker version of yourself, as well as every mistake, ridicule, and rejection. Therefore, your total portfolio of self-images is negatively skewed by the many earlier self-images you carry, despite your growth and improved abilities. Progress depends on being able to free yourself from the influence of these outdated memories and to consciously update them for a more accurate picture of who you are now.

The Situation. A negative experience from the past has come to define you. In your efforts to survive and "make it" in the world, you are constantly seeking to define who you are, where you fit, and what to expect. The younger you are or the more dependent you are on those around you, the more deeply your environments influence your sense of self. You believe what you are told. If you are given positive role models, lots of love and acceptance, and the encouragement to be you, your personality naturally flourishes and matures into its unique excellence. More typically, however, the needs, pressures, and dysfunctions of your caregivers dominate. Your personal development is diverted to serve them; you become what they need you to be. That may be their perfect, sweet, smart, beautiful, talented, hardworking, high-achieving prize—if that's what makes them feel better. Or they may feel better about themselves when you are suffering and subjugated, filling you with negative self-images.

It is not difficult to stand against all that to discover your own way and assert yourself; instead, your own internal voice has perpetuated these messages, which come to define you. By the time you are finding your place at school among peers, these early memories have shaped your strategies for getting along. Your internal dialogue mirrors the earlier lack of support: "I don't know. I can't do it. I'm not good enough. I blew it. I'm no good at anything. No one wants me. I am so stupid, lazy, fat, ugly, poor, unpopular." These imprinted messages continue to define you against any proof to the contrary. All that you learn and achieve with time and experience doesn't de-throne those established beliefs. Your abilities are, to some extent, stunted, as if that earlier, weaker, less capable version of yourself is actually running the show now. Those diminished results continue to confirm your inadequacies.

The Solution. Rather than coming to rely on your inherent qualities and qualifications, you have adopted survival strategies and coping mechanisms in order to survive with this defective self. You charm others, please them, act cute or sexy, work hard, hide, bully them, or rebel and dominate. Rarely do you excel just for the joy of experiencing your full self. But it is there—your distinct uniqueness is always there to be realized and used at any time.

First, you need to distinguish "me" from "them" and your actual self from all the past impressions. Cutting away the web of misdirection that has pulled you off your path will clear the way for you to emerge. Only then will you be free to regain control of self-image and replace false self-concepts with your reality. With that, you will become the only true hero who can save you and take care of you—You!

Cut Negative Past Impressions

Shame—any instance of feeling less than good and strong—is a call for cleansing. When you feel crappy, you need to eliminate not yourself but some belief about yourself that diminishes you. Every time you feel diminished and unacceptable, it is an opportunity to do the self-defining work that wasn't possible when your sovereignty was attacked in the past. Any wound to your self-esteem that was left by selling yourself out can be healed now by using what you didn't know then. Your consciousness has been patiently waiting as you have learned to walk in your grace. It can be helpful to recall the incident, but more important is to identify the belief and the feeling that took hold at that time. Then let go of those beliefs and replace them with more accurate, empowering images of your current self.

❶ Begin with Getting Peaceful (page xi). Tune in with the Adi Mantra and continue.

❷ Emotional Resilience: Cutting the Negative Thoughts.

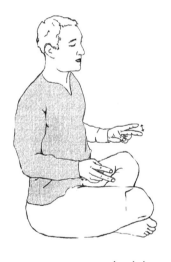

a. Press your elbows into your ribs as you extend your forearms pointing in front of you, parallel to the ground. Tightly hold the ring and little fingers of both hands with your thumbs. Spread the straightened index and middle fingers into a "V." Your palms should be facing each other, with the fingers pointing straight ahead.

- Fully open and close your fingers, like scissors. Do this quickly for 3 minutes. After 3 minutes, begin continuously pulling your most negative thoughts from your subconscious. You are cutting your bad luck, your bad thoughts, your misfortune, your everything. Even in spite of that, you will feel miserable. The faster and fuller you do it, the better the result will be. Keep scissoring your hands and cutting up those negative thoughts for 11 minutes.

- Continue moving the fingers and begin Cannon Breath through the mouth without roun ding the lips. Do this for 90 seconds.

- Keep moving the fingers, but now begin to create a "Pa pa" sound with your breath. Don't speak; just form the natural sound from the

278

movement of your lips. Continue to bring up negative thoughts and cut them as you do this for 90 seconds.

- Keep moving the fingers, but now imagine that you're abusing someone with your mouth and lips. Silently speak; become obnoxious and then abusive in your thoughts. Pull the negative, obnoxious, abusive thoughts up to the surface and release them for 90 seconds.

- As you cut, call on thoughts and feelings of shame; call on every memory, thought, and feeling and all your reactions to them. Just dig it out and let it fly. The pain in your fingers may help you access some anger about it all. Use that anger to cut and eliminate all your memories of anything that you feel bad about, any one or any thing that hurt you, your own smallness. Cut out all that's not serving you, all that is not your highest self. When the intensity diminishes—or in the final few minutes if it doesn't diminish—fill the space you created with all that you recognize as good, strong, and pure.

- To finish, inhale and exhale to relax.

b. Remaining seated, clasp your hands behind your neck. Move your elbows in and out as you dance from the waist upward. Be forceful, angry, and wild while your lower body remains a solid base. Use some drum music. Continue this movement for 6 minutes.

Really shake, release, celebrate, and exalt yourself.

c. Inhale and immediately bring your arms straight overhead. Spread your fingers wide; don't let your hands or fingers touch each other. Hold this position as you do Cannon Breath for 60 to 90 seconds. Inhale deeply and stretch up more. Exhale. Inhale. Stretch up even higher and hold for 20 seconds. Inhale. Stretch and do Cannon Breath quickly for 15 seconds. Exhale. Inhale. Hold the breath in for 20 seconds as you stretch and pull up every bit of you. Exhale and relax.

You can now feel your great intrinsic worth. There's no work to it; it just rises up for you to see and enjoy. Reside delightfully in it; sit and enjoy who you really are, without any thought at all. The message of Shame from your Soul has done its job and will now retreat until needed again to further polish and clarify your essential diamond nature.

❸ *Reflection.* Can you see connections from the past to your present attitudes, abilities, habits, and achievements? Has the past enhanced or limited your fulfillment? How could you rearrange your life to drop the old and match the new you? Which early messages and concepts are you carrying that have sabotaged your happiness? Can you take back control of your life and eliminate them in order to feel good about yourself again—or maybe even for the first time? What is separating you from others, from love, from feeling good about self and life, from your excellence and peacefulness? Get back onto your own side, stay loyal to yourself, stand strong and defend your home, repair the damage. Separate the external values of others; feel your own internal values and come into alignment with them. Write what you learned about yourself in that experience.

Elaine Cuts Free

Feeling like I'm a bad person has been with me all my life. I work hard, but no matter how well I do, it's not good enough. The first thing I learned by paying attention is that when I feel this way so strongly, I need to release it in some form—whether it be crying, screaming, or just going for a long walk to move my muscles and breathe fresh air into my lungs. I feel lighter after taking action, instead of suppressing and ignoring the message like I used to do.

The concept of bringing up the feeling of shame and using the SOS method of inquiry helped me realize how much Shame I had stored in me. This exercise brought up a lot of memories and experiences from the past and showed me how shame has affected many aspects of my life.

The meditation was tough. While I was cutting the negative thoughts, it brought up so many negative thoughts from my childhood to the present. I was surprised at how much I was holding onto. Just this awareness made me want to consciously cut through those thoughts and emotions. It was hard to process so much, and I felt really uneasy after doing it. Toward the end of the meditation, while practicing the Cannon breath, I felt some kind of release that helped me feel a bit lighter from the weight of those thoughts. I felt a slight release from the tightness I had been holding on to. I now feel lighter, like I have shed a layer of something from my body.

I realized that my feelings of shame had accumulated from past experiences and do not serve me anymore. Living with Shame seems to have become such a habitual way of feeling, thinking, and doing. But now I am consciously choosing that I don't need to continue this feeling from the past. I choose to shift Shame into acceptance of the past and of the way things are and how I can make the best of it all today.

Moving on from the Past

Any part of your self-image that is based on earlier downgrading impressions is inaccurate and debilitating. Whatever old self-concepts you are carrying can be dropped. You were not in control at the time they occurred. When you allow traumatic memories to rule you, you do not have the freedom to be yourself. Healthy personal development requires moving from external direction to internal control of how you know and see yourself and what you choose to do with it all. That is the next step in strength and stability. Be a new

Healthy personal development requires moving from external direction to internal control of how you know and see yourself and what you choose to do with it all.

and improved you as often as you like. You don't have to try to be good or great or anything else. Just drop the story that something is wrong with you. See yourself as whole and perfect, exactly as you are. Shame is meant to help you find yourself, and those memories will remain until you do. Enjoy the lessons learned. Clear the fogginess that keeps you from seeing your magnificence as a unique, human being, blessed to be who you are, as you are, where you are. Even if you are not yet sure who you are, break free and start taking that risky, worthwhile adventure to discover it. Don't have your unique voice silenced by influences from the past you couldn't control; instead, take over your own makeover.

> Even if you don't know what you want, buy something, to be part of the exchanging flow.
> Start a huge, foolish project, like Noah.
> It makes absolutely no difference what people think of you.
>
> ⇢ Rumi

The Third Source of Self-Esteem
Internal Validation: Self-Determining Your Self-Esteem

Self-image is built on information that is internal and sustainable, free from past impressions. Internal validation creates its own sense of Self by knowing the full range of qualities, interests, and skills within you and choosing those that best serve you. This capability is in each of us, though it is more active for some people than others, depending on how well it has been encouraged and reinforced. Self-validation reflects stronger will, the emergence of personal empowerment and self-determination. Just as in every inspiring story about "overcoming the odds," you too can find the ability to make your way, write your own ticket, and prevail over circumstances. Many of us struggle for years amid conflicting messages. But when we rise toward accomplishment and leadership, we gain significant control of our internal narrative about who we are and who we want to be. However, this ability to self-validate can run wild into fantasy, distorted self-importance (falsely inflated ego), misuse of privilege, abuse of power, arrogance, and cruelty, which unfortunately are more common than not in the stories of a rise to power.

The Situation: Ready to define yourself. When you are free from the past, you are empowered to use outside influences not to *define*, but to *find* yourself. This balance requires strength of will, which gives you the power to choose what works for you. By putting that balance of power in your own hands, you can put judgments, present and past, in perspective. You can validate yourself—isn't that handy?! Self-determination can start with the encouragement of a parent or teacher, or

> **You are empowered to use outside influences not to *define*, but to *find* yourself.**

it may come through defiance against someone or something that has harmed you. Initially your goals may have formed in reaction to others, but then you begin to take charge to create your value. Only then can you begin to truly know yourself and be in a position to follow your heart and experience real fulfillment.

The Goal and the Solution. The goal is to establish a strong, sustainable identity that comes from you. You can find your value by knowing your values. Create a space for yourself that is free of outside pressure and internal turmoil. Once relaxed, simply pay attention to yourself in a strong, caring way. The pure qualities that make you *you* have been there from the beginning; it feels so right and good to recognize and live in them that they rise to the surface. That's all it takes—the ability to pay attention and feel yourself directly. The process is often initiated by "trying on" the qualities you aspire to or that you admire in others. Heroes, leaders, and role models give you clues about the qualities within that you are trying recognize and express.

A Self-Directed Self-Image

❶ *Begin with Getting Peaceful (page xi). Tune in with the Adi Mantra and continue.*

❷ *Overcoming Your Shortcomings.*

a. Stretch your left arm straight out to the side at shoulder level with the palm facing down. Extend the right arm out to the side with the elbow bent, palm slightly cupped and facing forward. Sweep your right arm inward pivoting from the elbow, leaving the upper arm straight out and parallel to the floor as you make a circular inward motion as if the right hand were scooping up water and bringing it toward your face. The right wrist is relaxed and active. Purse your lips into an "O." As your right hand moves toward your face, inhale through the mouth, completing the inhalation when the hand reaches the level of the mouth. As the hand moves away from your mouth back to the starting position, exhale powerfully through your nose. Consciously create a very full breath to open up your chest cavity. Continuously and smoothly breathe with the movement. One complete circular movement (inhale and exhale) should take about 2 seconds. Bring the power you need into yourself. Give yourself power. Continue for 19 minutes.

- Your left arm out with palm down embodies all the external messages you receive from the world. You will feel that pain and the challenge of holding yourself up against beliefs that pull you down. Remember all the takedowns, rejections, detractors, and tormentors. Surrender and accept that it happens, that you do have imperfections; but hold strong.

- The right arm represents your ability to act and project, to feed and uplift yourself. Focus on great qualities. Who have you admired? What was it about them that you admired? Would you like to have that quality? Can you find it in yourself? What do you value in yourself? Remember a time when you achieved, took control, made it happen; when you did something that made you feel good; when you got positive external feedback and you approved of it. Go deeper into what it was about it that you value. Is this what you value? Own it.

- Bring forth all positive qualities and strengths; feel them abundantly within you. Expand into it. Radiate excellence. See others acknowledging who you really are. It takes will and determination to be self-determined. This ability to feed and nurture yourself makes you self-reliant and able to rise above the dark side.

- Hold the two polarities in balance. Use the confrontation on the left to bring forth your power from within to win, and use that incoming power on the right to help you manage the left. There is no need to push, resist, or hide. Feel full, just the way you are, the way you are meant to be. Commit to knowing and living this. Love and enjoy this self that you get to live with. This is the real you that can sustain you and take care of everything.

b. Place your open palms, one hand on top of the other, at the Heart Center (the center of your chest). Breathe long, slow, and deep through your nose. Relax, calm down, and go into deep meditation for 2½ minutes. Sit in self-awareness of your highest possible viewpoint. Be with Soul. Feel your strength and clarity.

c. To end, inhale deeply, expanding your chest. Hold the breath for 10–15 seconds as you stretch the spine upward and press your hands against the Heart Center as hard as you can. Direct the energy all the way up the spine. Exhale through the mouth like Cannon Fire. Repeat this breath sequence 2 more times.

❸ **Capture Your Gains.** Record your experience. How do you feel? What do you know now to be true about you? Will you vow to live in your excellence? Write the qualities you affirm and use them to create your new life—the good life.

Take care of yourself. Everything is for you. You are an absolutely complete unit.
→ **Yogi Bhajan, October 27, 1992**

The Fourth Source of Self-Esteem
Universal Validation: Infinity Within

Healthy personal development and spiritual growth require exertion of your will to rise above previous degradations. Recognizing, releasing, and replacing demoting conceptions and actions can be a long but rewarding and healing process. To move beyond being outwardly directed to internally motivated and self-defined is an essential step toward a fulfilled life. Once you know how to be what you want to be, you will begin to extend your power and test your limits. Self-determination brings new challenges; let's face it—there are defects and limitations to every personality. Expansion will increase your best and worst qualities. External input serves as a reality check for the ego. However, the opinions of others have already proven unreliable or disastrous; so where do you go for a touchstone that is more trustworthy than the agendas of others or your own fluctuating mind?

The sovereignty of self-determined self-esteem is a pinnacle of personal development that too few of us enjoy. May we all get there! But once the ego has helped us get there, the ego can become a limitation. This pinnacle is like a glass ceiling to the vast resources beyond the individual self, and it is certainly a barrier that is invisible to us much of the time. But there is a step beyond.

After gaining control of your identity, the next step is to tap into the vast ocean of all virtues; to access the "Internet cloud" of virtues, not just those from your own local files. The entry key is a neutral and elevated perspective from which you can see beyond yourself. When memories, mind, and ego soften their firm grip, the greatest "self" you can assert by personal effort pales and disappears. This may be for just a moment at first, but it still reveals all that is possible to be and experience. From that clarity, you can embrace and unify the highest angelic virtues and lowest animal characteristics within yourself, resulting in a truly complete human being. This is where your personal goals for yourself, your destination, and your destiny become the same.

Accepting human frailty and failings gives you the capacity to choose your excellence, courage, nobility, and grace. These timeless qualities, these more noble virtues, are an expression of your angelic nature.

Sensitivity, openness, and surrender replace your former methods of achieving what you want. Accepting human frailty and failings gives you the capacity to choose your excellence, courage, nobility, and grace. These timeless qualities, these more noble virtues, are an expression of your angelic nature; they arise effortlessly, without your ego having to prove or possess them. Your consciousness moves beyond judgment, comparison, lower, and higher and simply sees all, embraces all, is one with all. You transcend both thoughts—"I am unworthy" and "I am great"—to attain "I am that I am." Your all-encompassing essential nature serves as the basis for self-image, self-worth, and self-esteem. Your individual value is equal to all values. This highest basis for Self-Esteem—known as Universal Validation—is a recognition of the highest transcendent qualities that exist in all creation. Feel them within and without.

The Goal: Let Divinity Be the Source of Your Identity

Your sense of self is created by the Universal and Timeless qualities within you, within all of us.

Shame is all about rejection; its lesson, its cure, is acceptance. The natural urge is to turn away in disgust from all that is awful and ugly; to hide, cover, and deny the dark side of life. But there is no escaping it, for we live in a world of polarity: There can be no beauty without the ugly, and both are in every person and every atom. You cannot throw away one side of a coin; the two sides stay or go together. Any imperfection that cannot be faced means that its opposite perfection cannot be embraced. Compassionate understanding and acceptance of every fault and frailty are required to fully accept your greatness.

Where Shame is found, the shortcut to finding your inner hero may be to come to terms with all that you despise about yourself. Some call this Shadow Work, which is appropriate—you can't lose your shadow, so you might as well not be afraid of it. A shadow simply means there is also light somewhere, and that light allows you to see it. This Shadow Work is simply a prelude to Shame's ultimate gift: Self-Love. Here is a powerful practice to welcome both the high and low in you.

Embracing the Finite and Infinite Self

❶ *Begin with Getting Peaceful (page xi). Tune in with the Adi Mantra and continue.*

❷ *Accept and Exalt Yourself.* Use slow and uplifting music with the following movements:

a. Bring your arms up as if you were holding a baby, holding opposite forearms near the elbows with your hands. Inhale through the nose in 8 equal "sniffs," while gently swinging the arms from side to side in rhythm with the breath and to the beat of the music (as if rocking a baby).

I suggest a slow movement of 2 seconds per swing and sniff. Cradle and nurture that memory of you and that part of you that was confronted. Be real with what you feel. It's okay to feel weak, sad, lost, vulnerable, alone, miserable.

b. Exhale through the nose in one long, continuous breath as you lower your arms to Gyan Mudra on your knees.

As you exhale, call on any bit of strength and confidence you find within. Call on and expand the qualities you needed then and enjoy now. Call on any source of inspiration and embody it as your own.

c. Continue inhaling and exhaling in this way to the music at your own pace for 11–31 minutes.

As you continue alternating these two experiences with the breath and posture, hold and heal yourself and your forgotten qualities; give love and understanding. Can you find kindness for every ugliness as you accept and feel peace with it all? Slowly expand your dignity and feel the perfection of every imperfection. Exalt yourself and see that your dark and weak sides are all part of your divinity.

❸ *Follow-Up.* Can you surrender to and accept all the worst and best in you? Can you feel equal affection for all aspects of you? The more accepting of your shortcomings you are, the more tolerant you will be with others. The more accepting of your gifts, the more you will see and enjoy the gifts of others. You didn't make any of this life up yourself; you were made. All you have to do is use it, watch with fascination, and enjoy it all. This means the end of striving, the beginning of the end of stress. It's a foreign paradigm, that's certain, but it can be learned. "I am, I am" is easy; just be. Your identity becomes infinite.

What Your Soul Desires

Here is a well-known poem, the title to which could be translated, "The Desire." It speaks of what the Soul wishes for you to experience. Enjoy it now with all you know about Shame and Self.

La Desiderata

> Go placidly amid the noise and the haste,
> and remember what peace there may be in silence.
> As far as possible, without surrender,
> be on good terms with all persons.
> Speak your truth quietly and clearly;
> and listen to others,
> even to the dull and the ignorant;
> they too have their story.
>
> Avoid loud and aggressive persons;
> they are vexatious to the spirit.
> If you compare yourself with others,
> you may become vain or bitter,
> for always there will be greater and lesser persons than yourself.
>
> Enjoy your achievements as well as your plans.
> Keep interested in your own career, however humble;
> it is a real possession in the changing fortunes of time.
> Exercise caution in your business affairs,
> for the world is full of trickery.
> But let this not blind you to what virtue there is;

many persons strive for high ideals,
and everywhere life is full of heroism.

Be yourself. Especially do not feign affection.
Neither be cynical about love,
for in the face of all aridity and disenchantment,
it is as perennial as the grass.

Take kindly the counsel of the years,
gracefully surrendering the things of youth.
Nurture strength of spirit to shield you in sudden misfortune.
But do not distress yourself with dark imaginings.
Many fears are born of fatigue and loneliness.

Beyond a wholesome discipline,
be gentle with yourself.
You are a child of the universe
no less than the trees and the stars;
you have a right to be here.
And whether or not it is clear to you,
no doubt the universe is unfolding as it should.

Therefore be at peace with God,
whatever you conceive Him to be.
And whatever your labors and aspirations,
in the noisy confusion of life,
keep peace in your soul.
With all its sham, drudgery, and broken dreams,
it is still a beautiful world.
Be cheerful. Strive to be happy.

→ **Max Ehrmann, 1927**

> The fact is there is nothing more beautiful, more worthy, or more conscious than you. The time has come of self-value. And the question is not "To be or not to be;" the statement is "To be, to be." "I am, I Am." The time has come not to search for God, but to be God.
>
> → **Yogi Bhajan, August 2000**

The Gift of Shame: Self-Love

In your vital search for Self and Worth, you will use all four sources of self-esteem: External, Historic, Internal, and Universal. The proper proportions for a healthy and sustainable Self is quite the reverse of what is most commonly found. Your primary source of self-knowledge must be the most expansive and most complete: Universal. Next, use your ego sense to internalize and materialize these attributes. Only when Love, Truth, and Peace are embodied in you, valued by you, defended and promoted by you can they become manifest here on Earth to be enjoyed by everyone. You are the translator, making virtues understood through action. With all of this as your base, External Validation, when used as a garnish, gives you a reality check when you lose touch with Soul. In time, your memories come to serve and confirm all of this, locking it in positively.

Where are you on that epic passage from worthless to priceless?

Where are you on that epic passage from worthless to priceless? Whenever you are out of integrity; whenever your thoughts, feelings, and behavior don't properly represent and elevate you; whenever your inherent purity is not recognized, respected, and acted upon; whenever you need to improve your ability to love and honor who you are—at all of these times, Shame will be there to poke and provoke you back to your true home in the Self. Stand strong and tall in purity and worthiness.

It might go like this: The conflicts of competing expectations and the inner you-on-you war become exhausting and lonely. You can't win by contorting and conforming, so you give up. When you surrender to what is and accept who you already are, you experience a tremendous relief. Acceptance, being willing to see, and being okay with reality allow connection, which leads to compassion. Compassion, or to have passion felt between you and you, is self-love. With that self-love, you can face any corruption; you can leave the Garden of Eden with your innocence intact. You realize that there is darkness but without forgetting you can choose the light.

Don't be surprised if Self-Love is not available immediately or abundantly at first. When your self-criticism and overt harshness soften with a bit of acceptance, you can open the heart a bit further with compassion. For me, the job was too big to take on all at once. I had to start with a smaller step, and that was simply being kind. Just diminishing the suffering-causing habits and offering myself other acts of kindness "as if" I were worthy helped me feel more deserving. I tried to be a better friend to myself, to speak more supportively, and then to actively appreciate that nurturing. I can tell you firsthand that when you don't feel worthy of love and can't offer and accept your own love, you will not feel much of it from anyone else. They may be right there loving you, but you will be blind to it; you may even leave them, believing they didn't love you. Every relationship is a reflection of that all-important relationship with yourself. So if you are in the Lonely Hearts Club, it's not about who you are or about who wants you or doesn't; it's all about you. So, start with you. If you are one of the many who gives and gives to others, wondering why you never get enough in return, just remember that you can't buy love! It's abundant and free; you have but to dip into it, give it, and receive it—but *to yourself first*! Here is Yogi Bhajan making a rather strong point of it in *On Compassion for Self*:

The highest status which a man can enjoy in a human life is self-compassion. I am not asking you to be compassionate to others. I am asking you folks to be compassionate to yourself. This is the last thing a person has ever learned. The key to happiness, gate to happiness, is self-compassion.

If you have this misunderstanding that you should be compassionate to others, you are fooling yourself. Compassion does not mean anything to others. That is your trauma and your act. And it is meant for you. Be extremely compassionate to yourself and do not indulge in any unnecessary nuisance and tax your nerves, your mind, and your life.

There is no school, class, or college for it. Nobody talks about it. People all say: Have compassion. What are you trying to do? It is the most stupid thing to do. If you ever want to be compassionate, be compassionate to yourself. Others can handle their life. It is your life which you are supposed to handle, and that is called divinity of god. Every religion teaches it. And they openly teach it. Be compassionate to others—a deadly mistake. Definitely be serviceful to others, be kind to others, but always be compassionate to yourself. Be good to others, be helpful to others, and be friendly to others. All such adjectives are right; but never be compassionate to anybody. When you are not compassionate to yourself, you are totally a hypocrite. That means when you are not real. And you are pretending to be real when you are not real. It will happen only when you are not compassionate to yourself.

The Fourth Center guarantees that you will be either compassionate to yourself or passionate to yourself. It does not allow this for anybody else. Passion and compassion are two sides of the same coin. They are there for the Self. I am passionately in love of myself. If I am not passionately in love of myself, I cannot or shall not truly love anybody else. I will be a hypocrite. If I am not compassionate to myself, I will understand nothing. Period. Your friendship won't last, your relationship won't last, your marriage, this and that won't last. Because if you do not have a true passion for life and real compassion for the self, you do not know what life is.

Self-Study

Shame and poor self-image can cripple a life and are traditionally slow to heal. Honesty to your feelings, leading to conscious self-inquiry, will accelerate your elevation. Use the powerful practices in this chapter regularly, one at a time, for 40 days each in succession or in your own intuitive combination. Don't overdo it; just keep at it. Approach it not like a bulldozer but more like the slow, sure polishing of your gem quality.

Life Project

Reduce the influences and environments that don't support you. Spend more time with people and ideas that inspire your best. Remove the reminders of what you used to be, the naysayers that only point out your faults. Find uplifting environments that reinforce your best qualities and that expect and demand your excellence. Make commitments that require that excellence. Be a teacher and role model for others. The upward curve is continuous and life-long.

Chapter Eleven

Healing Your Wounds
Emotion's Essential Role in Clearing Trauma

If you jumped to this chapter first, looking for some relief, you are not alone. I hope you will find Hope—and valuable help—for your own journey of recovery.

You were born with all the equipment you need to heal, to become strong and whole. It takes work—from minutes to many years, depending on the damage—but each little bit of relief, every moment that you feel a little better and brighter, is incentive to keep going for more. My thanks to all who have shared their pain with the intention to heal it; who suffered and nearly died, but lived to rebound; who lived to tell their tale of survival and thereby help others do the same.

If you have been working your way through the book experimentally, I trust you have experienced for yourself that heavy emotions are not a problem. Instead, they bring helpful information and solutions. Every painful feeling brings welcome gifts: Fear leads to Coziness, Grief to Love, Shame to Self-Esteem, Anger to Empowerment. We have found how each emotion works with memories so that we can learn from the past what will assist us today. This is one of the most valuable ways that emotions have evolved to help and heal: traumas and their resulting patterns are our greatest teachers. That is the focus of this chapter.

Wounds and Scars

Every experience that touches your life leaves an impression. In an effort to keep "bad" events from recurring, the subconscious mind holds these memories to create automatic survival-based behavior. The subconscious is powerful in its influence, but it is not smart. Without coordination with the more advanced discriminating capacities of your mind, these learned reactions can do as much damage as good. An example is avoiding *all* intimate relationships due to childhood abuse. The degree to which a harmful event changes you increases with the intensity, the degree of harm done, the unexpectedness (such as sudden fright or betrayal), the intensity of emotion present during the event, the frequency and duration of events over time, and especially your ability to understand what is happening. This is called trauma.

Trauma:

- A body wound or shock produced by sudden physical injury, as from unexpected violence or accident, or the condition produced by this

- An experience that produces psychological injury or pain, or the psychological injury so caused

---

This definition, which includes the event and the lasting effect, recognizes that trauma occurs on the physical, mental, and emotional levels. These events leave a mark on all parts of our sensory system. When functioning properly, our system has the means to not only recover but also use the wound to reach a stronger condition. A cut to the body can repair itself with no trace. A deeper wound may leave a scar that is tougher than the original tissue. If improperly cared for, infection or reinjury may delay or prevent healing and may lead to death. But not creating the conditions for natural healing to occur does not mean the system cannot heal itself, as might have been believed before infection was understood.

Just like a physical scar, healed wounds make us stronger or wiser in some way than we were before the event.

The same is true regarding mental and emotional wounds. These aspects of our being also have built-in self-healing functions. We are now learning to work with them to create conditions for recovery from all traumas. Just like a physical scar, healed wounds make us stronger or wiser in some way than we were before the event.

Unripe Protective Equipment

The younger we were and the more intense the trauma, the greater the impact. Ideally, we would like to have challenges come to us as we are equipped to handle them. We hope to be protected by our parents and environments until we have the full-grown ability to run, speak, and protect ourselves. When immature, our body, mind, and emotions, and therefore our ability to get what we need to defend ourselves, are not ready for intense trauma. Early in life we are much more fragile, sensitive, and dependent; thus, some level of trauma is certain, and the impact can be significant. As life assails us, emotions rush forth, both as sensors of something gone very wrong and as providers of information about what is needed to protect us. Emotions like Anger and Fear are there to help; however, our mind is not yet trained to interpret and use the information to assist us. Of course, this can be true at any age. To make matters even more challenging, in our youth, there is often no one to teach and support us in sorting out the complex tangle of emotions. With proper guidance, however, our feeling equipment is there and can serve us, even at a very young age.

The next best option to knowing how to protect ourselves is to get protection from harm with the help of our elders. The worst and most common situations occur when those elders, our guides and protectors, are the very source of trauma. As Epictetus said, "On the occasion of every accident that befalls you, remember to turn to yourself and inquire what power you have for turning it to use." This is good advice. Even if the accident happened long ago, it's never too late to learn.

Pain Is the Remedy

Recurring post-traumatic memories and behavioral patterns are an ingenious healing system, as effective as a healthy immune system. When emotion is called forth to serve but its purpose of improving well-being is not achieved, the loyal emotion persists and grows stronger, as long as is needed to accomplish its Soul-appointed task. An emotion's insistence makes it even harder for us to channel consciously; the emotion speaks directly, acts out, fails again. When we belatedly begin to listen, a flood of emotions pours forth. Conscious techniques to relieve the backlog help us return to manageable, useful levels of emotional intensity. This process will take us ever deeper, revealing whatever remains to be addressed and purified. All wounds call upon emotion to move us steadfastly toward healing.

> **All wounds call upon emotion to move us steadfastly toward healing.**

Emotional Healing

Our fear response to danger has been in place from the earliest age, but it was not able to protect and prevent early trauma; we were just too small to stop all harm. This inability to protect ourselves at an early age can establish a pattern that leaves us, as adults, feeling danger but not acting to remove it. Under duress, the unprepared child in each of us "takes over," just when we need our most advanced adult capabilities to take care of things—a subconscious reaction when a conscious action is needed.

Damaged Healing System

When our body-mind-emotion equipment is not able to handle the impact of an event, whether due to youth or lack of awareness, some type of dysfunction is created and remains until healed. Impairment of our emotional equipment comes in different forms: perhaps as a disconnection from emotions via numbing and distraction, or maybe as a highly emotionalized state in which much is felt with no progress or benefit. Either way, we are less able to deal with current events; there is turmoil and confusion, with churning emotion trying to bring healing to no avail.

Fear and Anger Play Key Roles

Fear and Anger are natural "senses" designed to warn and protect us. But a young victim is not able to use Fear and Anger to obtain safety and other needs. (As adults, we may be equally unprepared and unable to do so.) As we mature, our latent Fear and Anger, which were unable to protect us earlier, are continually trying to right the wrong. Without conscious processing on our part, these two emotions surface in unproductive ways in response to what appears to be normal situations. When Fear and Anger appear to the traumatized adult, they have a dual purpose: to handle the immediate harm and to heal the past wounds.

Trauma and Emotions' Role in Healing

All emotions serve to guide and heal. As our warning and protecting energies, Fear and Anger play vital roles in handling current events, protecting us from future harm, and dealing with and healing from trauma. We have all suffered trauma at varying degrees, even if not at the hands of a wrongdoer; there are also accidents and even some welcomed events, like birth or a first date, that are traumatic by nature. Those experiences affect our well-being in ways known and yet invisible to us. We are diminished; something is lost and damaged. Emotions help remove the damaging effects and return us to a whole state, with added strength and wisdom.

In this book, we have taken the broadest perspective we can imagine to create a useful context in which to learn—that is, the viewpoint of the Soul. I defined *soul* simply as a feeling of profound peace, clarity, and completeness. The Senses of the Soul guide you to that experience. From that vast and timeless perspective of Soul, no temporary pain on Earth is too great a price for the wisdom and majesty, the undisturbable serenity, that is the endgame of your education. It is said that each soul chooses its natal circumstances, whatever will serve that soul's awakening. You may think, "Why would I choose alcoholic abuse, abandonment, illness, and ignorance?" But people *choose* the rigors of medical school, a hard yoga class, a brutal Olympic trainer; they pay lots of money for the "abuse" that will help them reach a goal, achievement, or victory. The same is true of your life. Soul chooses challenges in order for you to grow and expand, to become stronger and more conscious. For the possibility to know fearlessness, you may go through decades of danger and living with anxiety. Every challenge has in it something you must develop, know, or grow in order to solve, just like any good puzzle or videogame. This is not a belief you need to adopt, but it is a viewpoint that offers an empowering way to approach any difficult history and circumstance. It's a view of self-responsibility and possibility. All emotions serve this process and play an essential role. Healing the wounds of the heart, of emotional and psychological trauma, or of post-traumatic stress cannot be done without emotion. Emotions are an essential missing link that makes possible more rapid and complete healing and that takes you beyond recovery to advanced levels of consciousness.

> From the vast and timeless perspective of Soul, no temporary pain on Earth is too great a price for the wisdom and majesty, the undisturbable serenity, that is the endgame of your education.

Soul knows no limit of time and space. Whenever you were traumatized, there was some awareness, skill, knowledge, or consciousness unavailable. If you had acquired that skill or knowledge, you would have been able to prevent or resolve the incident. At the time, however, you didn't yet have or know that which the Soul wants you to know; so instead, you suffer. Soul is on a mission; so the traumatic mark remains as a placeholder or reminder. It is a serious pebble in your shoe. You get used to it and forget it for a while. But until the pebble is removed, until the consciousness is gained—no matter how long it takes—any time that same emotion from that original trauma is felt for any reason, the opportunity to learn that lesson and thus heal the trauma is awakened. Wounds remain open, like unsolved cases, like sore spots. When they are touched by that same emotion, it's like a portal through time and space, reaching back through many events to the first (and beyond that into past lived lives, if you please) and reaching forward to your completed lesson's wisdom.

Healing is always available to you. This is the nature of the Soul and the greatest gift that emotions bring you. Largely fumbled through and sometimes stumbled upon, this information holds a promise of an innate system for the mental-emotional healing we so badly need. Before our understanding of germs, many people suffered and died. They may have cursed God and died wondering why the body lacked the ability to heal itself. But the body doesn't lack anything; it has a brilliant immune system, always within us. But until we know how to work with that system—by keeping a wound clean and protected—it cannot work and bring us back to health.

Likewise, our emotional healing system needs a bit of cooperation—and that is simply the awareness and willingness to feel and listen and respond. The answers are all within for you to find. I hope the many approaches in this book will help you find them. Once your emotions are not so intimidating, once you know your way around them, you can handle them. They won't confuse you. Their sophistication won't seem so complex. All emotions will work together fluidly to show you how to take care of yourself and others, in this life and beyond it.

Separation from Soul: The Mother of All Traumas

What if the Soul were to call forth Trauma to bring life experiences and challenges, whether mild or devastating, in order to lead you to an unfailing connection to Soul? This creates the stuff of saints: unassailable honor, dignity, peace, kindness, fearlessness, deathlessness. It is not, however, saintly to carry around the suffering and pain from trauma. You will find that all wounds, all emotions, all experiences lead back to Soul. You are here healing from the trauma of being human—namely, the feeling and belief that you are separate or have no access to your Source.

All wounds, all emotions, all experiences lead back to Soul. You are here healing from the trauma of being human—namely, the feeling and belief that you are separate or have no access to your Source.

Healing from trauma occurs by doing just what you have already been practicing. By following the steps to allow, listen, and act, you can deal with a smaller immediate event quickly, with no "residue." Afterward, you will be wiser and better off than before. With open awareness, you will find an issue or ongoing event that has been bothering you, and you can use the same steps to resolve that ongoing situation. You may also be led back to an older, stronger trauma-causing event. The same process, with the assistance of all that you learn along the way from the milder and recent events, will eventually bring you to a peace, a wholeness that is stronger and wiser than before this long cycle began. The same process of healing will also lead to "existential healing"—or the healing of the Trauma of Incarnation.

The Soul's Role for Trauma

Have you ever experienced the vast, pure, sacredness of your essential self? We call it the Soul, but it's actually a simple, natural experience that's easy to access with guidance and practice. Take a moment to become peaceful and feel it right now.

Contrast the experience of Soul with all the hurt, abuse, and pain that life can bring. Imagine the trauma of when a beloved person or place of pristine purity is violently despoiled. It happens every day on Earth! When you remember how very sensitive and sacred we are, the harsh and profane experiences to which we are subjected can be seen with compassionate pain. The peace, poise, and dignity of the Soul are *never* shaken. So Trauma does not pierce the Soul. But Trauma does distance your everyday experience from contact, remembrance, and the feelings of the Soul. It fixates you on Self or Ego, making you feel separate and less powerful. This is commonly called *stress*.

Trauma begins with your actual birth onward. The greater the trauma, the more "stranded" you appear to be from the unshakable safety of being connected to Source. The Senses of the Soul patiently serve to bring you forward, through the pain, to reunite you with your healed, whole, honored Self. In the process, you become strong. Unfailing connection to the Soul can weather any storm peacefully. There is a rare but achievable human ability to live beyond fear and anger. The stepwise path to reach this saintly consciousness is to fully use emotions and all your sensory equipment to deal with what is confronting you now. That is the path to attaining your most elevated status.

Let's work with Fear, Desire, and Anger to see how your emotional system can repair the past and restore you to safety today. Remember that when a wound from the past serves to make you safer and wiser today, that means healing has occurred. We could say that the Soul's purpose for that experience has been served, and you can move on to new learning. But you must create a safe environment in which to heal old wounds to release you from limiting behavior and patterns of suffering.

The Trauma-Healing Cycle: An Example

Something came out of nowhere and hurt me when I was young. Fear did not see it coming. Anger was not prepared to run. I was too small to defend myself. So BOOM! I was hit in the body and heart. Emotions swirled in to repair and prevent more harm; Anger and Fear have built up; and I have become constantly vigilant. But I don't know how to use my emotions to save myself; so they just haunt me. I adapt a variety of coping mechanisms—I become numb or busy to distract me from the original and added emotional pain. Compulsive or addictive behaviors, deadening depression, and other endless creative but ineffective substitutes develop. I have life in a pieced-together holding pattern that allows some degree of "carrying on" through life. I'm as "normal" as I can manage; I am even highly functioning; but I am not whole.

Anxiety persists and intensifies, and I don't know why or how to stop it. Anger springs up in surprising ways for "no reason." If I attend to my emotions, as we have now practiced, and deal with whatever is in front of me now, these emotions can lead me to the ability to take care of myself from now on. When I learn how to prevent and handle the situation that hurt me long ago (and I begin to do so in smaller but similar everyday affairs), healing can be completed. I now know what I didn't know before, and I can rest assured about the future, trusting of my ability to be well. The peace and honor of my Soul are returned to my human experience, and this peace cannot be taken away, no matter what happens. I am in control of my destiny.

When I learn that I can trust myself to fully get what I need, the past is healed, because the purpose of emotion is complete. This healing starts with whatever is happening now. Handling today heals yesterday! Remember, when emotions are caught up with all of their current and past healing tasks, they merely stand by to serve you by smoothly keeping watch and then making sure you handle all your affairs. You can get there!

Gather Gifts from the Garbage

❶ *Begin with Getting Peaceful (page xi).* With eyes closed, create a feeling of vastness and safety as you continue with the guided meditation:

a. Choose and recall a traumatic incident from the past. Remember from the perspective of yourself at that age and time. Allow thoughts and feelings to arise.

b. Replay the memory in detail, but this time from the perspective of your current, grown-up, most advanced self. Imagine your current consciousness inside the head of that earlier you, watching it all happen. Again notice and allow the feelings and thoughts that arise.

c. Name every emotion that arises. Each one was there then to inform, solve, and improve the situation. The fact that the memory calls the emotion now means that emotion is still waiting to serve you; it is waiting to heal now what it couldn't prevent then. Start with the emotion that is calling the strongest.

d. From your now-broader adult perspective, feel your information-gathering Fear. How familiar has that feeling been? What calls it forth? Don't judge. Just observe, as a curious scientist would—in full awareness of all the data.

e. Ask your Fear questions: Was Fear arising to warn you in advance of the full impact? Explore how much you did or didn't see the danger coming. How has this scenario repeated or been avoided? Has Fear achieved its purpose in regard to keeping you safe in all similar situations ever since? If not, ask what it needs you to know or do to be forever safe.

f. Your Fear is protecting a Desire. What is that Desire? Feel the urgent urges that are in your memory and still present today. Reach clarity on the needs that were threatened or violated in the trauma. Use your skills with Desire to go to each deeper level. Make notes as you go whenever it will not disturb your focus.

g. Follow the thwarted desires to Frustration; follow the hurt and harm to protective Anger. Let it bloom. Name the specific harm done on every level of need to the body, mind, attitude, beliefs, heart, feelings, honor, dignity, your future. Let Anger—like a loving mother, protective father, superhero friend—rise up to protect you. What does it want to do to stop the hurt, to mend the damage, to restore honor, to ensure the future? Make notes as needed to capture this information.

h.   Use all of this information to mentally rewrite the scene based on what you have learned. Start with the same situation coming to you, but use every advantage of your current awareness to change how you handle it, including skills beyond your age at the time. It's your story, so see the perfect outcome. If you first need to attack and avenge yourself, play that out and feel your satisfaction with the results. Watch your movie now, having learned a better way to handle it all. Try several different outcomes, from the outrageous and fantastic to the practical. Creatively explore all of the possibilities and see them play out just as you wish. Assume the role of your strongest, wisest, most skillful self, and let that self lead you to several ideal outcomes. This "rehearsal" can open a new pattern of behavior. Record the best practical possibilities to come from this exercise.

i.   Once more, meditate and imagine current-day and future situations in which you use the knowledge, skills, words, and behaviors you have found. See how nicely things work out for you now.

❷ *Capture Your Gains.* To create lasting change, wherein these advanced behaviors become your new normal, you must play out these visions in real life. Experiment with your new tools in daily situations and observe the results. Start in easier situations first, or take on big problems that require immediate attention. With practice, your new way of being will become automatic the next time something more intense occurs. Even if you don't get it quite right, you'll know how to go back and make it right as soon as possible afterward.

Was the Lesson Worth the Price?

Healing from wounds occurs in its own time. Once you take proper care of a cut, you have to let it work in its own time. Emotions are the same. No one can tell you how fast you should "get over it." But permanent, irreparable Trauma is not nature's way. Rejuvenation and rebirth always follow loss. Recovering Hope, Love, Trust, Joy, and even Forgiveness and then feeling that it was all worth it are forms of rejuvenation (becoming young and fresh again) that indicate when full healing has occurred. They are worth the work to get there. *Trauma leads to strength and wisdom!*

We're All Recovering from Something!

The impression of every experience contributes to forming our person-ality. Through life's lessons, whether unconsciously on an evolutionary time scale or by "instant karma," we learn from today's mistake how to avoid tomorrow's problem. Adaptations that sabotage growth and do harm are the correction we seek in trauma recovery. There is no one who doesn't have this work to do; so let's be compassionate with ourselves and be patient with each other. Let's set a high bar on our recovery to gain the use of our full potential, complete self-actualization, and fulfillment of our destiny. Healing spans a wide range. The ecstatic pain of the saint, who suffers from any single moment of disconnectedness from the bliss of Soul, is at the high end. That may seem far off to those with severe anxiety or depression, but we just never know how close we are until the fog clears. Each of us must deal authentically with whatever is our next step. When we are intuitively in touch with our Soul and its many senses, we will know what to do to take care of ourselves. Here are a few post-traumatic conditions that are common today.

Inner Anger: Enemy of the Self

When Anger is repressed or misused, it is unavailable to work toward protective solutions externally or toward constructive strengthening internally. You remain in harm's way, with nowhere to go with all that energy. You may see yourself as the problem and thus misdirect the Anger into self-destruction, self-sabotage, and slow deterioration of health and happiness. (See more in Chapter 6.)

Numbness: The Silent Shield

Traumatic experiences bring intense emotions. The more outsized the damage, the stronger the energetic response. When there is no outlet for, understanding of, or control over the feelings, they faithfully remain swirling inside, looking to achieve their all-is-well purpose. The younger you are, the more certain this is to happen. Living with that persistent pain is difficult, compounding your problems. It feels like you are being attacked from the inside. An exertive response brings Expressed Anger or Inner Anger. If that energy is unavailable to you, or if it is punished or disallowed, you may discover that you feel nothing. You focus elsewhere, in fantasy or thought; you invent a better story and live in another world. You may become highly focused, cerebral, and intellectual, or perhaps you become dull and uninterested. Maybe you disassociate with the body, not caring for physical needs or overindulging without satisfaction in food, sex, or self-inflicted pain. When these become obsessive and addictive, there is a whole lot going on that distracts attention from the awful feelings. Of course, there is also a great array of legal and illegal drugs to numb the feelings.

This adaptation works may have helped you survive the "war zone" that caused the trauma, but it is at a cost. Avoiding those painful sensations deadens the same sensors that bring you the good stuff—the juice and joy of life. You live in shades of gray, with the living dead, in zombieland, which can get depressing after a while. This is a form of Depression, but with an insidious built-in defeat mechanism. You have to *feel* Apathy before it can rejuvenate you. From all that you now know about the vital role of emotions, numbness leaves you without your emotions' essential guidance. You lose the ability to know what you need and the energy to get it. Recovery can be difficult. Here is a story to illustrate that recovery *is* possible.

Stephanie Safely Feels Again

I have lived with so much fear, but I was surprised to find numbness too. I was so afraid of my fear that I was extremely hesitant to do this work. But you started me out slowly, safely dipping into it. After several weeks of practice, I had a surprising first-time vision of myself as a young girl, balled up and cowering in a corner under my mother's attack. I'm not sure if she was hitting me or just screaming at me; I'm not even sure it really happened. But she was definitely, manic with huge mood swings, and I do remember her chasing me around the house with a butter knife (not sharp, but it is definitely scary when you are little). It was so awful; I withdrew and became distant as a way to survive the pain. I was smart and read a lot, alone. I'd hide in a closet and read. There were bugs in there, which was horrible, but they were better than what was out there. To this day, I am freaky scared of any bug; if one is in the room, I am petrified but do nothing to get rid of it.

I'm just now tapping into how much fear was there all those years, even though I don't remember feeling it at the time. Come to think of it, there was no happiness either; no pleasure at all. Damn, it's still like that. I now realize how many signals are flashing—good and bad feelings—that I have been ignoring. My relationship is kind of the walking dead. Although I often felt unsafe with my boyfriend, I couldn't identify it as fear, and I never did anything about it.

Slowly, privately, I have begun exploring emotions that I have numbed and hidden so well that I didn't know they were there. I hadn't cried forever, and finally doing so felt good. The most surprising experience is that allowing those emotions didn't kill me, nor did they take from me. Instead, they made me much more centered, clear, focused. I am coming back into my own power. I feel like I have myself back again.

Cold Depression: Emptiness and Overstimulation

Imagine a nightmare in which you are perpetually chased by a huge monster. You are afraid and exhausted, but you can never stop. This is the prevailing psyche in our times of constant and rapid change, relentless information overload, constant demands, and pressure of time. Individually and globally, we are living a modern version of Sisyphus, who was condemned to an eternity of intensely struggling to roll a boulder uphill, only to have roll back down to start again. It seems we cannot match the demands of life, and yet there's no way out. Our energetic reserves are exhausted; our glandular and nervous systems are depleted. We lose confidence and connection to our Self. All of this is creating a combination of Fear, Depression, and Numbness called Cold Depression. All the conditions of Numbness are present and decay into Hopelessness, but the Fear drives us on. We seek the energy to keep going through any form of stimulation; we go into hyperdrive to feel alive. We go to extremes to feel a power that we don't believe in and that indeed proves unable to solve anything and bring rest. Exhaustion continues, but we dare not stop.

As with any chronic condition, the effects of habit accumulate over time. Habits must change, and still it will take time to heal the damage. Many lifestyle changes must be made to regain control and restore resources. You already have a list of things you know and "should" do that would work better. Anything that nurtures and strengthens will work. I recommend the many techniques of yoga, a system that has been around long enough to discover a wellness-promoting way to do everything a person does: eat, sleep, breathe, exercise, relax, have sex, think, give birth, and die. There is also a system called SuperHealth, which has seen very high success rates for addiction recovery through simple immersion in this yogic lifestyle.

It's hard to change habits, especially when the monster seems to be at your heels. Sometimes you bottom out before you can change habits. Your mental habits are at the core of solving not only Cold Depression but also all of your suffering.

Get Connected

The source of Cold Depression is alienation from Self, and the solution is to reconnect. You can start physically with the body—by feeling and caring for it. Then you can afford to address subtler issues. This entire book is designed for you to realize your true needs and what you can do to get them. Little by little, you feel better, cozier, kinder. Like a turtle slowly coming back out of its shell, you open up and connect with yourself. Then you can do so with others. As Peace and Joy deepen, you feel so good; that's what I call feeling your Soul. The entire work here with Senses of the Soul is based on Deep Listening, as introduced in the opening pages of this book. Deep Listening is our approach to feeling connected to the Self, others, and the Universe. Let's look at the importance of listening within as highlighted in cases of extreme danger.

Lessons on Survival

We have all experienced our own disasters but have lived to be here so far. But we want more than to survive; we want to thrive. We don't want to just live but also to feel strong, to enjoy our life experiences. We want to feel good. We can learn a lot about how to do that from survivors of disasters, and it turns out that there are people who study these survivors. In his book, *Deep Survival: Who Lives, Who Dies, and Why,* Laurence Gonzales draws lessons from studies of survivors from the World Trade Center, plane wrecks, mountain climbing and diving accidents, prisoners of war, and those lost at sea and in the wilderness. He combines their stories, analysis of those who die, and research on the brain with his own considerable outdoor experience and misadventures to answer the questions in the book's title. Here is my take on his findings and how each is represented and enhanced by working with your emotions to help you thrive in any hardship.

Faculties that Enhance Recovery from Disaster

Being present: Be here now, in your body and with your senses. Being too much in the head—with thoughts of where you want to be, what should be happening, stuck with earlier plans and future hopes, stuck in concepts rather than dealing with the current reality—fails every time. Dealing with what is real is especially vital when something huge has happened or when things are changing rapidly. Zen meditation calls it "Beginner's Mind." The ability to be present in each moment, rather than acting from old information and concepts, and having a responsiveness to what is actually happening are essential in a crisis.

> *The basic SOS premise and practice is to have conscious awareness of what you are feeling and why and then to learn to trust those feelings. Who you were before a trauma is gone; what you knew then is outdated. Emotions, which respond moment to moment with nuanced information, are intended to guide you.*

❧

Respect and humility: Hold a sense of wonder, awe, and healthy fear of the powerful forces in nature. The last act on Earth of many fit and well-trained "machos" is to underestimate the vast power within the beauty of the world.

> *Sit with the tremendous energies in your emotions, honoring their purpose and power. See them as coming from an even greater Source. Work with, rather than ignoring or resisting, that which is unstoppable.*

❧

Self-care: Be self-aware and sensitive to what you need, and then take care of it. Many people die of thirst or hypothermia and are found next to their fully supplied pack. When urgency to get somewhere has people ignore their basic needs, they suffer more than is necessary. Those who rest when tired, eat when hungry, and have a good cry when scared maintain themselves to outlast the storm.

The purpose of emotions is to bring attention to needs and to bring solutions and the energy to satisfy them.

🌸

Responsibility and initiative: Look to yourself for salvation. Some people accept their current mess and settle into the task of solving it. They find their way out of the jungle, while their co-survivors die, waiting to be rescued. Taking on the task of getting out of the mess works better than blaming and cursing fate or assuming you can't do it and someone else will.

Know that you are a complete self-healing system. You are the only one who can do the work. People can support you, but it is your life to handle and your feelings that guide you.

🌸

Hardiness and resilience: Build the ability to withstand pressure. This is a little about the strength of the body, more about the strength of the nervous system, and mostly about the strength of the mind. With practice, you can develop an attitude that you can handle things. Inner-city kids do better in the wilderness than their suburban peers, because they are used to bringing more effort to life and because they know they can take a lot. The fear and shock of heavy challenge—a weak inner fortitude—doom many who survive the initial impact but who must endure over time to reach safety. When you "practice hurting" in a constructive way, you become familiar with the inner game required to keep up with big demands. This is part of training systems like boot camp, martial arts training, and many spiritual systems, including yoga.

Emotions feel like an inner pressure added to external challenges. Discover that not only can you handle intense feelings, but you can also use them to shift from intimidation to comfort and then on to empowerment and elevation.

🌸

Hope and purpose: Have something to live for. In equally dire conditions, some give up, while others think of a loved one they want to see again or of something they are needed for that gives the extra push and endurance to get through to the end. Those who set about to assist others who are hurt more severely forget about their own injuries and find strength without thinking about it. Many of our greatest teachers and healers are doing just this—using their painful experience to help others and "paying forward" the help they are grateful to have received.

When you get a taste of the courage, serenity, or self-love that arise when you face feelings and let them work, that positive lift is a reason to live. You want more—you want to keep getting better, stronger, clearer. To feel that peace we call Soul becomes its own motivation; once this state is achieved, you'll tend to share it to help others.

♠

Connectedness: We need to be seen. It is a basic human need to be part of something. People lost in the woods face the possibility that they may never hear or be heard by another person again. To be all alone forever is so terrifying that it drives some into frantic desperate efforts that exhaust energy and drive irrational acts that make matters worse. Others despair and simply lay down and die, even when help is within reach.

When you listen within, when you are in touch with your thoughts and feelings, spend time meditatively talking with yourself to create a cozy inner world. This way, you're never alone. This familiar friendship with Self is not disassociation with the outer world, and it is the opposite of Numbness. Instead, it is a constant connection to Self. Self-compassion and self-love are to fully see and accept yourself.

♠

A safe place in the world: Know where you are. The brain dedicates a lot of resources to knowing where you are. From spatial proprioceptors to know where your body is to the use of memory and emotional signals to know where you stand in relationship to others, you are constantly navigating physical and metaphysical space. You maintain a mental map to feel safe on known territory. The further your mental map diverges from reality, the more you feel lost. It is an existential fear: the known is safe; the unknown is unsafe. "If I don't know where I am, I am not safe." Have you felt that flash when you realize you are not where you thought you were—whether in a city or in a relationship? That disorientation sends many people frantically deeper into the wilderness and away from people they love.

When your mental map includes difficult emotions, you won't feel lost in that sea of sensations. Locate yourself often by sitting down and just being at home right where you are. First-time meditators are often uncomfortable closing their eyes in public, while adepts go into that dark void with great relish and find contentment and joy in the emptiness. With practice, you are always at home, part of everything, wherever your body may be.

Manage your emotions. At least 75 percent of people in disasters get overwhelmed with fear and freeze up, go numb, or lose control in frantic acts that doom them. Survivors of catastrophes describe an intense effort to gain control of their powerful emotions. They remember talking to themselves while watching their world collapse, searching for a single thought of possibility, a hope to hold back thoughts of giving in to death, or an idea and an action that actually engage them in their own survival. The difference between life and death when under extreme duress often lies in one's ability to negotiate between rational mind and emotions. When fear or despair takes over, it's all over.

> *Relating to emotions as Senses of the Soul is to approach them as friends, wise mentors, and guides and to develop a positive working relationship with them every day. When there is no internal conflict with this vital part of yourself and their powerful forces are your allies, that alignment of internal resources can handle whatever life brings.*

Emotions are instinctual; they bring instant energy and action to match an attack on your safety. But they need your conscious guidance. Using metacognition to be aware of the feelings, the situation, and the solution takes some practice. But this essential skill can make proper use of your sophisticated sensory system, which is designed to help you fully take care of yourself equally on life-threatening days and in daily life.

Salvation: An Inside Job

Childhood may have been the disaster you survived. Traumas happen as instant earthquakes or as slow suffocations. Bad parenting, unsafe relationships, betrayal, devastating losses. Fathers leave, mothers get depressed, uncles molest, illness strikes, children die, love dries up, dreams go unrealized. The scars remain, but we are built to recover and survive. We have the capacity to thrive on challenge, crisis, and change. Emotions are essential in both prevention and healing.

It's a wild and wooly world, exciting and dangerous, full of adventure and challenge, pain and pleasure. How has your adventure been? Has it been a stroll in the park or an avalanche? You have the map and the compass to find your way out of the woods, a built-in sensory system that brings perfect guidance over smooth or rough terrain. Just put it to work! You have the power; you may just need some help discovering it.

The Self-Exalted Experience

When I was a young man finding my way, the world was both exciting and intimidating. I charged ahead enthusiastically, but then always held back in fear. I began a search for help, traveling the world and wandering through the world of ideas. Science was fascinating, but I needed something that helped me face life. I turned to metaphysics, the study of nonphysical things. My research led me to yoga philosophy—the most scientific and reproducible explanation of man in Universe I had found. The concepts were great, but I needed more. One day I sat in a room in Anchorage, Alaska, with about 60 other people for yoga class with an Indian master, Yogi Bhajan. He had us do some difficult postures. Under his firm encouragement, I pushed past the limitations that I imagined I had. I then had the direct experience of my strength and courage. It was nothing someone could have convinced me was true. That experience, along with revisiting it every day in some way in my personal practice, has given me a great life. That is the Self-Exalted experience. If you need help reaching it, as I needed my teacher to push me, use the recorded version available for downloading with this book or find your own access to that realization.

> *All therapies, and all help, and all knowledge are going to be absolutely obsolete. People need immediately self-exalted experience. And that is what the whole essence of human life is.*
>
> → **Yogi Bhajan**

Power and Peace

This short exercise has a powerful, immediate effect on the glands, as well as on the brain and its electromagnetic field. It gives you radiance and strength. It will prepare you for the self-healing visualization that follows. Participate with full strength.

❶ *Begin with Getting Peaceful (page xi). Tune in with the Adi Mantra and continue.*

❷

a.   Curl and tighten the fingers of each hand like a lion's claws. Keep the tension in the hands throughout the exercise. Extend both arms out to the sides, parallel to the ground, with the palms up. Bring both arms up overhead so your hands pass each other over the crown of the head. Bend the elbows so the palms face down. Then extend the arms parallel to the ground again so your hands are in the starting position. Start a fast-paced rhythmic motion in this way. Alternate which wrist is in front when they cross overhead. Create a powerful breath with the motion of the arms, inhaling as the arms extend and exhaling as they cross overhead. The breath becomes a steady Breath of Fire. Continue for 9 minutes.

b.   Without breaking the pace of the exercise, stick your tongue out and down all the way. Continue the arm movement and breath for 15 seconds more, keeping your tongue out the entire time.

c.   Then inhale, bring in the tongue, and fix the arms up and curved so that they form an arc around the head with the palms facing down about 6 inches apart above the head. The hands are still in Lion's Paws. Hold the breath for 15 seconds. Keep the arms fixed as you exhale and inhale completely. Then hold the breath for 30 seconds. Relax and let the arms down.

Enjoy your elevated status and bask in your excellence. In this energy state, you can handle anything. From here, things take care of themselves. Let your own system heal and take care of you. Meditate in stillness and then proceed with the visualization.

❸ *Timeless Tunnel of Wisdom.* Feel your body and have a mental picture of yourself sitting there. Hold internal sensations and an external viewpoint at the same time. You are the most advanced, cutting-edge version of you that has ever lived. Feel all your best qualities and virtues, your strength and excellence. There are always ups and downs. But even if you have had better days, you are the wisest and most experienced, the most conscious you have ever been. Accept, appreciate, and enjoy that for a moment.

You are in a tunnel of light that extends to your far left and your far right. Where you sit is the present; out to your left is the past. Stay where you are, but look to the left at yesterday, a year ago, 10 years ago. Each earlier time holds a less progressed version of yourself, learning its way toward your present self. You can go back as far as you want, seeing good times and bad.

Stop at any traumatic event or period. Go to a specific memory, a moment of pain or disaster. This is an earlier, smaller, weaker, less aware version of yourself. It is not you now. Go inside and visit his or her point of view. Relive the memory and allow feelings to flow through you. Fully feel until it eases up a bit. Have that younger you reach out through the tunnel to your current self, while you reach back and hold onto each other.

What do you know now that you couldn't have known then? Seeing all that you see from your present place, whisper a message to your former self about how it will be later. Give some comfort, support, and hope that your former self will get through it, grow up, and get more choice later. "Be patient now; it will be okay. There is this great version of yourself coming." Let the earlier self take this in and feel better. Stay connected as you come back to the present.

Now venture out to your right into the future. You have always been learning and growing. Imagine how much more will come in the next year. See yourself in 5 and 10 years, becoming ever stronger, brighter; everything getting better; you getting wiser and happier. Go further to the end of your life; see it fulfilled and complete, an exalted life. Go further into the realm of Spirit and Soul, where all wisdom and infinite peace come from. All of the other wise souls are there; God is there. Reach out and join hands with any and all of these images that reach to hold you. Let them whisper to your current self whatever you need to hear. Accept this wisdom from your future higher self, just as you helped your past. Sit with this knowledge and let it become part of your current consciousness.

See and feel the timeless connection of past, present, and future continuously and permanently available.

When you are ready, bring yourself gently back. Stretch and open your eyes. Make notes to record your discoveries. Remember what you learned—that wisdom can become part of your everyday consciousness.

Let your self be moved to sing an inspiring and uplifting song for several minutes. Yes, SING!

Reclaim Your Self

Each experience in life enriches you, whether you consider it good or bad. The difficult, scary, and traumatic events send a shock that separates you from yourself; you feel lost. Being lost—in the woods or from your own center, your soul—is not a physical condition. It is the lack of a mental map of who you are and where you stand in relationship to everything else. When you are on unfamiliar ground, unsafe, not at home, wandering, looking for safe harbor, then everything "out there" doesn't make sense, doesn't seem to support you; you don't fit in, don't know where you stand. It's a concept and feeling that can be assisted with external support, but it can only be ultimately remedied internally. In the dark night of despair, when you are staring out into emptiness and death, the only home is in the heart, the soul, the embrace of that infinity. As with any important relationship, with Self and Soul, it takes time, attention, and connection to get cozy.

You may not be able to control all that happens, but you can control how you respond. The events that touch you intensely, when met with consciousness, can expand your spirit and fill that deep reservoir that sustains life. Survivors of disaster speak of the exhilaration felt, the aliveness and exquisite beauty all around that is revealed in the midst of their darkest hours facing death. They gain an enduring reverence for life that takes them beyond fear of death. Most say they would not prefer that it had never happened. When you can go to the edge of your own darkness and face it, you will return with enduring light and peace. That fortitude can be developed and brought to face each day for each next test. If you can't find the strength, it's not just a matter of force. Your sensitivity and openness to the flow of feeling are equally effective powers. I hope by now that you have gained real skills and results in using your emotions—your use of the receptive side of power. We are all urgently in need of discovering it to bring balance to the psyche, to each life, and to world affairs.

Self-Study

❶ Know that all of your history can serve to make you wiser and stronger, to raise your consciousness. Set an intention to realize this and to reach that level of complete healing.

❷ Design a program and set a period of time that you can dedicate to your healing projects. For example: "I will focus for the next 12 months on completely healing from my family history of abuse. I will dedicate 30 minutes a day to practices, meditation, and journaling. I will clean up circumstances that maintain the patterns set long ago. I will take good care of my body during this time. I will get some support from friends, groups, and individuals or counseling and coaching as needed. This is the time to deal with it and move on."

❸ Make an inventory of the principal events in your life that have hurt you and left a lasting effect. Identify the strongest emotions relating to each memory. Use the information and techniques in the chapter on each emotion to let that emotion do its work for you.

❹ Use the techniques in this chapter as often as needed.

Suggested Reading

Karla McLaren, *The Language of Emotions: What Your Feelings Are Trying to Tell You* (Boulder, CO: Sounds True, 2010). I highly recommend this brilliant work to learn more about every emotion and the healing of trauma.

Chapter Twelve

Embracing the Sacred Self
The Answer Is Always There

A World of Hurt

There is a lot of suffering out there, as well as within our own hearts and minds. But there's reason for hope. Pain holds a cure that comes not by living with it but by listening to it, by letting it show us the problem and lead us to the cure. Like it or not, consciousness is expanding more rapidly. We are awakening with greater sensitivity. That means we'll feel more—the loneliness of elders we don't even know; the abuse of children far away; the terror of abused and mistreated people everywhere; the frustration, rage, and meaninglessness of those stuck in traffic right beside us. Worse will be the amplified sensations of our own inner darkness and disconnectedness. When we can't stand it any longer, we will work with what we have. When we feel, we can heal. It motivates us to solve.

If you have done even a bit of the work this book has offered, you have seen that when you go into difficult feelings and face them consciously, you come out feeling better. You will have discovered what we all need:

Sensitivity to know what is happening in and around you
Willingness to feel pain but not just put up with it
Ability to interpret your emotions and know what you need
Capacity to control your reactions and respond from consciousness

Responsibility for your own actions and results, as well as tolerance for the feelings and choices of others

Power to protect yourself and others

Surrender to accept what is and to allow things to take care of themselves

Innate healing that transforms trauma into strength and wisdom

Love that is always there when all the blocks to receiving it are resolved

Your pain brings sensitivity, which leads to empathy, which brings self-compassion, which leads to self-caring and self-kindness, which will encourage self-giving, which will create self-love. If that sounds very self-ish, you'll get over it when you begin to enjoy your life so much. You will be in such good shape that you'll have nothing left to do except help others do the same.

Your pain brings sensitivity, which leads to empathy, which brings self-compassion, which leads to self-caring and self-kindness, which will encourage self-giving, which will create self-love.

We've lived a long time inflicting pain and incurring trauma; now is the time to heal ourselves collectively by uplifting ourselves individually. The best thing you can do for world peace is to find peace inside. It's safe now to feel. Your sensitivity will become your strength. Use it to find your way home. Home is where the heart is—a place of love and safety. Your awareness will show you the way. Here are some examples of the wisdom that is always available when we take time to listen.

Art's Masterpiece with Anger

I used the SOS Method for Anger to understand why I was angry. I realized that I was being disrespected by some family members. I dug down to see what was hurt. Their words attacked me personally—hurting my feelings, my heart, and my sense of self. I could feel the power rising up to protect me. My confidence was shaken. What was the need? To be accepted. I dug deeper, looking for the root cause, and saw that I wanted to be loved. That level of clarity and honesty that led me to hear, "If you were to accept yourself in all dimensions and were happy with yourself, if you were to love yourself, would what someone else said or did still hurt your feelings? Their disrespecting you is about them; it is not your problem. When you are already getting what you need from yourself, you don't need external self-respect."

I saw that how I felt about myself could be based on external or internal sources. I kept asking and listening. "Why are you dependent on their approval? Is it because you're not accepting and loving yourself." Anger comes from the absence of love, and self-love took care of it. Once you have that, you are already fed, so you are not hungry and begging from others. I feel like I've found the Unified Field Theory of Life: Love is the ultimate power. If you are connected directly to Love, God, Soul—they seem all the same to me—then nothing and nobody can hurt you.

Ravi's Soul Speaks

Here is a self-healing experience that Ravi shared from her Timeless Tunnel of Wisdom meditation (page 315).

I reached back and could see her, my younger self, and I could comfort her. I have done this before, so it was familiar that I could go to her. I then reached the other way to see my future older self. It was very powerful to see myself as this kind, older, super-relaxed, full-of-love woman. And beyond her, I could see the fourth person in this chain—the purest part of who I am—my Soul. I could relate well to my older self, but I saw that she was relating to that universal self beyond her, and she was closer to the soul as she was getting older and closer to death. So I could see my soul beyond my older self, and although it was a reach, we finally touched. When we all joined hands, the tunnel exploded into a universal feeling of eternity; I'd call it God. The message I heard clearly was, "You are beautiful." My first thought was, "Well, that doesn't help me much." I wanted something that felt more encouraging. I just waited for another audible message, but nothing came; so I just sat in the energy and felt this overwhelming feeling wash over me that was love and support. And I felt very calm. It was an amazing experience.

Over the next 24 hours, I found myself often reaching to that future me, and the reaching got easier and easier until it wasn't so much of a reach; it became more normal to hold hands. We were close enough that I could feel her touch and feel her surrounding me with that overpowering sense of love and acceptance. Whenever I feel it now, I have a clear sense that my soul is right beyond that; it is the true source of that love. Just beyond my older self is my pure soul and we are always connected. I wanted love and acceptance so much as a child, as I still want it now. I was always searching for it, but I felt that nothing on this planet would ever satisfy me. But then I realized that I could just close my eyes and reach out to my older self as my mother; she could give me that pure satisfying love that I was looking for, knowing that the source of it is my Soul, which is beyond her.

The next day you had me doing the Cutting Negative Thoughts meditation (page 278) to cut away the negative things from my past—beliefs and neuroses that keep me disconnected from Soul. I was thinking, "I don't need scissors; I need a freaking machete to cut the pain from my past." It helped to imagine I was in a safe dome and that I was cutting back all that invaded my space. It feels like I've been beating it back forever. Then I started instead to focus on that relationship with my older self, with my soul, and on feeling that love. That's when I started to realize that I was finally feeling the fullest sense of love I had ever felt in my life. I realized that this is something I will have for the rest of my life: this relationship with my pure self and its love. The gratitude and my tears gushed out. What I had been looking for so hard all my life, it was just there. I wasn't focused on the pain anymore; I'd been focused on that for 40 years. It's amazing that the love was just right there all along. I can now be my mother to myself—how powerful is that? I can give to myself what I always wanted.

My husband, knowing how much pain I've gone through, was aware of my emotional breakthrough—all the tears of joy and sadness releasing all that past pain. He came and sat behind me and held me in a way that he's never done before. Before he was always unsure of what I need when upset, so he would give me space, which is not what I've really wanted. But this time he just held me. I had the realization that the lack of healthy love when I was young left me searching and that any bit of disappointment would always confirm the evidence that people didn't love me. So I never truly allowed the love that I do have in my life; I just couldn't trust it. Even though it was there, I couldn't feel that it was there. I thought I had, because I've worked on that over the years, and I have come a long way. But now, because of that experience of self-love, I could let more in. As I was feeling this overwhelming purity of love with my older self and my soul, it gave me the ability to feel it now, in the present, with the person who loves me the most on this Earth. I could see they were all connected: my self, soul, and others. I guess it's true what they say—if you don't love yourself, no one can love you.

It was like stories I've heard of people going through the death tunnel led by some entity to the light, an overwhelming feeling of peace and love. I had that experience, but I didn't have to die to experience it.

I realized that connection with my soul will always be there. I realized I have a way to have access love. In any moment of being confronted with negativity or my own anxiety, I can just close my eyes and tap into it. It all came from that voice: "You are beautiful." It wasn't the words but the feeling that touched and changed me. My essence is pure love.

The fact is, if a person has not experienced the love of his or her soul, within one's self, there is no chance that that person can go out and love, even though it is a faculty of love that you most powerfully need.

→ **Yogi Bhajan, July 29, 1996**

Getting Back Home

My spiritual teacher, Yogi Bhajan, once told me, and I am paraphrasing from memory: "All this religion, yoga, spirituality, teachings, practices, and efforts comes down to this: Sit down and work things out with yourself!" After five decades of searching, learning, and experiencing anything I could find that might help my happiness, I can say that what made the most difference was to calm down enough to pay attention, to talk nicely to myself and find out what was wrong, to respond with compassion, and to take care of myself. After extensive searching for things to fulfill me and for answers to help me, I am now simply coming to terms with being me—and it's actually quite nice. My internal Prodigal Son has been welcomed home, where the answer always lay.

I remember taking on the "project" of Self-Love. It sounded like a good idea. I thought it would be simple and would come automatically. But I found it surprisingly difficult, so I decided to start with an easier step: self-niceness. It's crazy how long even that took me to learn. Taking responsibility for every wrong thing in my life, I decided that wherever there was pain, suffering, difficulty, or things I did not like, then that was me not being nice to myself. I was nicer by eliminating the thoughts, people, and situations that felt bad. I didn't wait to feel that I deserved it. But as that cleanup left me in a world that treated me better, something deep inside me accepted that I must be worth it. Peace became the new normal. The positive momentum continued from self-kindness to self-compassion, through genuine self-affection, and on into Self-Love. It took a long time and a lot of work, acceptance, and surrender. But it was worth every last drop of blood, sweat, and tears.

My dream is that you and our future generations won't have to wander so long but will easily find the way to the Self. When that is so safe, comfortable, and cozy that nothing can disturb your peace, you will have found your true home.

There is nothing brighter, more beautiful, more bountiful than your own living soul. Get in touch with the warmth, the love, and the romance of it.

→ **Yogi Bhajan, from Aquarian Wisdom**

Sacred Self-Hug

Here is a simple thing to do as a daily practice or anytime you need it.

❶ Sit calmly and take a few deep breaths. Cross your arms with your hands holding opposite shoulders; left arm higher and right arm below it. As the hands hold on, relax the rest of your body—your face, neck, shoulders, and arms. The body language is a self-hug. If you have ever loved anything, you know the feeling of a hug; call it forth now. Feel cozy and loved within yourself. Breathe long, full breaths that slowly become effortless as you settle in to the hug. Have some gentle uplifting music playing softly, if you wish. Think any positive thought and image and evoke every warm feeling. Let everything else disappear until there is no thought at all, just the feeling that you are safe and loved. Let that melt you away until what is left is beyond feeling. All is well, all is perfect. Behold this awe and reverence for the vastness. Be in pure experience. It is Divine, sacred, pure consciousness.

❷ At some point you will be ready to "come back." Breathe deeply, stretch, and relax. Can you invite this experience to influence and alter your activity? When you visit it often, it will not be forgotten.

If you are reading these final words without having done the Sacred Self-Hug, back up and do it now for just one minute. I'll wait . . .

Good! I wanted to leave you there, in that external posture and internal position of embracing yourself fully. If you have you, you will be all right. May we feel what my son expressed in his high school graduation speech:

> I am exactly who I am supposed to be, and that is who I've always wanted to be, and I am completely in love with that person.

> ⇥ Har Narayan Khalsa, June 2012

Resources

The SOS Method: Simple Steps for Working with Emotions

Here is a fuller exploration of the SOS Method (page 42), which will help you discover the underlying cause of an emotion you are having or have had, resolve the situation triggering it, and bring you relief from both emotion and the problem it arose to resolve.

❶ **Stop and Feel.** Sit quietly in a place where you can relax and at a time when you can focus. It is best to practice in relative calm rather than when you are in the middle of the feeling, when you are upset and highly emotional. Spend several minutes creating calmness and clarity so you can take the position of observer of your thoughts and feelings. Anything that increases your clarity and safety is best: a trained guide, exercise, yoga, and meditation are good examples. Or use Getting Peaceful (page xi).

Now listen to the emotional messenger: simply call up the feelings you have strongest and most often—whatever is there right now. A memory of anything that bothers you will trigger the emotion. Relive that memory and pay close attention to your feelings—you will feel the same emotions in present time. Get interested in those emotions. Allow them; let yourself fully feel the bodily sensations. Sit with the discomfort and discover that you can handle it. Explore your own experience, as a scientist would. The sensations may be unpleasant, but they won't hurt you. Think of them as similar to getting into a hot tub; it is uncomfortable at first, but you know it will be good for you, so you slowly get used to it. The feelings will continue in strength and length according to the urgency and magnitude of the issue. This is how they get your attention and speak—they use information-packed feelings rather than words. As you allow them to flow through every part of your body, offering no resistance, they will "crescendo" and peak at some point, then begin to diminish to a lower level. Now that you are listening, they will back off a bit, just as you would go from shouting to someone across the street and then cross over to speak normally in front of them. You find your feelings are nothing to be afraid of; allowing them to pass through you brings relief. But don't stop there. Now that you see you can handle the feelings, put them to work.

❷ Find the Source. Now that you are willing to receive the message, listen to it and understand it. Address the sensations as you would in any intelligent communication. It helps to imagine the feeling as a wise person or spirit within yourself. Something has disturbed your well-being, so ask your feelings, "Why are you here? What do you want? What is wrong here that I need to know?" Ask any question that occurs to you. The answer often comes immediately, but don't expect it to come in words—it may be a feeling, an impression, an image, or a "sense." It may take a bit of practice to hear this subtle message directly before the mind steps in to analyze, judge, deny, or reject the message. Just trust what you hear and feel, even if it doesn't make sense to you or if initially you disagree.

❸ Ask for Solutions. Once you understand what's disturbing you, ask your emotions what they need for things to be right: "What must I know, do, or say to take care of this, for you, my bad feelings, to feel satisfied so that I can feel better? What will it take for you to feel complete?" If the answer is not clear, ask again. Learning to hear that quiet voice is part of the training; so, if it is not immediately clear, keep trying. Remember these solutions, whether or not they make sense and whether or not you think you can (or will) do them. Remember to listen first; ask the mind to wait to analyze and assist with a strategy, even if just seconds after the answers come. You will see that these amazingly accurate answers come from a place of higher knowing than your mind's thinking can access, and that is the proper use of the mind: to handle the details and execute the instructions of the soul.

❹ Take Action. Act on the needs and solutions you've gathered to resolve the situation. You will feel better! In fact, you will begin to feel better immediately, in Step 1, because the emotions back off a bit when they have succeeded in getting your attention. You will feel a little better again in Steps 2 and 3 as the feelings deliver their message. The downside of this immediate relief is that beginning to feel better can diminish the impetus to take action. But without completing this last step, the emotions will return again until you take action to lead to resolution. A lasting improvement in your feelings regarding this situation indicates that your corrections are working.

❺ *Repeat as Needed.* Continue this process whenever feelings arise, and continually create the improvements you require, leading to the fullest well-being possible.

Handle Yourself

This short set of exercises focuses on the solar plexus, your physical power center. It brings a quick boost to your confidence and self-control, and therefore a good preparation for all other exercises and meditations in this book. Use it as a daily practice to build a balanced use of your power. It can be done in 20 minutes at the full times listed, or reduce the times proportionately for a quicker lift. Take brief meditative rests between each exercise, or power right through for a more intense workout. Two cycles of the entire set will give you a good physical tune-up.

1. Sit comfortably on the floor with the spine upright yet relaxed. Curl the four fingers of both hands, then hook the right hand into the left with the right palm facing down. Push the side of the hands (right thumb knuckles) into your belly, just below the navel. Exhale completely and hold the breath out for 8 seconds with the abdomen holding firmly against the inward pressure of the hands. Then inhale and hold the breath for 8 seconds with the same two pressures. Continue this cycle for 3 minutes, then relax. Sit for a moment in calm self-awareness and feel your strength.

2. Sit on the heels and raise the arms overhead, pressing the palms flat together. Pull your navel in firmly as you powerfully utter "Sat" (pronounced more like "sut" in this instance). Then relax the navel as you calmly say "Nam". Continue for 3

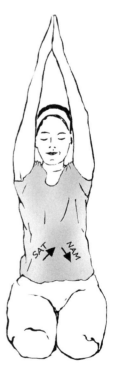

minutes, then inhale and squeeze the entire body tightly for 5 to 15 seconds. Exhale, relax everything and sit quietly observing your sensations for a minute or more.

❸ Stretch your legs out straight in front of you. Place the palms on the ground behind you. Raise both legs to 60 degrees and hold this position with a strong and steady Breath of Fire. Continue for 2 minutes, then inhale, exhale, and apply the lower locks (root lock). Then relax immediately into Easy Pose and belly laugh loudly for 1 minute. Sit calmly in self-awareness.

❹ Bring your hands into fists at the shoulders. Inhale deeply and suspend the breath, then begin alternately punching forward as if boxing rapidly. When you must, exhale, and inhale deeply to continue. After 3 intense minutes, relax and sit still.

❺ Alternate between Camel Ride and Shoulder Shrugs as follows. (a) Hold on to your ankles/ lower shins and inhale as you flex the spine forward, then exhale- extend it back and (b) Inhale – lift the shoulders up to the ears, exhale – drop the shoulders down. Find your rhythm with the breath. The pace is about 5 full cycles in 10 seconds. Continue this cycle with deep breaths for 3 minutes. Then inhale, exhale completely, apply the lower

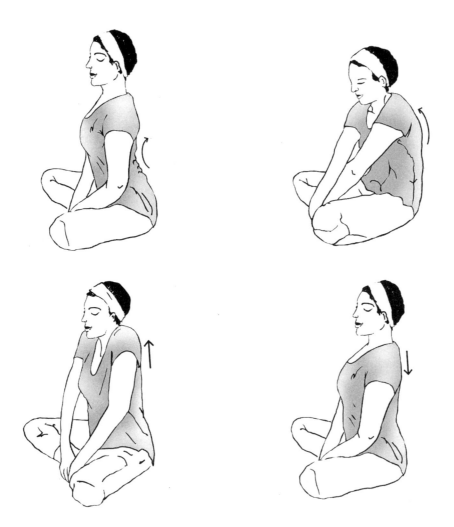

locks for as long as you like, then relax. Sit calmly and follow the sensations of energy and your own strength. Continue on to any meditation, or relax deeply on your back.

Immediate Recovery from Fear (and long-term care for modern life)

Ideally, when something causes an adrenaline spike, you act quickly and the danger passes. Your system then works to recover a relaxed metabolism which is energetically economical and sustainable. But when the shock is intense enough or the stressor smaller but repeated constantly you can stuck in high gear as an ever-ready defense. Either can deplete your energy and fatigue your nervous system and glandular systems, affecting your ability to respond. Then whatever danger was there remains, Fear continues, fatigue increases and the cycle escalates. As exciting as a busy modern lifestyle might be, your system treats it like non-stop danger, which exhausts the nerves and glands. When the danger is or seems relentless you remain agitated, get shaky and normal behavior starts falling apart.

Practice the Art of Relaxation

Relaxation is difficult for most people because of a subliminal level of emotional conflict or turmoil. Even as we go about our tasks, there is an inner emotive dialogue that generates patterns of anxiety, anger, hopelessness, or other self-defeating emotions. That is called "commotional living." It drains the reserve energy of the nervous system and creates defenses and armoring against the discomfort.

Your sympathetic nervous system is like your car's accelerator, but in you it is wired to be constantly on and ready to jump. It takes a strong activated parasympathetic nervous system, your brakes, to maintain equilibrium and not go out of control. Babies learn to "self-sooth" and so must you. The ability to calm yourself needs to be practiced, strengthened, and put to use. You must create peace for yourself on a regular basis to maintain health and happiness. Stimulation is the norm and comes easily nowadays. Relaxation is a learned skill you must prioritize; your well-being requires it. Simply said, reach Peace. The TV won't do the job. You must invoke the "relaxation response".

Try all of these for at least the time indicated; find which best address your source of fear and stress. Each has a unique approach using the body's self-healing capability. Use them when you need them most, but also as daily practices; the benefits are cumulative and enhance your ability to eliminate stress and the long-term effects of Fear. If Stress is great or long-standing, it will take time to recover, but you can. You wouldn't expect to get in shape at the gym in a few days. You need conscious relaxation as much as you need exercise, so practice personal peace; it might just be the greatest thing you can do for world peace!

Techniques to Bring Peace

Reduce Sources of Stress - Lighten Your Load

Being too busy, living in overwhelm, taking on too much of even the best goals is treated the same as living under an attack that is not your choice. And people often think they have no choice, perhaps until the doctor gives them the bad news ultimatum. But you can make a choice to change your circumstances, prioritize and then eliminate some time and energy commitments until the demands are equal to your capacity. Challenge and sacrifice can achieve great things, but it's possible to ignore the consequences until damage is done. In our culture this may take great acts of courage to make unpopular choices that better care for your wellbeing.

Release Fear from the Body

When there is no outlet to your readiness for fight or flight, releasing stress through non-aggravating activity and relaxing activities are both needed. Find a way that you enjoy to sweat every day, just to remain sane! Or at least get out and get going. But be sure you balance stimulation with relaxation. I see people walking intensely with their earphones that look anything but relaxed or vitalized. Stimulating exercise followed by deep relaxation is ideal, and this is in every Kundalini Yoga class. Walking in nature, time in beautiful and peaceful environments, uplifting music, hot bath, massage, relaxed meals, calming foods, supportive friends, meditation, laughter, fun, enjoyment, vacations, do what inspires you. Find what activities truly work for you by being aware of your immediate response, the after effects, and the long term results, and then put them in your schedule!

Long Deep Breathing - This is a basic and essential practice to calm body, mind and emotions. It can be practiced while sitting still as a meditation, in bed to help you fall asleep, and even as you work to bring calm in stressful situations.

- Inhale slowly and fully in a wave from belly to ribs to chest. Begin by expanding the abdomen, then expanding the ribs out and the chest up, and finally lifting the upper ribs and clavicle.
- Exhale equally slowly and completely from the top back down; dropping the upper chest, contracting the ribs, and finishing with the navel pulled way back to the spine, squeezing all the breath out.

Continue with deep, full breaths, controlling the movement like a wave washing up the beach then retreating back down. Once you get it all going, check for tension in your face and upper body and be sure to relax it all. Continue for as long as you like allowing the breath to soothe you with calm clarity. 3 to 31 minutes are suggested, the longer you do it the more the benefits. A regular practice builds long-lasting improvement.

Deep Relaxation. Train yourself to relax totally in a short time. The ability to let your body and mind go into deep relaxation and even sleep, releases tension and restores strength to the para-sympathetic nervous system. Just making that transition into what we call "falling asleep" helps break the habit and momentum of stress. A power nap of 11 to 20 minutes, reaching that state where you forget yourself is worth hours of sleep.

The Power Nap.

This exercise is from The Aquarian Teacher **level one Kundalini Yoga teacher manual, see References for complete details.**

- Start with a safe and quiet environment where you will not be interrupted. If you set a timer to end and awaken, choose a gentle alarm sound.

- Choose uplifting, calm music, nature sounds, or silence.

- Be aware of the particular frequency and rhythm of the mantra.

- You may want to cover your body with a blanket or shawl to keep warm.

- Lie down on your back with your arms at your sides.

- Rest your arms with the palms facing up.

- Feet are uncrossed.

- Close your eyes.

- Relax the breath. Let the belly naturally rise and fall.

- Let everything else go. The world will take care of itself – and you - for a while.

- Consciously instruct your body and mind to let go.

- Go through your body systematically and give permission for each part, limb, and cell to relax. Instruct each part of your body to lovingly release tension as you mentally say "relax, let go, all is well, I am safe, I am loved, or whatever is soothing to you. Here is a script that works well.

Letting Everything Go—Guided Meditation for Relaxation

This exercise is from The Aquarian Teacher level one Kundalini Yoga teacher manual, see References for complete details.

Lie down on your back with your arms at your sides on the ground. Rest the arms with the palms facing up. Close your eyes. Relax the breath. Let everything else go. You've done all you could and all you should. Prepare to heal, rejuvenate, relax, let go and let God. Consciously instruct your body and mind to be whole and let go. Go through your body systematically and give permission for each limb and cell to relax. Bring each part to alert by contracting it, squeezing it tightly for a moment and with love release the tension as you mentally say "relax."

Start with the feet. Feet relax. Ankles relax. Calves relax. Knees relax. Thighs relax. Back of the legs, relax. Hips and buttocks relax. Pelvis relax. Fingers and hands relax. Wrists relax. Forearms relax. Elbows relax. Upper arms relax. Shoulders relax. Shoulders and neck begin to relax. Neck relax. Muscles all the way down the spine and

back relax. All the muscles of the back relax. Buttocks, Navel Point and belly relax. Chest and ribs relax. Squeeze the face like a prune, relax. Click the tongue several times, relax.

Press the lips tightly, relax. Squeeze the eyelids closed, relax. Face and head relax. Now let the healing gaze of your inner eye and heart bless each inner organ and gland and give permission for even deeper relaxation. To heal, to rejuvenate, to lighten, to brighten, to heighten the glow of each cell and open the flow of life to all. Freely. Now, lungs relax. Heart relax. Thymus and the entire immune system, relax. Stomach, intestines, rectum, relax. Pancreas relax. Both kidneys relax. Adrenals reserve of inner fire, relax. Spleen, relax. Liver, the great cleanser, purifier, storehouse, relax, rejuvenate, heal. Sex organs, relax. Thyroid and parathyroid, relax. Upper glands of the brain: pituitary, pineal relax. The brain itself, relax. All thoughts flow smoothly, relax. Good thoughts. Healthy, Happy, and Holy. Let go. Let God. Now let the entire spine relax, bathe in the inner light and energy. Begin at the base of the spine. Feel a wave-like ripple relax from the spine throughout the regions of the body. All the zones of creativity and sexuality, relax, flow, connect. With the body relaxed, consciously and unconsciously, breathing rhythmically, smoothly, deeper and deeper. With each breath, leave the physical body to heal, to rejuvenate, to rest. Become light, weightless as if you could freely rise in a mental body and float a few feet above the physical, looking down to see it is safe, healing, deeply relaxed. Listen to the music and let yourself go to any radiant, ecstatic place. Be Blessed. Where every promise to God is fulfilled. A timeless place. Relaxed. Complete. Radiant. Peaceful. (After some time of silence.) Come back to full body awareness. Inhale deeply and stretch the arms up. Exhale. Rotate wrists and ankles. Rub the palms and soles of the feet together, vigorously. Hold your knees onto the chest and rock back and forth the length of the spine several times. Sit up and stretch the arms up. Shake the hands and arms.

Additional Terms and Techniques

Kriya

A combination of one or more elements of posture, breath, movement, focus and sound, or a sequence of such exercises which produce certain specific effects in the body and mental state of the practitioner. When repeated the benefits become stronger, more easily obtained and stable.

Easy Pose / Sitting Comfortably to Meditate

Most of the exercises in this book are done sitting and are enhanced by the ability to sit comfortably from 3 to 30 minutes, however you can do that. The main requirement is for the spine to be upright yet relaxed, so you can be attentive and calm, with a slightly straightened neck. Any effort, strain or pain will be a distraction. It may take some time to find your best posture, one that feels stable, well-balanced and comfortable to you. Sitting on the floor is ideal; padding and a cushion to lift the pelvis above the legs will help. You may also use a straight-backed chair with a firm seat, just don't slouch back, and have your feet rest equally on the ground.

Breath of Fire

This is strong, rhythmic, and continuously pulsed breath through the nose, unless stated otherwise. It is equal on the inhale and the exhale, with no pause between them, at about 2 cycles per second. Breath of Fire is activated from the navel and abdomen. Exhale by powerfully pulling the navel back (and slightly upward) toward the spine. It becomes automatic when you contract the diaphragm rapidly. To inhale, the upper abdominal muscles relax, the diaphragm extends down, and the belly goes out, capture an equally strong in breath. The chest stays relaxed and slightly lifted throughout the breathing cycle.

Neck Lock

Don't get carried away with the "lock" idea, this is a gentle straightening of the neck to enhance the effects of meditation, and is generally applied during all meditations and breathing exercises, especially when holding the breath in or out, unless instructed otherwise.

To do it, sit comfortably with the spine straight. Lift the chest and sternum upward, while you gently stretch the back of the neck as if a string were attached to the crown of your head and is pulling up. The chin moves slightly toward the back of the neck. The head remains level without tilting, and the neck and throat, face and brow remain relaxed.

Navel Point

In the martial arts as well as in yoga, the navel center is a key to physical movement, mental poise. It is a control point for personal power and subtle energies. The Navel Point is not the umbilicus, or belly button; think of it as a focus of energy centered 2 to 3 inches below the navel, and in closer to the lower spine. We learn to work with it by tightening the abdominal wall backward as if to withstand impact to the belly.

Root Lock – or "Lower Locks"

This aide to posture and meditation consists of three actions. To apply it, first contract the anal sphincter. Feel the muscles lift up and in. Next contract the muscles used to stop the flow of urine. Then contract the lower abdominal muscles and pull the Navel Point toward the spine. These three actions applied together into one smooth motion is called Root Lock. It may be applied lightly throughout an exercise of meditation, or quite strongly to end an exercise as directed. The breath can continue unimpeded when applied correctly.

Kirtan Kriya Research

There is a growing body of research on the benefits of Kirtan Kriya, a meditative technique using the sounds Sa-Ta-Na-Ma. See the following websites for more studies and applications to stress, depression, Alzheimer's and much more.

See the work of:
Helen Lavretsky, M.D., M.S.
Professor of Psychiatry
Director, Later Life Mood Stress and Wellness Research Program
Semel Institute for Neuroscience and Human Behavior at UCLA
http://www.semel.ucla.edu/latelife

Dharma Singh Khalsa MD
Author of Meditation as Medicine
President Alzheimer's Research and Prevention Foundation
www.alzheimersprevention.org.

Sat Bir Singh Khalsa, PhD
Director Of Research, Kundalini Research Institute
Assistant Professor of Medicine, Harvard Medical School
www.sleep.med.harvard.edu

Notes

1. SAMHSA, 1/19/2012

2. Centers for Disease Control and Prevention (CDC), March 31, 2011

3. Substance Abuse and Mental Health Services Administration

4. Anxiety and Depression Association of America, "Facts and Statistics," http://www.adaa.org/about-adaa/press-room/facts-statistics.

5. Northwestern National Life, ourstressfullives.com http://www.ourstressfullives.com/stress-statistics.html Northwestern National Life Insurance Company [1992]. Employee burnout: Causes and cures. Minneapolis, MN: Northwestern National Life Insurance Company.

6. AARP

7. U.S. Department of Justice Hate Crime Statistics 2010

8. Domesticviolencestatistics.org

9. Rennison, C. M. (2003, Feb.). Intimate partner violence, 1993–2001. BJS Crime Data Briefs. U.S. Department of Justice/Office of Justice Programs (NCJ 197838). Washington, DC: Bureau of Justice Statistics.

10. National Institute of Justice. (2000). *Extent, nature, and consequences of intimate partner violence: Findings from the National Violence against Women Survey* (NIJ Grant 93-IJ-CX-0012). Washington, DC: National Institute of Justice and Centers for Disease Control and Prevention. The Commonwealth Fund, Health Concerns Across a Woman's Lifespan: 1998 Survey of Women's Health, 1999

11. Tjaden, P., & Thoennes, N. (1998, Nov.). Prevalence, incidence, and consequences of violence against women: Findings from the National Violence Against Women Survey. *NIJCDC Research in Brief*. Washington, DC: National Institute of Justice and Centers for Disease Control and Prevention.

12. Silverman, J. G., Raj, A. Mucci, L. A., & Hathaway, J. E. (2001). Dating violence against adolescent girls and associated substance use, unhealthy weight control, sexual risk behavior, pregnancy, and suicidality. *Journal of the American Medical Association* 286(5).

13. Rennison, C. M. (2003, Feb.). Intimate partner violence, 1993–2001. *BJS Crime Data Briefs*. U.S. Department of Justice/Office of Justice Programs (NCJ 197838). Washington, DC: Bureau of Justice Statistics.

14. Strauss, M. A., Gelles, R. J., & Smith, C. (1990). *Physical violence in American families: Risk factors and adaptations to violence in 8,145 families*. (New Brunswick, NJ: Transaction Publishers. Carlson, B. E. (1984). Children's observations of interpersonal violence. In A.R. Roberts (Ed.), *Battered women and their families* (pp. 147–167). New York, NY: Springer.

15. Straus, M. A. (1992). Children as witnesses to marital violence: A risk factor for lifelong problems among a nationally representative sample of American men and women. *Report of the Twenty-Third Ross Roundtable*. Columbus, OH: Ross Laboratories

16. Centers for Disease Control and Prevention 2011

17. November 2011, pharmacy benefits manager Medco Health Solutions Inc.

18. National Institutes of Health

19. National Institute on Drug Abuse, August 2012

20. UN Office on Drugs and Crime. (2005). *World Drug Report*. New York, NY: United Nations.

21. InterventionASAP.com

22. National Association of Anorexia Nervosa and Associated Disorders, and CDCP '09-'10

References

The Teachings of Yogi Bhajan. See KRIteachings.org or a Kundalini Yoga teacher near you.

Gonzales, Laurence. *Deep Survival: Who Lives, Who Dies, and Why*. New York: W. W. Norton, 2004.

Hawkins, David R. *Power vs. Force*. Carlsbad, CA: Hay House, 2002.

Hawkins, David R. *Transcending the Levels of Consciousness: The Stairway To Enlightenment*. West Sedona, AZ: Veritas Publishing, 2006.

McLaren, Karla. *The Language of Emotions: What Your Feelings Are Trying to Tell You*. Boulder, CO: Sounds True, 2010.

Mackey, John, and Raj Sisodia, *Conscious Capitalism*. Cambridge, MA: Harvard Business School Publishing, 2013.

Mitchell, Stephen. *Tao Te Ching*, Harper Perennial Modern Classics. 1988.

Yogi Bhajan, PhD. *The Aquarian Teacher: KRI International Teacher Training in Kundalini Yoga, 4th Ed.*, Santa Cruz, NM: Kundalini Research Institute, 2007.

Resources for further information on research on the SaTaNaMa meditaton, Kirtan Kriya:

http://wholesomeresources.com/1862/1862/Meditation Effects on Cognitive Function and Cerebral ------Blood Flow In Subjects with Memory Loss: A Preliminary Study: www.alzheimersprevention.org/research_ucla_study.htm

Cerebral blood flow changes during chanting meditation: www.alzheimersprevention.org/JrnlofNucMedComms0909.pdf

Cerebral blood flow differences between long-term meditators and non-meditators: www.alzheimersprevention.org/research_ucla_study.htm

Meditation Use to Reduce Stress Response and Improve Cognitive Functioning in Older Family Dementia Caregivers: www.alzheimersprevention.org/research_ucla_study.htm

List of Exercises

This section lists every exercise contained in this book for your convenience and quick-reference.

Audio recordings for the meditations in this book can be found at the author's website: **www.sensesofthesoul.com**

Index